AF378535

The Sandon Guide to Royal Worcester Figures 1900-1970

The Sandon Guid
Royal Worcester F
1900-1970

o
res

David Sandon
John Sandon
and
Henry Sandon

The Alderman Press

Published by The Alderman Press
1/7, Church Street, Edmonton, N9 9DR
October 1987

Sandon, Henry
    The Sandon guide to Royal Worcester
    figures, 1900-1970.
    1. Worcester porcelain______Collectors and
    collecting
    I. Title   II. Sandon, John   III. Sandon,
    David
    738.2'7   NK4395

    ISBN 0-946619-18-2

The publishers wish to acknowledge and express their thanks
to the following;

for their photographic work — John and Joan Beckerley.
for their editorial endeavours — Michael Bruff and Julie Nelson.
for design and production — Bill Antrobus of Deer Park Productions.
for typesetting — Stone Associates Ltd.,
for origination, printing and binding — Netherwood Dalton & Co. Ltd., Huddersfield.

Printed in Great Britain.

Contents

Sources and Acknowledgements

Introduction

Index to Shape Names

Chapter 1   A History of Royal Worcester Figures.   1

Chapter 2   Twentieth-Century Royal Worcester Figures.   10

Chapter 3   The Making of a Royal Worcester Figure.   28

Chapter 4   The Modellers.   36

Chapter 5   Collecting.   52

Chapter 6   Marks and Date Codes.   57

Chapter 7   A Catalogue of Royal Worcester Figures 1900-1970.   60

Introduction and Acknowledgements

When I was Curator of Royal Worcester and the Dyson Perrins Museum I had long felt that a book dealing with Royal Worcester unlimited edition figures was badly needed. A booklet covering the Limited Edition figures of the Company was produced in the 1970s and updated several times in loose-leaf form, and this was of great benefit to the collectors of these fine models. My own book, *Royal Worcester Porcelain*, first published in 1973, illustrated some of the figures and briefly listed all of the shapes made by the factory. The interest generated by the book over the years has been staggering, and I realised how great was the need for a book about twentieth century unlimited edition Worcester figures.

For several years, I have been nagging two of my sons, David and John, to produce such a book. They had long been interested in Royal Worcester figures and had built up a great deal of knowledge about the subject from conversations with old craftsmen and collectors and by researching the factory records. But our busy lives prevented the project being started. Then, in the spring of 1985, on one of the BBC *Antiques Roadshow* television programmes, I discussed some Royal Worcester figures, and the wonderful close-ups in colour so impressed the publishers, Alderman Press, that they asked us to produce a book. This, the result, is the product not just of a year's hard work gathering the pieces from many sources, careful photographing and painstaking collecting together of material and putting the whole into a total and readable work, but also of the years of preparation that preceded it.

Our aim has been to include every figure and animal study introduced between the years 1900 and 1970, apart from those issued in Limited Editions. Some of the models that we have included quite probably did not go into full production but, where any details have been recorded, we have given them, as every now and again somebody does unearth a figure which we thought we would never see. We have not described in detail a large series of brooches, mainly of dogs and birds, but the shape numbers have been included in their correct place. It should also be mentioned that figures introduced before 1900 have not been included, even where they were continued into this century. The more important ones, however, have been referred to.

We would have liked to have illustrated every figure listed, but clearly this would have been quite impossible. Instead, we have concentrated on illustrating examples of as wide a range of models as we were able to find. It must not be assumed that if a figure is not illustrated it is a rare one. Conversely, we have illustrated many figures which are seldom seen. Where possible, colour illustrations have been used, but we have tried to fill the important gaps by reproducing black and white photographs, many from the factory archives. The colourings of the figures illustrated are not necessarily always the most commonly seen decoration of a particular model, and some figures were painted in a great variety of different colour schemes. Where an original intended colouring has been recorded we have listed this. Some figures were not given names when they were made and in cases like this we have used the names by which they have come to be most usually known.

Some figures have, in more recent years, been re-introduced, and we have mentioned this and pointed out all of the pitfalls known to us that collectors might encounter.

This book is truly a Sandon family guide. As well as the writing and main preparation done by my sons David and John and myself, with assistance from John's wife Kristin, the heaviest burden has fallen on my wife Barbara. She has typed most of the manuscript, organised and gathered the several hundred figures from one corner of Worcestershire to the other and borne, with great patience, the turmoil that the preparation of such a book entails. In particular, she began our interest in the figures of the 1910s and 1930s, especially the small animal studies. Her collection of these rare pieces, which she made twenty or more years ago, has proved such a godsend for this book.

There are an enormous number of other people whose help we greatly acknowledge. In particular we would like to thank the Managing Director of the Worcester Royal Porcelain Company, in Worcester, for freely allowing access to factory records, without which this book would not have been possible; Mr Peter Croser, the Public Relations Officer, for much information; the modellers, crafts-

men and staff of the Worcester Royal Porcelain Company, both past and present, not only for making these figures but also for being so free with information: in particular, if we have to single out one person, Mr George Morris; the Trustees of the Dyson Perrins Museum, and Mr Harry Frost, the Curator; the auction houses that have helped, especially John Matthews, Keith Baker, Fiona Baker and Anne-Marie Benson at Phillips, Michael Turner at Sotheby's, and dealers Geoffrey Godden of Worthing, Billy Buck of Steppes Hill Farm Antiques and Gabrielle Bullock of Bygones of Worcester. For their help in researching the modellers, we are grateful to Jennifer Opie and John Mallet of the Victoria and Albert Museum and Vic Meecham who has researched Stella Crofts. Miss Joan Burgess of the Zoological Society of London has spent considerable time researching the animals studied by Doris Lindner during the 1930s and we are very grateful for her work.

Many people who so kindly loaned their figures for photographing and study wish to remain anonymous; our grateful thanks go to them and to the following, whose names are recorded here alphabetically. Their joy in the possession of the figures will be doubled by the pleasure in sharing them with others, one of the delights of a true collector:

Mr J. Carr, Mr G. Clark, Mrs F. F. Cooper, Mrs P. Cullis, Mrs J. Dicks, Mr N. French, Mrs J. Fudger, Mr. D. Gibson, Miss N. Halliwell, Mr C. Harrison, Mrs J. Hartwright, Mrs F. Hepworth, Mrs A. M. Jones, Mrs V. Maynard, Mrs C. Metcalf, Mrs G. C. Naish, Mrs P. Robotham, Mrs B. Serrell, Mrs A. Starkey, Dr W. D. Steel, Mrs Uckfield, Pauline Walker, Mrs K. M. Walton

The colour photographs in the book are obviously of great importance in the understanding of the figures. The majority have been taken specially by John and Joan Beckerley, a number by Chris Halton and others have kindly been supplied by the owners of some of the figures. The quality speaks for itself and we are grateful for them all.

Finally, a dedication for this book. Perhaps it should be dedicated to all the members of the Worcester Royal Porcelain Company, past and present, for making these delightful figures with skill and love. Such an honour would be well justified, as without their dedication to their craft, often through the most trying times of the 1920s to 1940s, these models would not have been made. However, the number of craftsmen is very great and it is best to choose one person to represent all of them.

So, we dedicate this book to the memory of Miss Daisy Rea, painter and forewoman of the figurine painting department of the Worcester Royal Porcelain Company over many years. Her dedication to her craft, her consummate skill, her insistence on the highest standards in her own work and in that of her pupils, and her being just the loveliest lady that you could ever hope to meet, make it right that this book should be dedicated to her. Sadly she did not live to see it published, but to paraphrase the memorial to the designer of St. Paul's Cathedral: 'If you seek a memorial, look inside this book'.

Henry Sandon

Index to Shape Names

Aberdeen Toy Terrier, 2946
Admiral, 2661
Admiral of The Blue, 2661
Afghanistan Hound, 3425
Airedale Terrier, 2942
Airedale Terrier Standing, 3026
Alice, 3608
Alice in Wonderland Series, see 3608
Alicia, 3175
Alsatian (first version), 3295
Alsatian (second version), 3462
Amanda, 3620
Amaryllis, 3108
'A Merry New Song', 3252
Anemone, 3584
Angel Fish, 3475
Anna, 3174
Anne Boleyn, 2652
Ape, 2612
Applause, 3107
Apple of Your Eye, 3497
April, 3416
Argentina, 2936
Arita, 3171
At the Meet, 3114
August, 3441
Autumn 3341
Autumn, Bust, 3246
The Azori Cockerels, 3581-3584

Babes in the Wood, 3302
Baby in Dressing Gown, 2387
Baby on Cushion, 3009
Balinese Dancer, 3473
Balinese Dancers (small), 3550, 3551
Ballet Dancer (first version), 3186
Ballet Dancer (second version), 3192
Ballet Dancers Series, see 3171
Ball Players, 2673, 2674
Bal Masqué, 3111
Banbury Cross, 3165
Barbara, polar bear, 2900
Bather Powder Bowl, 2783
Bathing Girl, 3289
Battledore, 3471
The Beadle, 2322
Bear, 3110
Bears, Zoo Babies, 3265
Bengal Lancer, 3168
Betty, 2930
Bill, 2931
Billy Bluegums, Zoo Babies, 3273
Birds Series, small American, see 3645
Birds Series, small British, see 3197
Birds on Stumps, see 2662
Blackcock, 2622

Black Cocker Spaniel, 2944
Black Watch Soldier, 2109
Blue Angel Fish, 3574
Bluebeard, 2903
Bluebird, 3649
Blue Tit, 3199
Blue Tit on Plinth, 3383
Blue Tits on Stump, 3375
Boer War Soldiers, see 2106
Bogskar, 3330
Boleyn, Anne, 2652
Bonzo, 2855
Borzoi, 3426
The Bow, 3359
Boy and Dolphin, 3349
Boy and Rabbit, 2618
Boy on Boar, 2882
Boy with Donkey, 2894
Boy with Parakeet, 3087
Brer Fox, 3552
Brer Rabbit (first version), 2858
Brer Rabbit (second version), 3553-3556
The Bridesmaid, 3224
Brooches, see 2957
Bubbles, 3160
Budgerigar on Stump (Female), 2663
Budgerigar on Stump (Male), 2664
Bulldog, dog's head, 3320

Bulldog, English, 2945
Bullfinch, 3238
Bullfinch on Stump, 2662
Bull Terrier, Bill, 2931
Burmah, 3068
Buttercup, 2930

Cairn Terrier, Rats, 3350
Cairn Terrier, Toto, 3331
Calf, 2896
Calves, 3146
Canary on Stump, 2665
The Candlestick, 3222
Cantering to the Post, 3117
Cardinal, 3645
Cat Eating, 2897
Chaffinch, 3240
Chaffinches on Stump, 3364
Champion Spriggan Bell,
    Poodle, 3085
Chanticleer, 3561
Charles I, 2651
Charles II, 2672
Cheetah, 2606
Cheshire Cat, 3609
Children of the Nations
    Series, see 3066
Children with Lambs, 3147,
    3148
Child with Butterfly, 3157
China, 3073
Chinese Dancers, 3194, 3195
Chinese Family Group, 2848
Chinese Figures, Female,
    3419, 3420
Chinese Goddesses, 3481,
    3482
Chinoiserie Boy, 3354
Chinoiserie Children, see
    3348
Chinoiserie Figures
    Kneeling, 3397, 3398
Chinoiserie Figures on
    Plinths, 3385-3388
Chinoiserie Figures
    Standing, 3399, 3400
Chinoiserie Figures with
    Birds, 3446, 3447
Chinoiserie Girl Sitting, 3348
Chinoiserie Girl Standing,
    3362
Chinoiserie Sayings Series,
    see 3491
Circus Horse, 3684

Circus Horses Rearing, 3179
Circus Horses with Rider, 3180
Clarissa, 3607
Classical Lady with Lyre, 2659
Classical Lady with
    Tambourine, 2660
Clown's Head, 2468
Clumber Spaniel, 3231
Cockatoo Jug, 2852
Cocker Spaniel, 2944, 3033,
    3231
Coldstream Guards Officer
    (first version), 2635
Coldstream Guards Officer
    (second version), 2676
Coldstream Guards Officer
    (third version), 3675
Cole Tits on Stump, 3376
Colonial Trooper, 2108
Columbine (first version),
    2679
Columbine (second version),
    2681
Columbine (third version),
    2999
Coquelicot, 3583
Coquette, 2884
Cora, 2865
Corgi, 3243
Countries of the World Series,
    (see Children of the Nations)
Country Girls, 2732, 2733
Cow, 2609
Crawling Child, 3381
Crinoline Figure with Book,
    2621
Crinoline Figure with Cap,
    2620
Crucifix, 2619
Cupid, 'Good Luck to your
    Fishing', 3095
Cupid, 'Hit!', 3105
Cupid with Bow, 2103
Cupid with Sheaf, 2104
The Courtesy, 3360

Dachsund, 3294
Daisy, 3560
Dalmatian, 3293
Dance, 3088
The Dancers, 2949
Dancing Lady, 3086
Dancing Waves, 3225
Dandelion, 3084

Dandie Dinmont, 2943
The Days of the Week Series,
    see 3256, 3518
December, 3458
'Delicate Cowcumbers to
    Pickle', 3227
Delphine, 2906
The Dodo, 3613
Doe, 2874
Dog Ashtray, 3156
Dog Calendar, 3120
Dogs, Small Series, see 2941
Dogs Heads, 3319-3322
Dogs, Large Series, see 3425
'Don't let the cat out of the
    Bag', 3494
Double Birds in Tree Stumps,
    (first series), see 3363
Double Birds on Tree Stump
    (second series), see 3442
Double Mouse, 2636
3rd Dragoon Guards Officer,
    2675
17th Dragoon Guards Officer,
    2677
Dreaming, 2879
The Drum, 3154
The Drummer, 3154
Drummer Boy, 2723
Dublin Flower Girl, 2921
The Duchess, 3612
The Duchess's Dress, 3106
Duck, (first version), 2843
Duck Ring Stand, 2517
Ducks (second version), 3459,
    3460
Dutch Boy, 2923
Dutch Girl, 2922

Early Bird, 3498
Early English Lady and
    Gentleman, 2389
Edward VI, 2643
Egypt, 3066
Elephant, 3096, 3102
Elephant Jug, 2851
Elizabeth I, 2648
England, 3075
English Bulldog, 2945
English Costume Figures, 2374
English Springer Spaniel, 2944
Equestrian Series, see 3114
Evacuees, 3347

'Fair Cherryes', 3300
Falconer, 3679
Family Group, Mother and
    Two Children, 2615
Fantails, 3760
Farmer's Boy, 3433
Father William, 3614
Fatima, 2904
Fawn, 3122
Fawns, Zoo Babies, 3266
February, 3453
Female Chinese Figures,
    3419, 3420
Female Dancing Figures,
    2654, 2655
Female Nudes Seated, 2805,
    2806
Female Nudes Standing,
    2691, 2692
Female Nude with Mirror,
    2800
'Fine Writing Inks', 3299
First Aid, 3756
The First Cuckoo, 3082
First Dance, 3629
First World War Soldier
    Series, see 2582
First World War Soldiers,
    Sitting, 2646
First World War Soldier,
    Standing, 2645
Fish, 2611
Fish Series, Tropical, see
    3572
Fish Ashtray, 2484
Flamingoes, 2695, 2696
Flemish Man, 2105
Flemish Woman, 2105
Flower Girl (first version),
    2880
Flower Girl (second version),
    3099
The Flute Player, 2901
Foal, 3187
Foals, 3152
Fontainbleau Series, no
    shape number, see page 149
The Fortune Teller, 2924
Four-Eyed Butterfly Fish,
    3573
The Four Seasons, 3339-3342
Fox, 2950, 3387
Fox and Hound Menu-holders,
    2953-2956
Fox and Hound Pentray,
    3947

Fox Ashtray, 2872
Fox Head, 3024
Foxhound Calendar, 3188
Foxhounds Standing, 3385,
    3386
Fox Lying 3527
Fox Lying Straight, 2997,
    3570
Fox Sitting, 2993
Fox Tobacco Jar, 2925
French Marine Officer, 2629
French Soldier, 2582
Friday's Boy, 3261
Friday's Girl, 3523
The Frog, 3142
Funny Fish, 3493

Galloping Horses, 3466
Gamecock, 3562
Gentleman in Evening Dress
    with Cigar, 2632
Gentleman with Cloak and
    Opera Hat, 2633
George V, 3089, 3091
Giraffes, 2895
Girl and Rabbit, 2937
Girl Skipping Thro' Roses,
    3461
Girl with Beads, 3288
Girl with Kitten Powder
    Bowl, 3001
Goats, 3124, 3125
Goldcrest, 3338
Golden Retriever, 3230
Goldfinch, 3239
Goldfinch on Plinth, 3384
Goldfinch on Stump, 2667
Good Luck to your Fishing,
    3095
Goosey Goosey Gander, 3304
Grandmother's Dress, 3081
Grapes, 2799
Great Tit, 3335
Greece, 3069
Greek Figures on Plinths,
    2375-2380
Greyhounds, 2891
Guardsman, 2111

Hacking in the Park, 3296
Hamlet, 3448
Handyman, 2110

Happy Boy, 3010
Happy Days, 3435
Hare, 2892
Harlequin (first version),
    2680
Harlequin (second version),
    2868
Harlequin and Columbine
    Book-end, 2866
The Harpist, 2898
Heather, 3543
Hebe, 2101
Hedge Sparrow, 3333
Hen Party, 3501
Henry VIII, 2637
Hesitation, 3289
Highwayman, 3166
Historical Figures Series, see
    2634
'Hit!', 3105
Hog Hunting, 3164
Holland, 3074
Horseman Book-end, 2875
Hound, 2951
Hound and Fox Menu-holders,
    2953-2956
Hound Ashtray, 2873
Hound Head, 3025
Hound Lying, 3528
Hound Lying Straight, 2998,
    3571
Hound Sitting, 2994
Hound Tobacco Jar, 2926
Huntsman and Hounds, 3115
Hush, 2844

The Immaculate, 2625
Imperial Forces Soldier, 2106
Imperial Yeoman, 2107
India, 3071
Indian Brave, 2908
Indian Chief, 2907
Indian Squaw with Child on
    Back, 2909
Indian Squaw with Child on
    Shoulder, 2910
Infant Faun and Putto
    Powder Bowl, 2807
In The Ring, 3180
Invitation, 3698
Ireland, 3178
Irina, 3177
Isabella, 3538
Italy, 3067

January, 3452
Japan, 3072
Jay, 3248
Jay (American version), 3646
Jester (first version), 2213
Jester (second version), 3483
Jester Jug, 2856
Joan, 2915
Johnnie, 3433
Joy Ride, 3496
Jubilee Statuettes, 3089
Judy, 3489
July, 3440
June (first version), 2906
June (second version), 3456

Kate Greenaway Boy (first
    version), 2725
Kate Greenaway Boy (second
    version), 2727
Kate Greenaway Girl (first
    version), 2726
Kate Greenaway Girl (second
    version), 2728
Kate Greenaway Figures (new
    versions), 3809, 3810
Kids at Play, 3153
Kingfisher, 3235
Kingfisher on Stump, 2666
King George V, 3089, 3091
The Kiss, 3040
Kittens Group, 3141
Koala Bears, Zoo Babies,
    3273
Kookaburra, 2821-2823

Labrador Retriever, 3233
Ladies in Mob Caps, 2616
Lady and Gentleman on
    Rococo Bases, 2523
Lady Bountiful, 3097
Lady with Fan, 2911
Lady with Mask, 2650
Lady with Mirror, 2649
La Fleur, 3586
La Miroir, 3588
Large Dog Series, see 3425
Lavender, 2930
Leopards, Zoo Babies, 3263
Le Panier, 3585
The Letter, 3382
Lily, 2930

Linnets on Stump, 3365
Lion, 3100
Lion Book-end, 2876
Lions, Zoo Babies, 3264
Liserion, 3581
Little Boy Blue, 3306
Little Dancer, 2883
Little Dancer Powder Bowl,
    2938
Little Jack Horner, 3305
Little Miss Muffet, 3301
Little Rock Temple, 3504
L'Oiseau, 3587
The London Cries (first
    series), see 3227
The London Cries (second
    series), 3541-3543
'London Gazette Here' 3271
Long-haired Cat, 3615
The Longies, see 2898
Looking over Shoulder, bowl,
    3127
Lough Neagh Mary, 2920
Lucky Spider, 3492
The Lute Player, 2899

Mack, West Highland Terrier,
    3355
Mad as a Hatter or Mad as a
    March Hare, 3502
Magnolia Bud, 3144
Mandarin, 2568
March, 3454
Mare and Foal, 3170
Marguerite, 3582
Marigold, 2930
Marsh Tit, 3336
Mary, Queen, 3090, 3092
Mary Queen of Scots, 2634
Masquerade Boy, 3359
Masquerade Girl, 3360
Master Mariner, 3755
Maurice and Sonia, Tigers,
    3274
May, 3455
Mayflower, 3656
Maytime, 3123
Mephistopheles, 2850
Mermaid, 3161
'A Merry New Song', 3252
Michael, 2912
Mick and Mack, Bears, 3265
Military Figures Series, see
    2629 and 2675

Mischief, 2914
Mischief Powder Bowl, 2928
Miss Muffet, 3301
Mock Turtle, 3610
Monday's Boy, 3519
Monday's Girl, 3257
The Mongrel Pup, 2916
The Months of the Year
    Series, see 3416
The Mother, 2885
Mother and Two Children
    Group, 2615
Mother Machree, 2924
Motorist, 2489
Mouse, 2610
Mouse Ashtray, 2827, 2828
Mouse, Double, 2636
Mrs. Toby, 2841
Mr. Toby, 2831, 2832 and 2840
Music, 2391
My Favourite, 3014

Naiad, 3030
Natasha, 3176
The Necklace, 3288
Nelson and Norah, Leopards,
    3263
Nell Gwynne, 3006
Netsuke Animals, see 2604
Nightingale, 3337
Noel, 2905
November, 3418
Nude Bather Kneeling, 2698
Nude Bather Reclining on
    Plinth, 2690
Nude Bather, Seated on
    Plinth, 2697
Nude Boy, 3371
Nude Boys with Cornucopias
    (first version), 2704-2707
Nude Boy and Girl with
    Cornucopias
    (second version), 3373
Nude Boy with Dolphin, 2702
Nude Boy with Fruit, 2694
Nude Boy with Roses, 2717
Nude Boy with Seaweed,
    2703
Nude Child Seated on Plinth,
    2687
Nude Female Leaning on a
    Pedestal, 2688
Nude Females with Slippers,
    2689, 2693

Nude Girl, 3372
Nude Girls Seated with
    Roses, 2719, 2720
Nude Girls with Garlands,
    2715, 2716
Nude Girl with Roses, 2718
Nursery Rhymes Series,
    3301-3306
Nuthatch, 3334

October, 3417
The Old Goat Woman, 2886
Oliver and October, Lions,
    3264
One Circus Horse, 3684
Only Me, 3226
Over The Sticks, 3116

Paddy, 2857
Pansy, 2930
Parakeet, 3087
Parroquet on Stump, 2663
    (female), 2664 (male).
Paul, 3479
Peacock Menu Holder, 2537
Pekinese, Dog's Head, 3322
Pekinese Puppy Group, 3118
Pekinese Sitting, 3034
Pekinese Standing, 2941
Pelican Ashtray, 2893
Pelican Jug, 2853
Penguins, 3093, 3094
Peter Pan, 3011
Philip, 3557
Piccaninny, 3559
Pick-a-Back, 2887
Pied Woodpeckers on
    Stump, 3363
Pierrot (first version), 2682
Pierrot (second version),
    2869
Pierrot Book-end, 2867
Pierrot Group, 3202
Pierrot Puff Bowl, 3126
Pierrot with Ruff and
    Companion, 2393
Pigeons, Wings Crossed,
    3421, 3422
The Planter's Daughter, 3138
Playmates, 3270
Playtime Series, see 3747
Pointer, 3229

Polar Bear Ashtrays, 3184,
    3185
Polar Bear Eating, 3062
Polar Bear Looking Up, 3063
Polar Bears, Sam and
    Barbara, 2900
Polly Put the Kettle On, 3303
Polo Player, 3163
Poodle, Champion Spriggan
    Bell, 3085
Poupée, 3754
The Powdering Mask, 3140
Priscilla, 3480
Psyche, 2102
Punch, 3488
Puppy, 3133

The Queen in the Parlour,
    3193
Queen Mary, 3090, 3092
The Queen's Beasts, 3503
Quail, 2623

Rabbit, 2607
Rabbit Flower Holder, 2514
Rabbit Herald, 3078
Rabbit Wilfred, 2842
Raleigh, Sir Walter, 2668
Ram, 2613
Ranter, Standing Hound,
    3356
Rats, Cairn Terrier, 3350
Recollections, 3139
Red Hind, 3572
Red Indian Series, 2907-2910
Red Ribbons, 3699
Red Riding Hood, 3510
Regency Figures, 3414, 3415
Repose, 3272
The Rescue, 3346
'Ripe Speragus' 3250
Robin, 3197
Robin (American version),
    3647
Romeo and Juliet, 3449
Rose (first version), 2930
Rose (second version), 3541
Rose Maiden, 3224
Roses, 2798
Royal Artillery Officer,
    2658

St. Joseph, 2626
Salmon, 3031
Salvage, 3370
Sam and Barbara, Polar
    Bears, 2900
Saturday's Boy, 3524
Saturday's Girl, 3262
Sauce, 2881
Scotland, 3104
Scots Guards Officer, 3677
Scottie Cigarette Box, 3162
Scottie, Dog's Head, 3319
Scottie Terrier, 2946, 3029
Sea Breeze, 3008
Seaforth Highlander Officer,
    2657
Seal, 3013
Sealyham, 2932, 2934, 3028
Sealyham Cigarette Box,
    3119
The Seamstress, 3569
Sea Scout, 3491
Seasons, The Four,
    3339-3342
Seated Nude Boy with
    Flowers, 2684
Seated Nude Girl with
    Flowers, 2683
Seated Nude with Leaves,
    2801
Sea Urchin, 2917
Seaweed, 3353
September, 3457
Sergeant-Major Fish, 3575
Setter, 3228, 3463
Setter on Plinth, 2871
Setter without Plinth, 2952
Sheep, 3155
Shepherdess, 2214
Sheriff, 3757
Short-haired Cat, 3616
Shuttlecock, 3472
Siamese Cat, 3714
Siamese Dancer, 3474
Siamese Dancer, (small),
    3551
Sir Walter Raleigh, 2668
Sister, 3149
Sitting Child, 3380
Sleeping Baby, 3009
Sleeping Doe, 2874
Sleepy Boy, 2918
Slow Coach, 3495
Small American Bird Series,
    3645-3650

Small British Bird Series,
    see 3197
Small Dogs Series, see 2941
Snail, 2605
Snake, 2608
Snowy, 3457
Soldier of the Black Watch,
    2109
Soldier of the Imperial
    Forces, 2106
Soldiers of the Worcestershire
    Regiment, 2591, 3535
Song, 2391
The Song, 2902
Southwind, 3388
Spade Fish, 3579
Spain, 3070
Spaniel, Dog's Head, 3321
Spaniel Puppy Group, 3130
Spaniel Puppy, Tony, 3361
Spanish Beauty, 3654
Spanish Lady, 2936
Sparrow, 3236
Spitfire, 3352
Sporting Dogs Series,
    see 3228
Spring (first version), 3012
Spring (second version),
    3342
Spring, Bust, 3247
Spring Morning, 3546
Squirrel Jug, 2854
Standing Nude Boy with
    Flowers, 2685
Standing Nude Girl with
    Flowers, 2686
Stowaways, 3369
Summer, 3339
Summer Day, 3547
Summer House on the Hill,
    3505
The Summit, 3143
Sunday's Boy, 3256
Sunday's Girl, 3518
Sunshine, 3083
Surprise, 3655
Sweet Anne, 3630
Sweet Nell of Old Drury,
    3006

Taffy, Welsh Corgi, 3366
Take Cover, 3351
Tamara, 3172
Tangles, 2919

Tatiana, 3173
Terrier on Plinth, 2870
Terrier Powder Bowl, 2927
Terrier Sitting, 2942
Terriers Standing, 3026, 3027
Territorial Soldier, 2588
The Thief, 3145
Thrush, 3234
Thursday's Boy, 3260
Thursday's Girl, 3522
Tigers, Couchant, (first
    version), 2780
Tiger (second version), 3101
Tiger (third version), 3121
Tigers, Zoo Babies, 3274
Toad, 2624
Toby, Mrs., 2841
Toby, Mr., 2831, 2832 and 2840
Toby, Paddy, 2857
Tommy, 2913
Tony, Sitting Spaniel Puppy,
    3361
Tortoise, 2604
Toto, Cairn Terrier, 3331
Treasure Trove, 3748
Tropical Fish Series,
    see 3572
Trout, 3032
Tuesday's Boy, 3534
Tuesday's Girl, 3258
Two Babies, 3150
Two's Company, Three's
    None, 3499

Victorian Musicians,
    see 2898
Violets, 3542
Vivandière, 2724

Wales, 3103
Wandering Minstrels, 2161,
    2162
Wartime Series, see 3346
Water Baby, 3151
Watteau Figures, 3402-3405
Waxwing, 3648
Wednesday's Boy, 3521
Wednesday's Girl, 3259
Wednesday's Girl (new
    version), 3638
Weighed Out, 2388
Welsh Corgi, 3243
Welsh Corgi, Taffy, 3366

Western Tanager, 3650
West Highland Terrier, Mack,
    3355
Westwind, 3396
White Boy, 3558
White Rabbit, 3611
Wild Horses, 3466
Wilfred, 2842
Will You, Won't You?, 3720
Wind, 2617
The Winner, 3671
The Winner, with Stable Boy,
    3667
Winter, 3340
Wire-haired Terrier, 2942
Wire-Haired Terrier,
    Standing, 3026
Wise as an Owl, 3500
Witch, 2543
Wolf, 3511
Woodland Dance, 3076
Woodpecker, 3249
Wood Warbler, 3200
Worcestershire Regiment
    Soldiers, 2591, 3535
Wren, 3198

Yellow Grunt Fish, 3576
Yellow Hammers on Stump,
    3377
Yonder He Goes, 3167
Young England, 3747
Young Entry, 3169
Young Farmer, 3433
Young Foxes, 3131
Young Foxhounds, 3132
Young Horse, 2877
Young Huntsmen, 2734, 2735
Young Spotted Deer, 3266,
    3529

Zoo Babies, see 3263

Chapter One
A History of Royal Worcester Figures up to 1900

From earliest times man has used clay to make images of gods, animals and buildings. Ceramic figure-making has risen and fallen with civilizations: the Greeks were famed for their terracotta, the T'ang dynasty in China is synonymous with powerful models of horses and soldiers, and in Mexico and Peru finely-modelled portrait vessels showed tremendous skill used by primitive potters. Most of these fine achievements were for religious use or were buried in tombs, and it was not really until the eighteeenth century, with the development of porcelain, that figures were made purely for ornament in the home.

The Meissen factory in Germany must be credited with inventing the modern porcelain figure. J.J. Kändler's harlequins, shepherds and shepherdesses, orientals, and crinoline ladies were in great demand, and factories across Europe strove to compete. Elsewhere in Germany, Franz Anton Bustelli at Nymphenburg mastered the rococo style. In Italy and England, Giuseppi Gricci at Capo di Monte and Joseph Willems at Chelsea made important contributions using soft-paste porcelain bodies. By the 1750s figures were being made in England at Chelsea, Derby, Bow and Longton Hall, all heavily influenced by Meissen.

The Worcester Porcelain Company, founded in 1751 by Dr John Wall and a group of businessmen, had a considerable advantage over its rivals. Its teapots did not crack nor craze when hot water was poured into them, a problem which seriously affected the other English factories. This gave Worcester a virtual monopoly in the making of useful wares, and they concentrated on fine tea services, avoiding almost totally the figure market. From the factory's first fifty years less than ten different figure models are known, none of which can be numbered amongst its finest products.

Worcester had taken over Benjamin Lund's short-lived soft-paste factory at Bristol, and it was at Bristol in 1750 that the earliest figure was made. A standing Chinaman in white glazed porcelain, imitating the 'blanc de chine' imported from China, it seems crude and primitive, reflecting a factory in its infancy, but has considerable charm.

The earliest figure which we know to have been made at Worcester itself is 'Cupid at Vulcan's Forge', a somewhat clumsy model on a misshapen rectangular base. Made about 1757, it is a poor relation of Chelsea figures of the same period. The figures made in the 1760s all have a family likeness and are probably the work of a single modeller, John Toulouse, who occasionally marked his moulds 'T', 'TO'

Fig. 1. A figure of a Turkish lady, c. 1765, richly decorated with gold highlights. (Private Collection, formerly Geoffrey Godden)

or 'IT'. Pairs of Sportsmen, Gardeners and Turks are reminiscent of Bow, but in spite of good-quality colouring, they somehow lack sophistication (for the Turks see Fig 1). The most successful is a group of two canaries in the branches of a tree with flowering apple blossom, clearly copying Derby or Bow, but again not quite getting there. The figures were an attempt by the factory to compete in the London market, but it really should have stuck to useful wares, as in no way are they a credit to Worcester.

Sometime in the 1770s, John Toulouse moved to Bristol, where he modelled for Richard Champion's hard-paste factory. He also spent some time at Caughley in Shropshire before he turned up again at Worcester in the 1790s working for the Chamberlain manufactory. The Chamberlain family had left the main Worcester factory and set up their own rival establishment, again producing mainly teawares with a certain number of rich ornamental pieces. Geoffrey Godden has shown that 'Old Toulouse' modelled, in his usual style, a figure of Apollo with his lyre, and a pair of kingfishers. These were supplied in white, or with simple colouring and gilding, and were sometimes mounted on shell centrepieces for holding sweetmeats (fig. 2), or with a clock case behind. These crude models could in no way compete with contemporary Derby figures and consequently very few were made.

It was not until about 1815 that Chamberlains produced figures whose quality could rival that of their contemporaries. Their unglazed white biscuit models, such as 'Cupid in a Chair', or cottage-shaped pastille burners, show the fine modelling of which they were capable. Their most successful figures were a series of portraits of stage personalities of the day. Madame Vestris is modelled in her role as a broom seller, probably based on an engraved music sheet. When the Rainer family from the Tyrol toured England in 1826 with their song and dance act, they took the country by storm. Chamberlains were quick to seize the opportunity and from a published engraving they produced a set of five figures of the singers in their colourful costumes ornamented with the regalia presented to them by King George IV. Not only were these the first commemorative figures made at Worcester, they were also the first figurines that formed a set.

To our knowledge, the main Worcester factory, under the direction of the Flight and Barr families, produced only one figure of a classical lady, this being made in biscuit porcelain. While finely detailed, the figure is an uncomfortable model and deserves to have been a failure. Thomas

Fig. 2. Early Chamberlain Worcester figure of Apollo mounted on a shell sweetmeat stand, modelled by John Toulouse, c. 1795. 9in. high. (Geoffrey Godden Collection)

Fig. 3. A Chamberlain Worcester figure of a schoolgirl, c. 1825. The fine quality of the decoration raises this above the contemporary Staffordshire figure. (Geoffrey Godden Collection)

Baxter is known to have modelled horses as handles for Flight vases, and it is not inconceivable that he modelled the classical lady figure, though there is no evidence to support this.

Meanwhile the Chamberlains and the third great factory in Worcester, Graingers, made a wide range of animal models. Small studies of dogs, cats, deer and rabbits, mounted on simple mound bases or on tasselled cushions, were produced as cheap 'toys' or novelties. Lacking in fine detail, these animal models possess a primitive charm and are consequently very collectable today. Graingers used their white biscuit porcelain to make a number of figures in the 1830s and 1840s. Single figures of ladies with somewhat exotic titles such as 'Haide' and 'Persephone' are curious but not great works of art. They were expensive to produce and did not sell well, so now are among the rarest figures of all. Graingers' best work was on a smaller scale. A fine figure of a baby in a crib was made to commemorate the birth of the Princess Royal in 1840, the factory's first royal portrait commemorative. Two groups of putti building an arbour and encrusting a gothic arch with flowers allowed the factory to combine moulded figures with hand-made flowers of the highest quality. These were the most successful Worcester figures to date, but were very expensive to produce and led to Graingers abandoning figure production.

The 1840s found porcelain-making in Worcester at a low ebb. The Flight and Chamberlain factories were forced to merge in 1840, and the new company lacked drive or initiative. At the Great Exhibition in 1851 factories such as Minton were able to show superb figures in the new parian body, but Worcester could exhibit nothing to compete with these. In 1852 W. H. Kerr and R. W. Binns bought the ailing factory and realized that they had to breathe new life into the works.

They made two important contributions to figure-making at Worcester. Firstly they introduced a fine parian body. Parian, a durable material with a high felspar content, was capable of very detailed modelling and did not need to be glazed to be kept clean. When it was glazed, it had a warm creamy look and could be enamelled and gilded very successfully. Parian was used for virtually all Worcester figures up until the 1920s. Secondly, Binns realized the importance of the modeller. Previously, Worcester had used its own factory modellers for anything that was needed. A trained sculptor, however, could produce an original model of a much higher standard, and Binns brought to the factory

4

William Boyton Kirk, the son of a Dublin sculptor and a very talented modeller himself, who had built up a high reputation in London. Kirk was commissioned to produce a series of twelve figures and groups of characters from Shakespeare's *A Midsummer Night's Dream*, to form part of one service for display at the Dublin Exhibition in 1853. Produced in the unglazed parian, Binns' designs and Kirk's finely detailed modelling caused a sensation and set the course of the factory over the next thirty years. (see fig. 4).

Fig. 4. A centrepiece from the Shakespeare Service by William Boyton Kirk, 1853. The unglazed parian body is ideally suited for Kirk's delicate modelling. (Dyson Perrins Museum)

W. B. Kirk, E. J. Jones and Charles Toft were the factory's principal modellers during its revival in the 1850s and 1860s. Their work followed the popular styles of the day with classical subjects and draped and veiled female forms predominant. Busts of royalty and eminent personages were the speciality of Jones, his study of the Prince of Wales being a particularly fine portrait. The display put on by Worcester in the 1862 London Exhibition was highly commendable and alongside the parian was displayed 'Ivory Porcelain', the creamy glazed parian painted in soft enamel colours in the style of Doccia and Naples porcelains from Italy, known at the time as 'Capo di Monte'. The factory called this finish 'Raphaelesque' as a selling point, and the numerous small figures and groups which were made in this style particularly those of chubby-faced putti, were highly regarded both then and now. The major contributor of models from about 1870 was James Hadley, whose skill and understanding of the material made him the most important person in the field of porcelain figure modelling in the last quarter of the nineteenth century.

It is not known exactly when James Hadley joined the Worcester factory, but by 1875 he was invaluable to it. Although he left the works in 1875 to work freelance, it seems that Mr. Binns bought every model he produced. He was capable of almost anything and, as well as producing figures and groups in any size required, made relief-moulded plaques and a great many vase shapes. He was able to work in any style: classical or Middle Eastern, rococo, or Japanese, Hadley was able to master them all, and over a period of thirty years his output of designs and models was staggering.

Mr. Binns knew how important it was to keep up to date with the latest changes in fashion and taste. The classical forms of the 1860s were 'old-hat' a decade later. Raphaelesque gave way to Japanesque, and following the first displays of Japanese art in Europe in 1862 and 1867, Binns bought a vast collection of Eastern ceramics, eventually numbering some thousands of pieces. These he displayed in his own museum and they inspired James Hadley to emulate them. The public did not want direct copies. They had their own romantic idea of what Japan was like and the figures they asked for were more akin to Gilbert and Sullivan's comic opera '*Mikado*' than to true Japanese art. So successful were these Japanesque wares that eventually even the Japanese copied them to sell to Europeans. Hadley's masterpiece is his pair of figures of a Japanese lady and gentleman, both standing by a carved table supporting a vase. They look magnificent whether stained all over to imitate ivory or bronze, or fully decorated in a mixture of ivory and metallic tones. James Callowhill, a great all-round decorator and a particularly fine portrait painter, was responsible for colouring this pair, and the Japanese faces are so accurate that is hard to believe such pieces are the product of the Worcester factory, as far removed from Japan as it is possible to be.

Public taste changes fast and Japanesque was becoming old-fashioned itself by the 1880s. The Aesthetic movement led by Oscar Wilde and his contemporaries

Fig.5. Two figures from the series of Down and Out London characters modelled by James Hadley, intended to be used as menu-holders holding sandwich boards, 5½ in., c. 1880. (Sothebys)

became all the rage. Hadley produced to Binns' design a teapot in the form of an Aesthetic man and woman, inspired by the opening production of Gilbert and Sullivan's *Patience* in 1881. While short-lived, the style developed into the romantic imagery of smartly dressed children made famous by the drawings of Kate Greenaway and others. It was in this 'Kate

Greenaway' style that James Hadley felt most at home. During the 1880s he produced probably his best work, humorous studies of boys and girls, prim and proper and often mischievous, their curly hair peeking from below smart bonnets and boaters. He modelled single figures and elaborate groups, often fitted up as candle-sticks or lamp bases, or gathered round a basket to form a table centrepiece. His models of 'Smile' and 'Frown,' inspired by the writings of Goldsmith and depicting two schoolboys seated on a bench, are superb studies in miniature. Modelled in 1887 and only 4in. high, the charm and quality of these groups sum up the work of James Hadley. (see fig. 16).

Probably the best known of all James Hadley's work are his Middle Eastern subjects, the pairs of Water Carriers and figures in tribal costumes, such as the Bringaree Indians. Mostly introduced in the 1880s and often made in several different sizes, they proved to be tremendously popular and some were still in production in the 1920s and 1930s. (see fig. 8). The fascination that distant places had for the Victorians is evident in the popularity of the set of figures of the Countries of the World. Conceived as a set, the twelve figures are all of similar size, and on identical bases. (see fig. 7). In 1881 Hadley modelled figures of an Irishman, a Yankee, a Chinese, an Hindoo, an Italian and a Negro, and later the same year a figure of 'John Bull' was issued to represent England. The following year a Scotsman and a Russian were added to the series. Ireland and Wales were not represented until fifteen years later, when figures of an Irish girl and a Welsh man and girl were modelled, these last possibly not the work of Hadley, though closely following his style. The figures were not sold as a set but could be bought individually, and some sold better than others. The Irish man and girl were the most popular, followed by the Welshman and the Yankee. John Bull was, surprisingly, less popular, but the figure looks down, always a bad selling-point. The Russian and

Fig. 6. Smile and Frown: two groups of Goldsmith's Schoolboys modelled by James Hadley, c.1890. Only 4in. high, these represent James Hadley at his very best. (Sothebys)

Fig. 7. John Bull and Paddy: figures representing England and Ireland from the Countries of the World series modelled by James Hadley. Date codes for 1892. (Sothebys)

Hindoo proved to be very unpopular and are rarely seen today. Like all of James Hadley's figures, the Countries of the World were issued in a variety of different colour schemes, depending on the taste and pocket of the purchaser. Some were left just in white glazed parian, usually because of some fault in the firing. The cheapest decoration was all-over 'old ivory' and this was sometimes heightened with gold. Others were decorated in 'blush ivory', a richer-shaded matt effect in apricot and ivory tones. 'Shot enamels' were used to strengthen further the shading with bronze and coral tones and more shaded gold. Some figures were issued with naturalistically-painted faces and hands, the costumes being left just white with details picked out in gold. Only rarely were fully naturalistic colours used for the faces and costumes. Later, in the 1910s and 1920s, new effects such as under-glaze powder-blue were used in conjunc-

Fig. 8. A pair of figures of Eastern tribesmen modelled by James Hadley, decorated in ivory and 'shot silk', 13in. high. date codes for 1890. (Phillips in Edinburgh)

tion with 'blush ivory', and occasionally in the 1930s Hadley models were revived in the full bright colours of the period, often looking totally out of place on a Victorian model.

James Hadley's links with Royal Worcester were severed in 1896 when he established his own factory in Worcester, producing a distinctive style of vases and a certain number of figures and moulded plaques, often in earthenware and strongly coloured clays. His departure left the factory's figure-making department without real drive, and few exciting new figures were issued in the late 1890s. Hadley's pupil Charles Noke had left Worcester in 1889 to join Doultons, where he built up a rival figure-making department using ivory colouring, and it is ironic that he was to be responsible for introducing at Doultons so many series in heavy competition to Worcester figures. The first new series Worcester produced in 1900 will be discussed in the next chapter.

One final nineteenth-century concept, the effect of which continued well into this century, is the idea of small figurines used to douse the flame of a candle. The hollow-based single figures called candle extinguishers start in the eighteenth century when crude Staffordshire models of ladies in long open skirts were made in salt-glazed stoneware and cream-coloured earthenware. By the 1830s and 1840s extinguishers were being made at Meissen and were copied in England by Minton and other smaller Staffordshire factories. At Worcester, during the 1850s, Kerr and Binns moved into the production of candle extinguishers in a big way. They proved very popular and some have continued to be made to this day. They were not made as one great set and most were single models, although there are some which form pairs or small series, such as the three characters from John Habberton's book *Helen's Babies*, children dressed in adult clothes far too big for them. Some of the models are clearly the work of James Hadley, for example the figures of Town Girl and Country Girl in the 'Kate Greenaway' style. Many are humorous and depict popular characters from books or the stage. Jenny Lind, the singer known as the 'Swedish Nightingale', was caricatured as a pair of models with birds' heads, 'Confidence' and 'Diffidence'.

Mr Caudle, a popular humorous character from Victorian literature, was modelled with his night cap pulled over his ears to shut out his wife's nagging tongue, a scene familiar to many people and a popular ornament to keep beside one's bed. Some of the extinguishers, such as Mr and Mrs Caudle, the French Cook and Granny Snow, proved tremendously popular and continued to be made well into the twentieth century. Two models, those of a monk and a nun, are still being made today, more than 120 years after their introduction, and a number of Victorian models were reintroduced in the 1970s, again proving to be very popular. But just as some extinguishers are very common, others are exceedingly rare and consequently very much sought-after today. Mr Punch and his dog Toby are surprising rarities, considering how popular the characters were in Victorian England. The sensational criminal trial of the Tichborne claimant captured the public's imagination. Arthur Orton, an Australian butcher, claimed to be the long-lost heir to the Tichborne fortune. Orton was modelled as a candle extinguisher and sits on a butcher's block. The lawyer, Coleridge, is also modelled as an extinguisher and fits over the top of Orton, thus extinguishing his claim to the fortune. It is a subtle piece of humour and the quality of the modelling shows it was aimed at an educated market.

Only four new candle extinguishers were introduced after 1900. In 1909 was issued the rarest extinguisher of all, Motorist (shape number 2489), a model of a lady dressed in a long coat and goggles for a drive around the Edwardian countryside. We only know of one original of this model surviving, although one would think it would have appealed in its day. Hush (2844), issued in 1927 is another surprising rarity, while Witch (2543) and Mandarin (2568), introduced in 1912 and 1914 respectively, proved to be popular and are consequently more common. Candle extinguishers offer a great scope for collecting. If you cannot afford the high prices which the rare extinguishers now command, you should look for the better-painted early examples of the more common models, perhaps collecting a model such as French Cook in as many different colourings as you can. So popular has the collecting of extinguishers now become that in recent years Royal Worcester has reintroduced a number of the Victorian models, including some of the rarities.

Chapter Two
Twentieth-Century Royal Worcester Figures

1900-1930

The spread and appreciation of the Art Nouveau style, which first gained prominence at the Paris Exhibition in 1900, encouraged artists throughout Europe to try out new forms of expression. In England the craftsman potter was experimenting with new styles of modelling and decoration. As the Art Pottery movement grew rapidly in strength the exciting new designs attracted the interest of the art-buying public. Ceramic figures were becoming more stylized, concentrating on simplicity of form and losing the Victorian extravagance and concentration on detail.

Worcester, however, was very slow to adapt to the changing fashions following the passing of R. W. Binns, whose death on 28th December 1900 was undoubtedly a considerable blow to the factory, and the end of a great era. Binns had always kept abreast of the latest fashion trends and had been quick to copy ideas which had brought success to rival manufactories world-wide. The departure of James Hadley in 1895 could have heralded the way for a complete change in style but, with only a few exceptions, the new figures introduced prior to the First World War were so heavily influenced by Hadley that they could easily have been his own. Perhaps this is not altogether surprising, as the remaining modellers, principally George Evans and his sons Ernest and Sydney, had been either directly trained by or had worked alongside Hadley.

At the 1904 St. Louis Exhibition, Worcester offered nothing new, quite content to show the Hadley figures which had brought them success for so many years; in fact, from 1900 to 1910, an average of only three or four new figures were introduced each year. We do see a hint of a break in style with a model of a Jester (2213) introduced in 1902 and a pair of Pierrots (2393) from 1905, the year which saw the greatest number of new figures. A set of Greek figures (2375-2380) do reflect a feeling of Art Nouveau, but were placed on Japanesque bases of thirty years earlier, quite spoiling the effect. There seems to have been a great reluctance by the factory to try something totally new. Worcester's customers were probably not yet ready to accept the Pierrot figures, and in 1908, at the Franco-British Exhibition in Shepherds Bush, the Worcester stand featured Thomas Brock's 'Bather Surprised', modelled in 1875, and many figures by James Hadley.

Perhaps the most interesting of the figures from the first ten years of the twentieth century were the six Boer War soldiers of 1900 (2106-2111), rather stiff in design but very finely modelled. Although not models of great beauty they reflect the patriotism then sweeping through the country. Expensive to produce, they were aimed at the wealthy families of the day, who would have taken great national pride in displaying these fine figures in their lavish homes. The Boer War soldiers sold relatively well, although it is interesting to note that the least-often seen of the six today is the Handyman (2110), which is undoubtedly the best model of the series, not being as stiff and formal as the others and more of an attempt to depict a life-like ordinary soldier.

Remembering the Boer War series, the Company brought out a group of three First World War soldiers in 1914 and 1915 (2582, 2588 and 2591). These were still in the Victorian style, very stiff with expressionless faces, and, not surprisingly, nobody wanted to buy them. This seems, at last, to have brought home the realization that the old-fashioned figure style could not merely be updated but must be completely changed. The following year saw the introduction of two further First World War soldiers (2645 and 2646), modelled by William Pointon, and it is refreshing to see that the stiff, formal figure has at last been dropped and a genuine attempt made to produce a life-like study. One soldier sits lighting a cigarette whilst the other stands, his kit-bag under his arm.

An unusual flower-holder in the form of a rabbit (2514) had been introduced in 1911 along with a ring-stand modelled as a duck (2517). At about the same time a tiny tortoise, modelled by George Evans in 1878 as part of the base of a birdcage, was tried as a separate model and sold in great numbers. This did not have a shape number, having formed only a small part of the earlier model. Its success encouraged Worcester to bring out a series of small animal, bird and fish studies (2604-2613, 2622-24 and 2636) based on Japanese Netsuke and other ivory carvings. The Worcester models resemble so closely the Japanese originals that the moulds may even have been cast directly from them.

Like Netsuke, the charming little studies were delightful to pick up and hold and here lay their popularity. The most natural decoration was Worcester's 'Old Ivory', exactly imitating the originals. Numerous other colourings were used, including attempts to imitate jade and hardstones. Perhaps the Snail (2605) and the Snake (2608) were destined to be unpopular with the public, whilst the Cow (2609) and Fish (2611) were awkward to produce and, it must he said, rather ugly. Fairly popular were the Ape (2612) and Ram (2613), but undoubtedly the best sellers of all were the Rabbit (2607) and Mouse (2610), both remaining in production until the 1950s. To the collector this series has long been very desirable and, as so often happens, the unpopularity of some of the creatures at the time of their introduction has resulted in great scarcity of these same models today, and causes considerable frustration to the collector.

During the First World War the Board of Trade encouraged British manufacturers to produce crafts which would compete with products previously imported from Germany. The Worcester factory wanted to show that Britain was perfectly capable of making delicate porcelain figurines and they introduced in 1916 a small group of figures in the style of traditional German crinolines. Two figures of ladies (2620 and 2621), probably designed for use as bells, accompanied two gentlemen in evening dress (2632 and 2633), and in a similar style were two rather pretty groups of ladies with children (2615 and 2616). This series of figures was a commercial failure, although three other series introduced at the same time, again to compete with German products, were not only immediately popular but continued to be so for many years to come.

The Regimental and Historical series were an indication of the very fine standards of modelling that were once again to provide great recognition for the Worcester factory. Both were quite heavily influenced by Continental models, as several German factories had been making historical and military figures. Worcester felt that they had the ability and craftsmanship to produce much finer figures than their Continental contemporaries and, even though they might now be considered stiff and formal, the figures were a complete breakaway from the tradition of James Hadley, not least in the fact that they were painted naturalistically and in bright colours. The Regimental Series was probably aimed almost totally at the individual units represented, who would perhaps buy them for presentation to a member on retirement, or display them proudly in a showcase. The modeller was Fred Gertner, who had joined the factory only a year earlier in 1915, quite possibly being brought in initially to design these two major sets. The Historical models, commencing with Mary Queen of Scots (2634), had the general appeal which the Regimental Officers lacked and, despite being on the expensive side, were to sell very well. Earlier examples are not often seen now and are well worth looking for.

In 1917 Gertner modelled a series of birds on stumps (2662-2667) which were intended to be made in the cheaper 'Crownware' body. Crownware was a high-fired earthenware introduced at about this time and required figures that were simple to produce without detailed modelling. The birds were again made to replace the German porcelain bird models which had enjoyed enormous popularity in England and were no longer imported because of the war. Designed also for Crownware was a range of small nude figures of girls and boys produced between 1917 and 1919 which were, once again, almost exact copies of Continental originals produced a little earlier. They were probably conceived to be arranged in groups as table ornaments, or placed in the centre of bowls surrounded by floating flower petals. It is quite likely that Gertner was responsible for these figures, which, with the possible exception of the larger female nudes, did not prove popular. To some extent the unpopularity of the Crownware body may have been to blame for the failure of the

figures, although one or two were also made in glazed parian. Worcester unwisely decided to return once again to the Hadley style, a range of figures (2723-2728 and 2732-2735) being either slightly adapted versions of James Hadley's original models or new figures imitating the Hadley style. F. Clemencin, a freelance French modeller, was asked to produce four figures (2798-2801) but it was now quite clear that the public was no longer interested in the outdated style and demanded something new.

The necessary inspiration, however, seemed to be missing at Worcester and some of the existing shapes were tried in new forms in an attempt to sell them. The popular Mouse appeared on a pair of ashtrays (2827 and 2828) and a Kookaburra, presumably aimed at the Australian market, was placed not only on a pair of ashtrays (2822 and 2823) but also on the cover of a powder bowl (2821). Also finding their way on to powder bowl covers were some of the nude girls that had proved less than successful as figures and were now tried as useful items, again with limited popularity.

A range of Toby jugs was produced in the late 1920s and had a mixed reception. Traditional Tobies (2831-2832, 2840 and 2841) sold very well in small and miniature sizes, but the larger versions, and some novel jugs such as Mephistopheles (2850) and Jester (2856), failed miserably. Possibly this was because the public expected Toby jugs to be made in thick Staffordshire pottery and considered fine porcelain unsuitable. Another range of small jugs was formed as animals and birds and could also be purchased as salt and pepper pots. Cheap and simple to produce, as well as being charming and humorous, these delightful models were, sadly, unable to breathe new life into the Worcester factory, which had for some years been going through a severe financial crisis. Mr C. W. Dyson Perrins, who had injected a considerable amount of money into the Company during the 1920s, was advised in 1927 that a receiver should be appointed, but continued with his generosity to keep the factory going until the receivers did eventually move in on 24th July 1930. The works were shut on the following day.

The 1930s

The closure of the factory was a devastating blow to the men and women who had devoted all their working lives to the china industry. It was not uncommon to find several generations of a Worcester family continuing the tradition in a city where fine porcelain had been manufactured since the middle of the eighteenth century. As was the case in the Potteries in Staffordshire, where factories were equally badly hit by the recession, there were few other industries in Worcester. The prospects for the Worcester workers looked hopeless.

One can imagine the great relief felt by the workforce when the factory was reopened on 12th August 1930 under the guidance of Joseph Gimson, who was appointed Works Manager two days later and subsequently promoted to Managing Director. Production slowly restarted, and Mr Gimson began a major review of output, making significant changes in direction in an attempt to steer the factory through the difficult period. Crownware and earthenware bodies were withdrawn, to be replaced by revolutionary high-fired porcelains. Ornamental products were considerably behind those of Worcester's competitors in variety and quality of design, and it was in this area that the greatest changes were to be made.

In the nineteenth century many artists had worked alongside industry in the creation of manufactured works of art, but with William Morris came a new attitude towards mass production which caused artists to shun the factories and work on their own in small workshops producing hand-made objects for those who could afford them. During the 1920s a number of independent modellers, particularly in the artistic Chelsea area, were producing ceramic figures, fired, painted and glazed by themselves. Some of these potters were no longer hostile to factory-produced

goods and Doulton, ever the leader in commercial art, commissioned wares from artists such as Charles Vyse and Phoebe Stabler. Meanwhile Doulton's factory modellers had been keeping up with the times and were very much influenced by some of the figures on sale by the independent potters in London. Doulton was producing a wide range of different figures and selling them. Worcester, in Mr Gimson's eyes, had a lot of catching up to do. Dramatic changes were needed and by the end of 1932 some ninety new figures had been introduced with dozens of earlier figures reintroduced in new and up-to-date colourings.

Realising that the factory's own modellers lacked inspiration, Joseph Gimson naturally looked towards London for his new figure models. Having made the acquaintance of a group of young, mainly female, sculptors at the many cocktail parties which formed part of the London social scene, Joseph Gimson asked them to show him examples of their work with a view to breathing new life into the traditional Worcester figurine. Those employed ranged from unknown artists, often quite new to the ceramic medium, to fully established modellers who had already made a name for themselves either in their own workshops or by modelling for other factories.

Rather than put all his eggs in one basket, Mr Gimson decided that he would be best served by experimenting with the new styles while at the same time retaining a degree of safety across the range of productions. He realized that the best way to discover what the public wanted to buy was to offer them as wide a range of different models and styles as possible. Figures which proved popular were to stay in production for many years to come, and he was quick to discontinue any model which did not sell in sufficient numbers.

The Beaux Arts Gallery in London was a showcase for the new styles of ceramic art. Run by Jules Lessore, son of Emile and a member of a leading family of ceramic artists, the gallery was happy to launch

Worcester's new styles. In 1931 an exhibition was mounted giving the public their first view of the new look Worcester figures. It was 'make-or-break' time for Joseph Gimson, and thankfully the response was encouraging enough to show that the factory was on the right track.

The historical and military figures of Fred Gertner were, of course, much to the fore, but virtually everything else was new. The models included the work of the young Doris Lindner, who was to prove to be one of the most successful Worcester modellers of the twentieth century. Mr Gimson had seen her work on sale at Heal's department store and had been particularly struck by the distintictive Harlequins and Pierrots, designed as book-ends, made by Miss Lindner in brightly painted plaster. Her dancing girls (3086 and 3088), although somewhat stiff in design by modern standards, displayed her ability to capture movement in a subject.

The models of Ethelwyn Baker and Eric Aumonier were as far removed from the accepted Worcester figure of the past as it was possible to conceive. Miss Baker's Victorian Musicians (2898-2899, 2901 and 2902), known by the paintresses as the 'Longies' for the long thin shape of their faces and bodies, were presented alongside the same modeller's book-ends formed as the polar bears Sam and Barbara (2900). If these models seemed strange in the eyes of the public, then the work of Eric Aumonier must have seemed even more so. His very stylized animal studies (2874-2877) were a source of great amusement to the paintresses at the factory, who gave them rather impolite nicknames and could not understand them at all. They must surely be considered the strangest figures ever to have been made by Worcester, and now rank among the rarest.

Less of a gamble were the models of Phoebe Stabler who, together with her husband Harold, had worked independently in London and was connected with the Poole pottery of Carter, Stabler and Adams. Because of her links with Poole,

Phoebe seems to have been reluctant to give the factory anything totally new. The figures she provided were similar to models already made elsewhere and may have been lying around in her workshop when Mr Gimson paid a visit. Flower Girl (2880) and The Old Goat Woman (2886) had both been marketed by Doulton as early as 1913 under the names 'Lavender Woman' and 'Milking time'. Worcester enjoyed a certain success with Miss Stabler's models but did not commission any further work from her.

Stella Crofts had gained a reputation in London for animal studies in glazed pottery made and fired in her own kiln. Worcester produced seven of her models in porcelain, the most impressive being a fine study of Giraffes (2895). The models were really more suited for glazed Art Pottery and did not work well in porcelain, even though the quality of modelling and painting was particularly high. Bluebeard and Fatima (2903 and 2904) were elaborate and rather striking figures modelled by Sybil Williams and Jessamine Bray, but were costly to produce and the modellers enjoyed far more success with their much simpler and charming pair of Noel and June (2905 and 2906), produced in two sizes. These were immensely popular with the buyers and sold in great numbers, remaining in production some twenty-five years later.

As was perhaps to have been expected, the new range of models contained rather more disappointments than successes. The work of one new artist, however, was so well received that she was to become the most important figure modeller for many years to come. Freda Doughty had the ability to capture the innocent charm and naturalism of children, apparent from her very first group of four models; Michael, Tommy, Mischief and Joan (2912-2915) were an immediate success, Tommy, with his mischievous grin, and Joan selling in particularly large numbers. Freda's early models also included the delightful and popular Sea Breeze and My Favourite (3008 and 3014).

Fig. 9. Left: shape 2910, Indian Squaw, modelled by Frederick Gertner, puce mark, dated 1930. Right: shape 3142, The Frog, modelled by Gwendoline Parnell, puce mark, dated 1938.

The models of Margaret Cane were rather similar to Freda Doughty's children but although they proved to be more popular than the work of many of the other freelance modellers, they seemed to lack the realism that Miss Doughty was able to capture so consistently and Mr. Gimson, therefore, was faced with a simple choice between the two. Other notable models from 1931 and 1932 included a set of four Red Indians (2907-2910) by resident modeller Fred Gertner which did not prove very successful, probably because they were true to life and did not represent the Indians the public knew from Hollywood Westerns. Doris Lindner produced the first of what was to become an extremely popular series of small dogs, establishing herself as a superb animal modeller. She preferred the curious Art Deco figures that she had modelled the previous year, but these did not sell and she had to change her style and sculpt subjects that would sell. Responding to Mr. Gimson's orders, she was to become the factory's principal animal modeller. She may have been responsible for some of the large number of brooches introduced in 1932, designed to adorn hats, but these met with only limited success.

In 1933 the opportunity was taken to review the successes and disappointments of the previous two years and few new models were introduced. Mr. Gimson

15

decided to retain the services of Freda Doughty and Doris Lindner for their children and animal studies respectively, but he did not ask the experimental modellers for any further figures. He concentrated on developing the new style of 'Worcester Children' which was to become ever more popular and he looked for new ways of selling the other, less-successful, models.

Marketing of the figures was of great importance and the factory still aimed to offer the public as wide a choice as possible. Previously Worcester figures had been available in a very limited range of colours, mostly the drab ivory and bronze effects favoured by the Victorians, but the new figures were issued in as many as ten different colour schemes. Fortunately many of the original colour designs survive in the factory records and from these can be seen the different ways in which some of the figures were tried. It seems that the general practice was for the modeller initially to indicate to the factory how he or she would like the figure coloured. Eric Aumonier intended his models to be painted with curious coloured shapes and spots with loop-like railings around the bases, although the paintresses thought this to be a waste of time. Doris Lindner conceived the Dancers (2949) and Dancing Ladies (3086 and 3088) as sculpture, to be decorated in mottled grey, simulating stone. Not surprisingly, the ordinary public, who wanted pretty figures, did not appreciate such subtlety and would not buy them. Mr Gimson asked Daisy Rea, the paintress, to design a new colour scheme and she gave the Dancers a black suit and flame dress which proved a little more successful. Some of the modellers' designs for colouring still survive. Anne Acheson gave detailed instructions as to how she wanted her figure Tangles (2919) to be coloured (*see* illustration on page 34). Doris Lindner first of all tried her designs in water-colour and then painted an unglazed biscuit model directly in water-colour as a guide to the factory paintresses. To increase the range of figures on the market, the factory brought out of its mould stores a great number of nineteenth-century figures, including Hadley's Joy and Sorrow, Eastern Water Carriers and Kate Greenaway children. The Down-and-Out menu-holders and a series of figures of Indian craftsmen modelled by James Hadley were all reintroduced, painted by Daisy Rea and her sister Grace in updated colouring. They particularly favoured a 'flame' colour using pink painted over orange, and boldly coloured faces. The strong character of James Hadley's modelling worked well in matt ivory tones, but seems strange in garish 1930s colours. Few were sold and the later versions are now much rarer than the nineteenth-century originals. The customers in 1932 seemed to want only pretty children and animals and the factory realized this from the sales figures.

In order to sell some of the larger, unusual figures such as the 'Longies', Argentina (2936) and The Old Goat Woman, an arrangement was made with the firm of Charles Selz of New Cavendish Street, London, to mount them as the bases of table lamps. The shades were often designed to match; for instance the Victorian Musicians were fitted with shades painted with bars of music. Some of these figures worked quite well as lamps and very occasionally turn up with their original fittings and shades surviving. Selling the figures in London was extremely important and many gimmicks were tried out. In November 1931 a Debutantes' Ball called The British Porcelain Ball, was held at Claridges in London. The young ladies who had come of age, each dressed as a china figurine, performed a specially composed 'Porcelain Ballet'. Four debutantes dressed up as Royal Worcester figures. Noel and June (2905 and 2906) were played by Miss Jean Hay and The Hon. Joanna Douglas; Miss Eleanor Gamble played Mary Queen of Scots (2634), and one of James Hadley's Victorian figures was played by Miss Lilian Payne. The event was extensively written up in the newspapers and in the pro-

Fig. 10. Factory publicity photographs for Royal Worcester figures mounted as lamps, the shades designed by Charles Selz of New Cavendish Street, London. Top: shape 2886, Old Goat Woman; shape 2881, Sauce. Bottom: shape 2936, Argentina; shape 2901, The Flute Player. (WRPC)

gramme for the Ball Worcester illustrated Noel as 'A new and beautiful statuette, just one of over a hundred charming subjects'. Virtually all were new and they filled the china shops in London alongside the products of Worcester's principal rival, Royal Doulton.

In this way the factory found out which style of figure was most popular with the public. After a brief period of consolidation Royal Worcester felt able to introduce new models once again. They began cautiously, adding to the most popular ranges of child and dog studies, but every so often trying out new and original types of figures. 1934 saw the introduction of Freda Doughty's first major series of children in the costumes of the Nations of the World. Ten models were initially produced, 3066-3075, Wales and Scotland (3103 and 3104) being added the following year with Ireland (3178) completing the set in 1936. Some of the figures proved to be more popular than others and are consequently seen in greater numbers today. The public now had the opportunity to collect and build up a set of charming and inexpensive figurines, the success of which led to the introduction of many other series in future years.

Freda Doughty's two most successful figures were introduced in 1935. Grandmother's Dress (3081) and Boy with Parakeet (3087) possessed just the right combination of grace and charm and sold in great numbers, continuing in production until the present day. Workers in the factory claim that at times during the 1950s these two figures were keeping the whole works going, being almost the only models that sold regularly.

The year 1935 also saw the introduction of the first Limited Editions. The idea of Limited Editions, usually involving the making of only a predetermined number of a particular figure before smashing the moulds, came from America. Alex Dickens, an American art publisher, had asked the factory to make sets of plates decorated

with birds after Audubon and these were made in 1934 in limited numbers with reasonable success. The following year saw the Silver Jubilee of King George V and Queen Mary and to commemorate this the factory commissioned Gwendoline Parnell to model a pair of statuettes of the King and Queen. Miss Parnell was one of the Chelsea modellers who had built up a considerable reputation in London with her society portraits. It was decided to limit production to no more than 250 pairs at a cost of 8 guineas a pair, and they were painted by Daisy and Grace Rea, the King in naval uniform, the Queen in Garter Robes, both looking majestic on their tall black plinths. The first pair was presented to and accepted by the King, the second pair to the Princess Royal and the third to the Duchess of York. The colouring had been taken from photographs and the Company received a request from Buckingham Palace that the King's hair should not be shown so silvery-white. Daisy Rea darkened it on all subsequent models.

In order for Miss Parnell to depict correctly the King's hand holding a scroll, C. W. Dyson Perrins' own hand was cast in plaster at the factory and sent to Miss Parnell to copy. The original cast of Dyson Perrins' hand is still preserved in the museum bearing his name.

Seventy-two pairs had been produced before the unexpected death of the King brought an abrupt end to the edition. No more were made and those already in the shops took a long time to sell, illustrating one of the greatest dangers facing makers of commemorative souvenirs. The statuettes were a little stiff in design and showed no attempt at the movement seen in later Limited Edition models. They were Gwendoline Parnell's first models for Worcester, to be followed by many others during the 1930s and 1940s. She became well known in Worcester; always well dressed, rather in the Victorian style, she was known as 'the Duchess', and was usually to be seen carrying a parasol. Many of her figures reflect this style, having colourful costumes painted with delicate flowers and patterns.

Following the Audubon bird plates, Alex Dickens approached the factory asking if they would make a series of Limited Edition models of birds of America. The factory's most popular modeller, Freda Doughty, was asked if she would be able to attempt these, but she declined, saying that her sister Dorothy was the one for birds. Thus began the first of a series of bird models that would bring business to the factory for forty years. The full story of the American 'Doughty Birds' has been told already*, and we do not propose to discuss these at length here. Their significance to us is that they opened up an exciting area of Worcester modelling and the skills painstakingly developed over the next decades were to be used in all branches of figure making. Initially only Dorothy Doughty's American bird models were produced in Limited Editions. Freda was not involved with Limited Editions and was happy for everyone to be able to enjoy her figures. Certainly to have restricted some figures to only 250 or 500 would have greatly reduced the factory's sales, whilst other figures barely sold a fraction of such numbers.

Doris Lindner, at this time, continued with her small animal models which were an important part of the factory's output. The predominance of fox-hounds and foxes was no chance happening. The wealthy classes in England tended to enjoy fox-hunting and could afford to buy porcelain novelties for their tables. Ashtrays, menu-holders and calendars, all adorned with foxes and hounds, found a ready market in the hunting, shooting and fishing fraternity and this led to the introduction of series of sporting dogs and fish. Always the factory needed to make what would sell and looked for new markets at home and abroad.

Worcester's stand at the British Industries Fair in 1935 showed an impressive display of their new figures (*see* illustration on page 20). Featured prominently were Doris Lindner's Dancing Ladies, Stella

Crofts' Giraffes, the more successful figures of the freelance modellers and a large selection of the work of Freda Doughty. Curiously, Thomas Brock's Bather Surprised and James Hadley's Joy and Sorrow, still in the ivory and shot gold of the nineteenth century, were displayed amongst the current range.

Apart from the introduction of Freda Doughty's popular figures, 1935 was notable for a wide range of other new models with enormously varying appeal. Gwendoline Parnell was seen at her elegant best with such figures as Lady Bountiful (3097), Amaryllis (3108) and Bal Masqué (3111). These were relatively large figures and to decorate them as Miss Parnell intended was time consuming for Daisy Rea and her girls.

The paintresses earned more for painting large figurines than for small models such as Tommy and Joan, which were a fraction of the size of Gwendoline Parnell's impressive studies, although it was possible for the girls to paint half a dozen small figures in the time that a model such as Lady Bountiful, with her delicately patterned dress, would take. Painting the smaller figures was therefore much more profitable for the paintresses and Daisy Rea remembers that, although considerable satisfaction was taken from the elaborate work on the larger models, when it came to payment at the end of the week her girls would wish that they had not spent so long on the difficult figures.

Two particularly charming figures of Cupid from Miss Parnell (3095 and 3105) were certainly different from the modeller's usual style and are subjects of considerable appeal; once again, it is surprising that they did not sell well. We must begin to wonder if, perhaps, some of the models were not really promoted in the shops to give them a chance to become popular – or was it that the somewhat mischievous faces given by the modeller did not have the same charm as the traditional Dresden Putto? Was writing 'Good luck to your Fishing' around the base a particularly sensible idea for such a feminine figure?

---

*George Savage, *The American Birds of Dorothy Doughty*, 1962; Henry Sandon, *Royal Worcester Porcelain*, 1973.

Fig. 11. Original photograph of Royal Worcester's stand at the British Industries Fair, 1935. Many of the new figures introduced in 1931 and 1932 have been dropped by 1935, while James Hadley's Joy and Sorrow and Thomas Brock's Bather Surprised, all from the mid-Victorian period, are still included.

Some interesting figures were provided in 1935 by Doris Lindner, including a group of four equestrian studies (3114-3117). These were on a smaller scale than the great equestrians she was to model many years later but they did point the way towards a whole new style of figure. The series remained in production for a long time, although they do not seem to have sold in vast numbers. This may have been because they were dearer to buy than the average figure, being quite difficult to produce, and also because they were so obviously susceptible to damage. When an expensive model is vulnerable in so many places one can imagine a prospective purchaser considering this very carefully.

A rather amusing pair of penguins was also modelled by Miss Lindner in a very much more formal style (3093 and 3094) and in the same year she was responsible for an imposing study of a poodle named Champion Spriggan Bell (3085). Although an unusual subject, this commission presented an opportunity for Doris Lindner to study and work with a specific animal until she had captured the individual features and character of the poodle. A great lover of dogs, Miss Lindner had always kept them as pets and she much enjoyed the chance of working closely with one of her favourite subjects. In the years to come she was frequently commissioned to model portraits of a particular animal, usually a horse or a bull, and here was an early indication of the modeller's talent in that direction.

In contrast with Doris Lindner's striking poodle and her equestrian studies, it is interesting to note that a group of small animal models was provided by one of the internal factory designers, E. Evans. The Elephant (3102) is notable for its simplicity and would surely not have been out of place if included in the series of little models of animals of some twenty years earlier. This, and the accompanying Lion and Tiger (3100 and 3101) are so rarely seen nowadays that once again we must wonder how many were made. It is likely that Evans was also responsible for the rather charming Bear (3110).

In 1936 Doris Lindner modelled delightful groups of dogs and foxes (3130-3133) and a group of kittens (3141). The same modeller was also responsible for various groups of farm animals, including the playful Maytime lambs (3123). The dogs and foxes were probably aimed at the hunting community and the young farmyard animals at farmers and country people, and seem to have been reasonably popular. The kittens, though, are very rarely seen and possibly failed because they did not meet the needs of that particular market. It is interesting to reflect that some of Doris Lindner's later greatest successes were with large models of bulls and cows in Limited Editions, showing that when Worcester's feet were planted in the farmyard, hunting field and show jumping arena it could do very well.

Freda Doughty and Gwendoline Parnell provided further studies typical of their popular styles. It must be said, however, that whilst Miss Doughty's new models were instantly successful, possessing her usual innocence and charm in just the right mixture, one or two of Miss Parnell's figures must have presented the Worcester craftsmen with considerable difficulties. Her incredible model of the Planter's Daughter (3138) was to be made for a number of years and the size and weight alone must have caused great problems in

firing and decorating.

Less successful models of 1936 were the farm animals of Bargas and the equestrian studies of Geraldine Blake (3165-3170). Both of these series may well have suffered from the growing popularity of Doris Lindner and it is not surprising to find that they were quickly discontinued. The Bargas models were somewhat stylized and angular, with nothing of the growing naturalism of Doris Lindner's.

Perhaps the most interesting failure of 1936 was the series of ballet dancers commissioned from Rachel Greaves (3171-3177). Miss Greaves had approached Joseph Gimson at the British Industries Fair in 1935 and shown him a photograph of a dancer. This led to the charming set of figures based upon dancers of the time. The Company made a full set of moulds but seemed to lose interest in them and returned the moulds to the modeller, who kept them in her garage for some forty years until they were brought to the attention of Henry Sandon, who suggested that they should be resurrected. The Company made five of them in the 1980s; these modern versions, in hard white glaze with a gold line at the bottom, differ totally from the originals, which were intended to be issued in soft grey colours. It is likely that none of the originals was actually put on sale, and we certainly have not seen any coloured examples.

In 1937 Eva Soper began a popular series of small birds to complement the earlier Fred Gertner bird models. These were to be an enormous success, most of them still being produced at the time of writing. Few other new figure subjects were introduced in the same year, but mention should be made of the seemingly strange models of Dorothea Charol, a freelance modeller. In the late 1930s she produced studies of ballet dancers and bathing girls, similar in style to her previous work for continental factories and certainly very different from the accepted Worcester figure. Her Repose (3272) and Hesitation (3289) may have been considered too risqué for their time and were not produced. Daisy Rea often said that she thought Mr Gimson was reluctant to allow on to the market revealing figures of young ladies. Certainly Worcester produced far fewer figures of that type than, for example, did Doulton, so this theory may be true. In the 1920s Worcester had made a number of nude models, but all of these had been discontinued. Like the Deco models of Aumonier, the style of Mme. Charol's work was perhaps just a little too old-fashioned in 1937 to succeed.

Two important series were modelled by Doris Lindner and introduced in 1938. The first was a series of Sporting Dogs (3228-3233) to complement her existing range of canine studies. It is possible that these were at first made with the export market in mind, as we have seen very few early examples of these figures in England. The second series was a slight departure from Miss Lindner's work to date, although it did result once again in her studying animals from nature. A number of young animals had been born at London Zoo and these had captured the public's imagination through photographs in the press. Doris went to the zoo to model some of the most charming figures to be made at any time by the factory. The Zoo Babies (3263-3266, 3273 and 3274) so beautifully and naturalistically capture the playful young animals seen by Miss Lindner that it is difficult to believe the series was not a success, yet very few were apparently sold. Fortunately the modeller recorded the names of some of the animals and where it has been possible to trace them, details are given in Chapter 7. In 1940 both the Zoo Babies and the Sporting Dogs were redesigned without bases, a move which did not please Miss Lindner, but it was a commercial decision.

Gwendoline Parnell's 'Cries of London', introduced in 1938, were ambitious figures in the style of old Chelsea. They were based on prints popular in the 1930s but failed to find the same general appeal when converted to porcelain. Very few of the 'Cries' were made, but in the same year was introduced by far the most important

series of figures produced at the factory to that date — the Days of the Week.

A popular nursery rhyme inspired Freda Doughty to model seven delightful figures illustrating the seven days of the week. The idea was that they would represent the character of a child born on a particular day of the week and customers would buy the figure appropriate to themselves or their friends. They were slow sellers initially, but by the 1950s were selling in great numbers, prompting the factory to issue a further set of seven in 1954, so that there was a boy and girl for each day. This series has proved very popular ever since, and at the time of writing all are still made. In the 1980s miniature versions were introduced, again proving very popular.

Meanwhile the 1930s were drawing to a close and the threat of war became a reality. We cannot say if it was because of the outbreak of war or merely a depressed home market but the factory seems to have taken this opportunity to review the range of products in preparation for noticeable changes in direction. Very little that was new appeared in 1939 as the factory prepared for the difficult times ahead.

The 1940s and up to 1970

The outbreak of war presented new problems to the Worcester factory in the form of restrictions which hit all manufacturers of ceramics. Whilst the country was at war, production of richly decorated wares and elaborate ornamental lines had to be halted and the saving grace as far as Worcester was concerned was the reputation earned in the United States during the 1930s.

The series of American birds modelled by Dorothy Doughty and produced from 1935 in Limited Editions of up to 500 was still much in demand. As it was vital for the country to earn dollars in trade with the United States, the Worcester factory was allowed to continue production of the birds, many orders having been received.

In addition, certain other fine quality wares were allowed to be made but solely for export, with very little for the home market.

Many of the factory artists and craftsmen became involved with the war, either directly as members of the Forces or working in factories producing war weapons. About a third of the Worcester factory was taken over by the Ministry of Aircraft Production and a special kiln was built for the firing of resistors for wireless equipment.

With many of their colleagues involved to varying degrees with the war effort it must have been a considerable strain on those remaining merely to continue the current editions of the Doughty birds. Further models by Dorothy Doughty were introduced during the war years and it must be said that not all were successful. The pair of Bob White Quails, begun in 1940, was intended as a cheaper Christmas present for sportsmen, with no flowers added to keep the price as low as possible. The sportsmen for whom they were intended would not buy them because Dorothy had modelled chicks with the mother quail, an offputting sight when you intended to go out next day and shoot the parents; and the ladies did not like them as there were no pretty flowers. Production was halted after only twenty-two pairs had been produced and they are now the rarest and most sought-after of all the Doughty birds. Other wartime birds sold much better, however, and this encouraged Worcester to persevere.

Instrumental in the designing of figures was Alex Dickens, who asked Worcester for a new range of dog models aimed at the American market. Aline Ellis produced a small series of dogs, the first being Toto (3331) from *The Wizard of Oz*, which was introduced in 1940 following the success of the film of the previous year. The Ellis models were made for export and often incorporated the special mark of Alex Dickens with the factory mark under the base. A new series of six nursery rhyme characters was modelled by Freda Doughty with a more universal appeal and 'Polly put the kettle on' (3303) was to prove particularly popular, continuing into the 1980s, although the others were discontinued after the 1950s.

Apart from a rather strange set of four dogs' heads (3319-3322), the other interesting figure from 1940 was a model by Doris Lindner of Bogskar, the winner of the Grand National of that year. This was the first major equestrian study from Miss Lindner and, although this one was far from being a success, it heralded the way for the introduction of many popular models to be made over the following decades. Neither the modeller nor the Worcester factory could have known in 1940 that the Grand National would not be run again until 1946. Whether the enforced absence of the Sport of Kings contributed to the failure of the Worcester model of Bogskar we cannot say for certain. It is possible that only two of the figures were made and the modeller later expressed the view to us that winners of annual horse races often lose their popularity by the following year. The poodle, Champion Spriggan Bell and now Bogskar had taken many months of work from the first modelling to the completed figure in the shops and the original subjects had been soon forgotten. The public did not want to buy an expensive souvenir of last year's champion and it goes to show how narrow a tightrope the Company had to walk between success and failure.

In the late 1930s Eva Soper had begun to model what was to become a large and extremely popular series of bird models of small size. Many new birds were added in the 1940s and, being relatively inexpensive, were widely collected by the public, keen either to have just one as a memento of a favourite bird or to collect many of the delightful studies to group together in cheerful arrangements.

Freda Doughty was able, as always, to produce more highly-saleable figures, such as The Bow and The Curtsey (3359 and 3360), introduced in 1941 and made for a number of years. Gwendoline Parnell continued with her series of London Cries and also, in 1941, modelled a set of figures representing the four seasons (3339-3342). Very few of Miss Parnell's models seem to have sold well and these disappointing new figures were no exception. Her last work for the Worcester factory was a model of a Chinoiserie girl (3362) completing a group of three similar studies.

Possibly the most disappointing set of figures, and certainly one of the most interesting, was the wartime series modelled by Eileen Soper, Eva Soper's sister, brought to the factory for this one set of figures. Seven were produced (3346, 3347, 3351, 3352, 3369, 3370 and 3382), and these captured so effectively the reality of living in wartime Britain as seen through the eyes of children, so poignantly depicted by the modeller, that they may well have seemed too sad and even rather frightening. Brought out when the terrors of war were hitting families all over the country they were intended to bring light-hearted relief to a very serious subject, to make people smile through the tears. In reality, they hit too close to home and were almost destined to fail. This is a great pity, because they must now be considered amongst the finest models of the period; perhaps, if they had been introduced after the war was over, they might have sold much better. Daisy Rea remembered that she and the other paintresses were each given one of the wartime series by the Company but she herself thought that they were very sad models.

During the last years of the war very few new figures were introduced. Production had been heavily concentrated on wares for export, with little available for the home market. Until the year 1941 a different yearly date code was incorporated in the trade mark on every figure produced but apart from special marks on certain 'American Market' models, no new code was used from 1941 until 1949. This spared the annual task of punching an extra dot into every copper plate mark to denote the extra year. It is, therefore, rarely possible to pinpoint the year of production of the

figures made at this time, but we suspect that very few models were actually produced from 1941 to 1948.

Two very unusual items were made during the war which were not given numbers and were not listed in the shape books. Perhaps only one or two examples of them were made. They comprise a pair of Toby Jugs depicting Churchill and Roosevelt, which were painted by Miss Rea, modeller unknown. Also proposed, but apparently not made, were a set of six Victory figures, such as Neptune spearing a German submarine, which we illustrate from the original water-colours, again modeller unknown, (*see* pages 210 and 211).

A prolific modeller of the later 1940s was Agnes Pinder-Davis, who produced a wide range of Chinoiserie boys and girls. Some of these were a little strange, to say the least, and none more so than her last major series of Chinoiserie Sayings (3491-3502). Agnes Pinder-Davis was capable of superb modelling work and her pair of Balinese and Siamese dancers (3473 and 3474) are two of the most impressive Worcester figures ever produced. They were a Limited Edition of twenty-five pairs only and, so difficult were they for the factory to make, that this edition took more than twenty years to complete. Financially they were a disaster and were sold at a considerable loss at the time, but it is sometimes necessary to reach for the stars with the production of prestige items. Mrs. Pinder-Davis' most successful Chinoiseries were the two pairs of complementary figures issued between 1944 and 1946 (3397-3400). Initially made just in white the set of four were among the few porcelain figures accepted for the 'Britain Can Make It' exhibition held at the Victoria and Albert Museum in 1948. In the catalogue was the note that these white models were only immediately available for export and would be on sale to the home market 'later'. Gwendoline Parnell had modelled three Chinoiserie figures (3348, 3354 and 3362) and Royal Worcester conceived the seven as one set. Miss Parnell took the paintress Daisy Rea to

Birmingham to see an exhibition of Oriental costumes belonging to the actor George Robey to get ideas for the colouring of the Chinoiserie Studies. After spending many hours looking at the fancy silks, Gwendoline Parnell decided that the colour of the bright green dress which Daisy herself was wearing was the most suitable she had seen, and it was this, combined with black, which made the series so distinctive. In return for her help in designing the colouring Miss Parnell gave Daisy a very special gift of an egg, finely gift-wrapped. Eggs were still strictly rationed at this time and Daisy always remembered this present.

Freda Doughty was asked to model a series of children to represent each month of the year. These she introduced between 1947 and 1949 and they have been in production ever since. Here we can see Freda Doughty at her very best. There is no doubt that she captured superbly the special quality of movement of children when they do not think they are being watched, most of the observation being from life. It has always been fascinating to meet grown-up people who say, quite proudly, that they were the model for a particular Freda Doughty child, drawn and modelled while they played at the Doughty sisters' homes in Goudhurst, Kent or Falmouth in Cornwall. Sets of figures can often be good for business as, once one of them is bought, the purchaser or receiver will often want to build up the complete set.

Doris Lindner provided, in the late 1940s and early 1950s, some unusual yet impressive large models of dogs. She also produced rather strange pairs of pigeons (3421 and 3422) and ducks (3459 and 3460). They cannot be considered beautiful, looking rather like wooden decoys, and it is perhaps a good thing that she concentrated on four-legged animals. At this time she was to concentrate more and more on Limited Edition equestrian studies, and her output of smaller models decreased. From her imposing 1949 study of Princess Elizabeth taking her first

Trooping the Colour in her uniform as Colonel-in-Chief of the Grenadier Guards and sitting on her horse, Tommy, Doris's equestrian studies were to become more and more remarkable, culminating in most striking models of the great racehorses, so full of movement that they seem almost real.

In 1953 a special presentation vase for the Coronation of Queen Elizabeth was made by the six members of the Fine China Association, of which Worcester was one. The great vase, 25½ in. high, 11½ in. wide and weighing 29lb. was designed by John Wadsworth, Minton's art director, and each factory was responsible for parts of the piece. Worcester's contributions were two of the ten Queen's Beasts, which fitted into niches on the ten-sided vase. Eleven copies of the vase were made for presentation by the Duchess of Gloucester to the seven leading commonwealth countries and the four home countries of the United Kingdom. It is possible that one or two extra models of Worcester's Heraldic Beasts were made and these are worth looking out for, not least for the fact that they were painted by Harry Davis, the master painter.

In the post-war years, and particularly in the early 1950s, the Rabbit and Mouse (2607 and 2610), so popular earlier in the century, were again in production. There would not have been a lot of money around at this time and it is easy to see why these delightful little models were produced once again. Another popular series dating back to the nineteenth century, and similarly cheap to produce, was the set of candle extinguishers. The models known to have been in production in 1955 were Japanese Girl, Dr. Fox, Mandarin, Witch, Owl, French Cook, Monk and Nun. These simple and inexpensive figures provided a total contrast to the increasingly adventurous and daring models produced in Limited Editions. The little animals and extinguishers were usually cast from one or two-piece moulds and provide an extreme contrast with Dorothy Doughty's incredible Magnolia Warblers introduced in 1947. These required more than eighty moulds weighing 4½ hundredweight.

In 1953, Ronald Van Ruyckevelt joined the design staff and worked closely with Dorothy Doughty, as the factory was concentrating heavily on her Limited Edition bird models. Ronald was a very talented modeller in his own right and in 1956 began the modelling of a series of fish studies, filling an obvious gap in the range of subjects available. Modelling large fish in Limited Editions, and also smaller, inexpensive models, he won a considerable following.

A rather strange series of figures was provided in 1956 by a modeller from Paris named Azori. The figures were undecorated and unglazed and, although they at first seem rather strange, the quality and appeal of the modelling is quite distinctive. These sold in rather low numbers, however, even though they were still on sale in 1970.

It was most unusual for a set of figures by Freda Doughty to prove unpopular, and considering the charm and interest evident in her *Alice in Wonderland* series (3608-3614) it is very difficult to believe that they did not sell well. This is apparent, however, from the fact that very few examples have been seen. We know of more models in collections in the United States than in Britain, and it is possible that these figures were intended for export. The seven delightful models included the Cheshire Cat and, in the same year, 1957, Freda modelled two other cats (3615 and 3616) which could be painted in various different ways. These single, seated, cat studies proved very popular. The failure of the Alice in Wonderland series may have had a lot to do with a significant change of direction in Worcester figure making. In 1957 or 1958 many figures were withdrawn. These included all of Doris Lindner's small dogs and animals and most of the work of Miss Parnell, Mrs. Pinder-Davis and the other freelance modellers. The only figures to remain in production were Freda Doughty's Months of the Year and Days of the Week along

with a few other models of children, the Historical figures and some of the 'unlimited' equestrian studies by Doris Lindner. Any new figures introduced in the late 1950s and early 1960s were in a different style, and perhaps aimed at a different market.

Clarissa and Amanda (3607 and 3620), modelled by Neal French in 1956/57, and Freda Doughty's First Dance and Sweet Anne (3629 and 3630) were modelled on a larger scale than previous figures and depict slightly more grown-up subjects. The factory was thinking along these lines for a new series of Limited Edition figures of young ladies in Victorian costume. Freda Doughty was not terribly keen on the idea of limiting the number of figures made, preferring to give as many people as possible the chance to buy her work. Neal French's ladies were perhaps not given much of a chance, but they proved very difficult to sell, and the factory therefore looked elsewhere for the new series. Ronald Van Ruyckevelt's wife Ruth showed a natural talent as a modeller of very feminine subjects and the first four of her Victorian Ladies were introduced in 1958 and 1959, all limited to 500. These were followed in 1960 by the popular Tea Party group. Perhaps not to be outdone by this, Freda Doughty tried her hand at larger and more adult figures during this period. Her Surprise (3655), Invitation (3698) and Red Ribbons (3699), and in 1961 Will You, Won't You? (3720) were much more ambitious than her children of the past. They were costly to make and to buy and somehow nobody seemed to want them. It seemed that the public who were willing to spend more on a larger figure preferred to have a Limited Edition with a certificate and the hope that it would turn out to be a good investment. It has turned out, however, that these large figures by Freda Doughty are now so much rarer than the Ruth Van Ruyckevelt models that they are becoming just as collectable.

Most of Freda Doughty's attempts at depicting older children seemed doomed to failure. Although Grandmother's Dress and Boy with Parakeet still sold in large numbers, her figures of Mayflower (3656) and Falconer (3679) were withdrawn soon after introduction. She clearly decided that this style was not for her and she should rest on her laurels as the factory's most successful modeller. Her Children were on sale in every china shop around the world and are a permanent memorial to her great talents.

Over the years Freda Doughty had seen the outlook of the factory change. The emphasis was no longer on commercial inexpensive figurines aimed at the general public, but instead the factory had shown with the development of the Doughty birds and equestrian studies that they were the world leaders in the manufacture of fine realistic porcelain sculpture. Each new Limited Edition was technically more superb than the last, culminating in the 1970s with Bernard Winskill's Military series and James Alder's birds.

Despite the enormous and continuing popularity of the Freda Doughty models Royal Worcester, for some reason, felt it necessary to look for alternatives. Neal French was asked to bring the Doughty children up to date and show children doing the things they really do in modern times. The result was the Playtime series (3747-3757). The Art Director proved to be wrong in his aim, underestimating the appeal of the Doughty figures. Neal, in fact, feels that he perhaps did not go far enough and should have made his children more mischievous instead of giving them toys and dolls to play with. The first of the six designed was Treasure Trove (3748) and was considered, unfortunately, to be on the expensive side to produce. Neal was told, therefore, that the rest must be cheaper and his modelling had to be done for the convenience of mould-making which, for a modeller, imposes restrictions that often produce less satisfactory results. He feels that the three

girls were better models than the boys. At the time he liked them, but looking at the figures twenty years later feels that he would rather not have designed them as they are not typical of his best work. He does consider that the series was not given a fair chance, although he accepts that it was probably destined to be a failure as the models were a compromise — a sort of half-hearted attempt to produce something different from Freda Doughty's children, which were selling in great numbers. They could not break away from the tradition and Neal regrets not having been able to be a little braver and produce 'tough urchins', more like real children. Neal's first child was born a year or two after he modelled the Playtimes and he accepts that he had no experience of children; indeed, at the time, he did not particularly like children, and he has certainly given the figures heads which seem a little too large, the children appearing to be older than intended. Very few sets were sold, although examples are known issued simply in white.

The same modeller produced a set of six different small figures in the style of Bustelli, the eighteenth-century German modeller, produced in hard porcelain in two separate colourings, making a complete set of twelve, all of them intended as table decorations. These were introduced in the early 1970s, and were again unsuccessful.

Although the period covered by this book may seem to have ended in the failure of newly-introduced small figures, these 'failures' are now highly collectable items. Royal Worcester poured its resources into the making of the fine Limited Edition figures and the established successes of Freda Doughty. We leave the Company in 1970, 220 years after its beginning, in the proud position of being one of the greatest porcelain companies and possibly the finest figure maker in the world.

Chapter Three

The Making of a Royal Worcester Figure

Mrs. Philip Lybbe Powys, a visitor to Dr Wall's factory in Worcester in 1771, described how she saw the workers making figures from moulds, with separate limbs and parts of bodies, sticking them all together with 'a kind of paste'. The 'paste' was, in fact, thick slip (liquid clay), used as a sticking-up medium, and if Mrs. Powys was able to visit Royal Worcester today she would find the process virtually unchanged, the only difference being that now the limbs, heads and bodies are slip-cast with liquid clay instead of the original method of pressing solid clay into the moulds.

During the years covered by this book Royal Worcester figures have been produced in the following basic sequence: modelling the figure; cutting up the figure and making plaster moulds from the parts; casting pieces from the moulds and fitting them up; firing the complete figure into a biscuit body followed by a 'glost' firing; decorating followed by one or more firings to fix the colours and gold. It will help to understand the finished figure if these processes are explained.

Modelling

The model is the original creation by the modeller. Normally made of plasticine, the model is sculpted with tools, often around an armature if the model is complicated.

Most modellers prefer to model from life, or a combination of life and photographs, in order to get greater accuracy and a sense of life in the finished piece.

Two particular complications present themselves to the modeller. The first is that the fired porcelain figure will shrink by a large amount, almost 50 per cent loss of volume, so the modeller has to scale up his model to take this into account. It is obviously no good including a mass of small detail which will become meaningless when reduced in size, especially when it will be further obscured by the covering of glaze. The second is that the model must not be so complex to manufacture that the cost of production is pushed beyond what the market will bear. A large number of separate arms, legs, bits and pieces, each requiring a separate mould, will not only increase the costs but create problems in firing. Extra firings to produce special decorative effects add greatly to the final price of the figure.

Internal factory modellers, like Gertner and the Evanses, would understand these basic problems and their models would reflect this, perhaps being somewhat 'safe' as a result. On the other hand, some freelance outside modellers, more used to working in pottery or making one-off models, found the problems difficult to understand until they had spent some

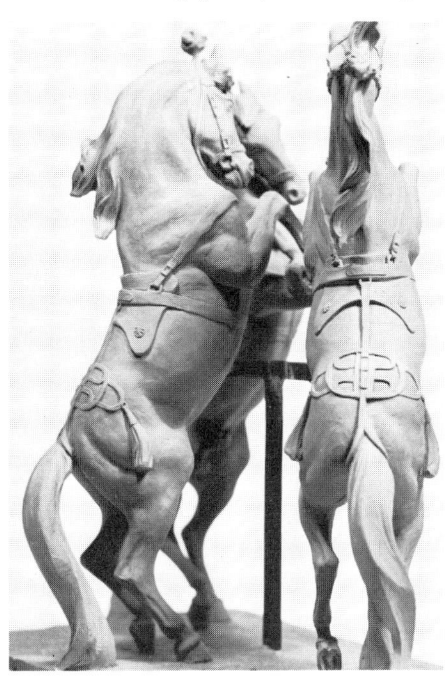

Fig. 12. Original photographs of the plasticine models by Doris Lindner for her circus groups; shape 3180, In The Ring, and shape 3179, Three Circus Horses Rearing. The metal armatures can be clearly seen.

time at the factory working with the company craftsmen and sales staff, who were always willing to help. Fred Gertner or Len Morris would show them how a figure had to be cut for moulding. Daisy Rea would explain the complications of painting with metallic oxides, so different from oils or water-colours. Doris Lindner, on one occasion, insisted on painting her own 'standard', to show exactly how the colouring should be. Daisy left her to it over the lunch time and, when she returned, found that all the colours had run down the figure as if it had been left out in the rain. The modeller had thought that one used the metallic oxides like water-colour.

There has always been a friendly working relationship between the freelance modeller and the factory craftsman. Many of the modellers were regarded with awe, as they often came from an exotic world, like London or Paris, but there is no doubt that they brought a breath of fresh air into the factory. Watching all this closely, from

the 1930s, was Joseph Gimson, who discovered most of the modellers and encouraged them. Mr Gimson could call on the wide range of expertise in the factory and Neal French explained to us the sequence of events that would precede the production of a series of figure subjects. Usually the modeller would first receive a directive which, in the case of Neal's own Playtime series (3747, 3748 and 3754-3757), was a request to up-date the 1930s children models. Told that six would initially be required, he started drawing and putting down more than twenty ideas to produce six final figures. Design meetings were held every few months, presided over by Joseph Gimson, with the other directors and design and sales staff in attendance. The Art Director would draw up an agenda and any proposed models could be shown, either in drawing form or, preferably, as a fired example. Neal found that an actual example was far more likely to convince the various directors than a drawing,

29

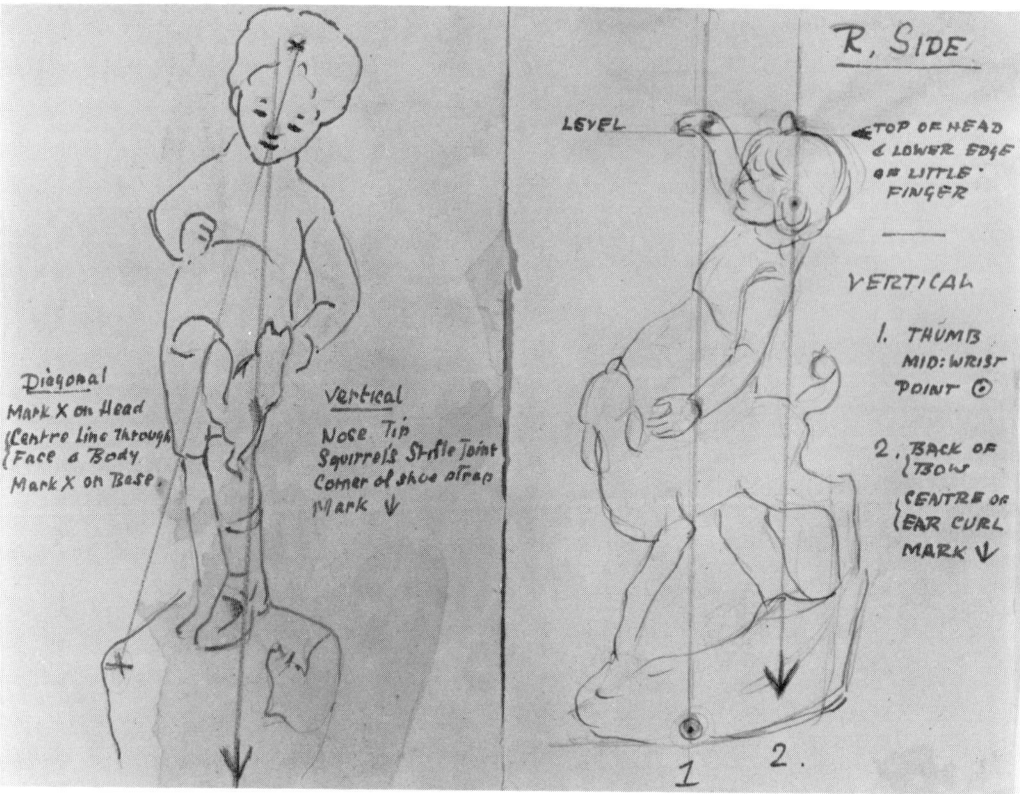

Fig. 13. Original sketches by Freda Doughty giving instructions to the casters for assembling two of the Months of the Year series. Left: shape 3417. Right: shape 3416. (WRPC)

but often found it very difficult to have one fired in the kiln without questions being asked by the director responsible for kiln firings, who was annoyed that such things were going through 'his' kiln. Neal had to persevere, however, and found that a modeller was always given a fair trial at the regular meetings.

Cutting up and mould making

The modeller's precious baby is passed over to the mould makers. The craftsman responsible for cutting up the figure has one of the most important jobs in the factory, as it is his responsibility to cut the model at the right places, with correct angles so that the cast parts will join together. Once cut up, a part can never be put back exactly, so a great deal depends on the job being done correctly. A decision has to be made as to how many pieces there should be. The more there are, the longer the casting and sticking-up job will be, and the greater the cost of making, but it is necessary to be able to take a part out of the mould without distorting it, so awkward angles and shapes have to be cut and moulded very carefully. An arm or hand pointing away from the body will need to be cut and separately moulded, although one still by the side might be made in one mould with the body.

Not everything goes smoothly at this stage, as Len Morris found with one of Doris Lindner's farmyard series, the calves (3146). After cutting up the parts he lost one of the heads and, frightened stiff of telling Miss Lindner, used the one remaining head for both animals. 'No one notic-ed', he told us. Some modellers liked to have their plasticine models back again, in pieces, so that they could use the plasticine again. Doris Lindner was a firm believer in the reuse of her plasticine, as she thought it was better to rework it. In consequence, virtually none of her original plasticine models survive. In recent years, some modellers, such as James Alder, have used a combination of plasticine and wax, this technique being able to produce some in-credibly fine detail – for example, on Alder's own great bird models.

The mould-making process is an ex-tremely difficult and time-consuming craft, the preparation of a set of working moulds from a complicated model some-times taking weeks. To watch a great mould maker, like George Morris of Worcester, produce a mould that will make a faithful reproduction of the model is a privilege that few have had.

Fine plaster of Paris is used, poured over the prepared part of the model in a box, in two halves to produce a 'block' of the shape. From this 'male' block a hollow, or 'female' mould is made, from which the porcelain part can be cast with slip. Because the detail in a plaster mould will wear away with a number of uses, the original master mould is usually retained carefully, and a second-generation master mould made from which the working moulds are produced.

A mould for the simplest piece, a head, for example, will be in two parts with a slip pouring hole in the neck. More complica-ted pieces, such as an animal body, may have to have three, four or five separate parts to the mould, in order that the cast body can be more easily withdrawn. If there is a lot of detail on a piece, such as hair on the head, the working mould can wear after a few dozen casts, so the mould maker is constantly in demand to make more working moulds from the second-edition block. Therefore, all figures pro-duced should be equally fully detailed, no matter how many hundreds of the model have been produced.

Casting and fitting up

From the mould makers the set of working moulds go to the casting department and it usually befalls the foreman of the department to make the first or 'standard' figure. When this has been approved, usually by the modeller and the Art Director, the standard is then used by the casters to follow, so that each model is as close to the modeller's intentions as poss-ible. This system of a standard was brought in to ease the problem of the freelance modellers not being around the factory very much to check the work in progress. It was rather like leaving a part of their own selves there.

The casting is done by pouring liquid clay, called slip, into the casting hole in the top of the mould, the parts of which have been bound tightly together with strong elastic bands to avoid seepage. The slip is allowed to fill the mould to the top and the porous plaster quickly begins to absorb the water, leaving a skin of solid clay forming on the inside of the mould. The longer the slip is left in, the thicker the resulting wall of clay, and for some very large pieces the level of slip has to be topped up. When sufficient thickness has been reached, perhaps after a few minutes, or even less for a very small part, the caster pours out the surplus slip, shaking the mould vigorously downwards to ensure that all has been removed. This then leaves the part inside hollow. The very tiniest bits, for example the end part of the Snake's tail (2608) can only have the slip in the mould for a moment (as the casters say, 'showing the slip to the mould') and are extremely difficult to make and take from the mould, as we know to our cost, having made many attempts at producing Snake's tail.

The moulds are allowed to stand and dry, and when the time is ready the scrap clay is scraped from the top of the casting hole and the triangular funnel and the bands are opened. The parts of the mould are then carefully opened and the cast piece can be removed. It is still slightly soft at this stage, with moisture in it, in a state called 'green' by the casters. When the piece is dry enough, the seams are removed. Each join in the mould will result in a seam, and these all have to be 'fettled' with a knife and moistened brush to remove them. A quickly or badly made figure will show seams, but they should not be visible on a piece from a good factory.

The separate pieces of the figure are assembled on a plaster bat in front of the caster. A figure looks very strange at this stage, almost like the end-product of being 'hung, drawn and quartered'. When the Queen, then Princess Elizabeth, visited the Worcester factory in 1951, she met Bob Bradley, the foreman caster, who showed the Princess her own figure as an equestrian study in a dozen bits and pieces, body and limbs and head all separated like a human three-dimensional jig-saw. Like Mrs. Powys in the eighteenth century, the Princess was very intrigued by this, crying out: 'Oh, Mr. Bradley, I hope you get me in the right order again!'

To fit up the figure, the caster joins one part to another with a small amount of thicker slip, and the whole figure is built up slowly, piece by piece, until it is complete. The surplus slip has to be carefully removed and any detail that has not come off very well improved. Particularly awkward parts have to be supported, and the supports must be cast of the same material so that they will shrink at the same rate as the pieces they are reinforcing. To stop the supports from sticking to the figure in the firing, a small dusting of alumina powder is used as a separator, a healthier material to work with than the crushed flint formerly used, which could give the caster a form of silicosis. Some of the more difficult figures have to have a considerable amount of complex supporting, which greatly adds to the cost of manufacture. Even for a figure that looks comparatively simple, such as Tuesday's Girl (3258), more material can be used in the support than in the figure itself; in the case of Tuesday's Girl, a drum-shaped surround holds long supports that prop up the outstretched arm so that it does not collapse when it shrinks in the firing. These supports can only be used the once, as they will not shrink again the next time, and when one realizes that the material is quite expensive, one is better able to understand the extra cost involved in the making of a difficult figure.

The completed figure in the raw clay is put aside to dry out naturally, when all the 'greenness' goes out of it and it becomes white. At this stage it is extremely fragile and a slight bang can cause it to collapse, or might set up stresses that could emerge as 'fire-cracks' after the firing. Many old casters would take their especially complicated figures to the biscuit kiln themselves, asking the kiln foreman to put it into a kind place in the oven, treating it as if it were their own baby – which, in a sense, it was. The set of moulds are put into a drying cupboard, with hot air fed from a kiln, to dry out and be used again.

Firing

Two initial firings are generally done, a biscuit and a glost. In soft-paste porcelain, such as parian and bone china bodies, the biscuit is the highest, about 1,250 degrees Celsius, followed by the glost firing at about 1,050 degrees.

Before the introduction of electric or gas-fired tunnel kilns, old bottle-oven kilns were fearsome things during their firing. The raw figures, vases, cups and saucers were put into saggars — fire-proof cases — and stacked up around the inside of the bottle in 'bungs' twenty or more feet tall. The door was sealed up and the firing was begun with coal being shovelled evenly into the eight fire mouths around the bottle. For several days the temperature would be slowly built up to the maximum, held there for some hours and then allowed to die down. When the kiln had cooled down sufficiently, the door was opened and 'drawing' commenced. Drawing the kiln — removing the fired pieces in their saggars — was a nasty job, particularly on account of the heat still in the kiln and the saggars. Old kiln men who worked in the days of bottle-ovens have told us that they could only stand fifteen minutes or so at a time before needing to recover in the air with liquid refreshment. They blessed the advent of the tunnel kiln, in which the wares are stacked on cars which slowly move through a long tunnel, the heat increasing until the middle of the tunnel is reached, from which point the temperature falls until the car emerges at the other end and cooling down commences. The tunnel kiln has been of great benefit and the firing time of four days in 1900 had shortened to two days in 1950, and has now been reduced even more.

The figures that emerge from this first firing are termed 'biscuit', a strange term which perhaps refers to their dry, white appearance. They are cleaned of their alumina powder, props are removed and they are inspected by the biscuit warehouse foreman. Some few figures have been sold in the biscuit and there is no doubting the lovely effect of fine modelling and form in this stage, uncluttered by glaze or colours (*see* Colour plate 11). The public, however, seems to have an antipathy for unglazed, and even glazed undecorated figures, perhaps thinking they are unfinished.

If there is any underglaze cobalt blue to go on the figure, it is put on at this stage, being the highest firing ceramic colour and able to withstand the glost kiln temperature. If no underglaze blue is necessary the figure goes ahead to the glazing department.

The glazer's job is to cover the figure with a thin, even layer of glaze, almost like glass. The usual method years ago was to dip the figure into a tub of glaze, shaking the figure vigorously to ensure that the glaze was spread evenly, and then putting it aside to dry. Nowadays it is more common to spray the glaze on with an aerograph gun. The figure then goes through its second firing, the glost firing, after which it emerges white glazed and ready, after inspection, for decoration or for selling as it is, in the white, undecorated stage.

Decoration

There are many and varied ways in which a figure can be decorated, not just by painting with a brush. Some areas of colour can be applied with a fine aerograph pencil, which in skilled hands can result in wonderful effects of flowing or shot silk colours. Some decoration can be done by transfer-printing areas of dresses, for example, with patterns produced by printing from copper plates onto thin sheets of paper. In recent years a growing amount of printing by the lithographic process has developed, in an attempt to keep down the cost of hand painting. Whatever the method, the raw materials used are metallic oxides — oxides of various metals which will fuse permanently into the glaze in subsequent kiln firings at lower temperatures than the previous biscuit and glost firings.

The hand painting of figures is one of the processes that all visitors to a porcelain factory particularly wish to see. The painter works from a decorating standard that has been painted by the foreman or forewoman or by the modeller, and which stands in front of the painter as the figure is painted. Many of the figures require their colours to be fired in sequence over several firings. In the early 1930s the figurine painting department was limited to Daisy Rea and her sister Grace, who always took great care over the painting and assumed personal responsibility for the figures, and would write the figure's name and that of its modeller under the base in puce. The numbers of painters grew until, by the 1950s and 1960s, at the height of popularity of the small figurines, there were as many as two dozen, mainly girls. Daisy Rea was the original forewoman and then Freda Griffiths took over. In the latter years most of the figurines had their factory marks and figure name and number put on by a print. Some of the Limited Edition figures, especially the Victorian series by Ruth van Ruyckevelt, were painted by the senior girls, but the others, such as the Doughty Birds, Equestrians,

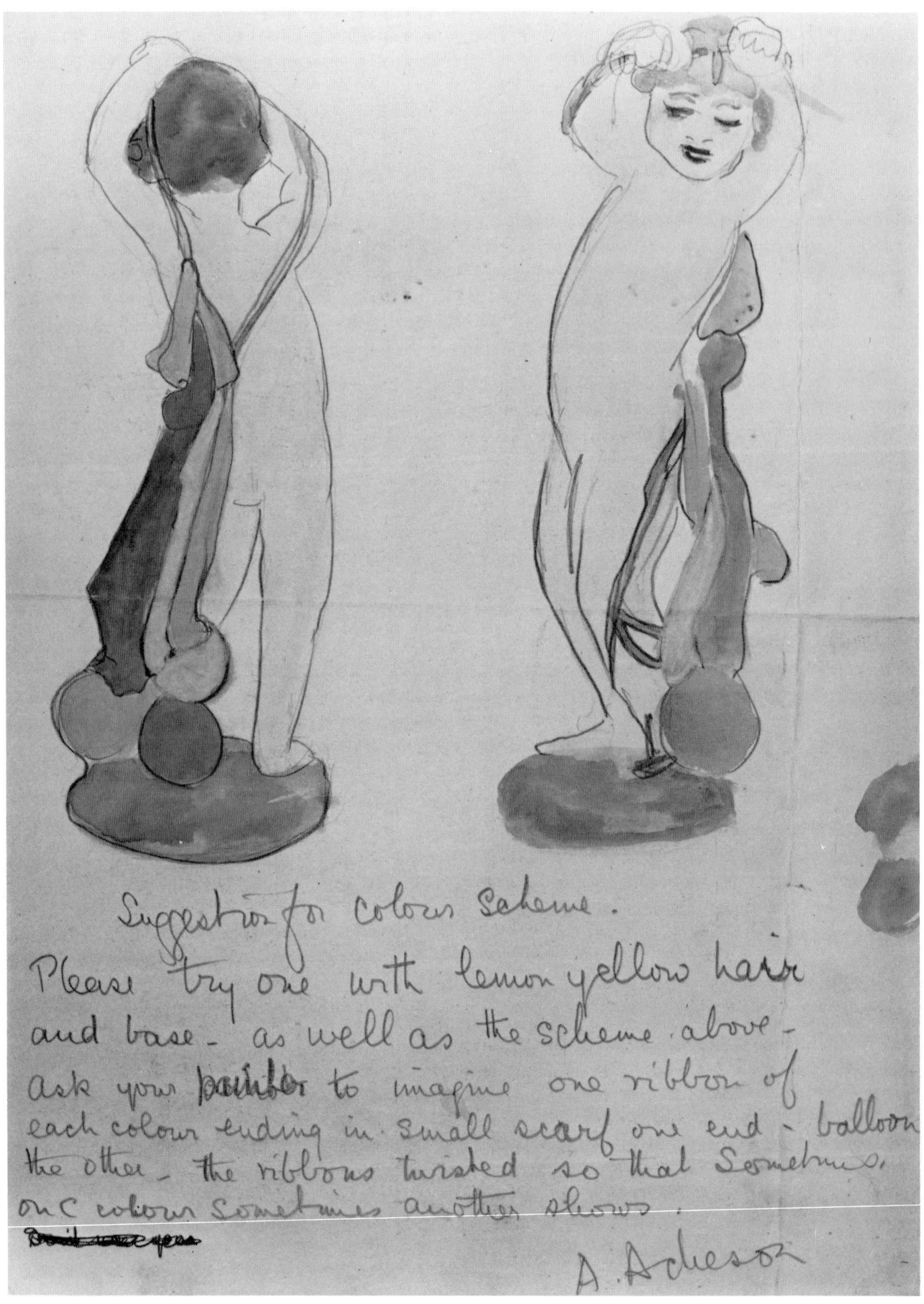

Fig.14. Original sketch by Anne Acheson giving instructions to the paintresses for colouring shape 2919, Tangles. (Worcester Royal Porcelain Company)

Birds and Fish, were painted by the men in a separate department.

The ceramic colour is fired in a smaller decorating kiln at temperatures around 760 degrees, and if there is any gold to be added this is put on by the gilder and the model fired again separately at a slightly lower temperature. Gold requires burnishing by girls after firing, unless it is to remain unburnished and dull. Then the figure is complete, needing a final close inspection before being ready for sale. If the figure is slightly defective, perhaps in colour or quality, it may be sold as a 'second' in the factory seconds shop, and this fact is sometimes noted by an incised cross cut into the base.

Chapter Four
The Modellers

One of the greatest joys of collecting Royal Worcester figures is that in most cases it is possible to find out the name of the original modeller. Knowing something about the modellers helps to breathe life into their figures, and so we have spent many years gathering information about the lives of the modellers themselves. We are fortunate to have been able to meet some of the modellers and talk with them about themselves. Other details have come through the recollections of workers in the factory who knew and worked alongside the modellers of the past. Some of the freelance modellers who lived in London never visited the factory, and our knowledge of them is based on exhibition catalogues, periodicals and other published books. In particular, we acknowledge the help of the following works:

B. Batkin, *Wedgwood Ceramics 1846-1959* (1982); R. Blunt (ed.), *The Cheyne Book of Chelsea China and Pottery* (1924); D. Eyles and R. Dennis, *Royal Doulton Figures* (1978); J. Hawkins, *The Poole Pottery* (1980); I. Mackay, *The Dictionary of Western Sculptors in Bronze* (1977).

Sadly our information about many of the modellers is scarce, especially on the early twentieth-century works modellers and some of the freelance modellers of the 1930s. We have recorded here all the details we have been able to uncover, and we realize that certain modellers deserve much larger entries. We hope that gradually, as more facts come to light, some of the gaps will be filled. Although not a modeller herself, we also include in this chapter details about Miss Daisy Rea, whose contribution to Royal Worcester figures was considerable.

Acheson, Anne C: Born in Portadown, Northern Ireland, in 1882, she was educated at Victoria College, Belfast, and later at the Royal College of Art, studying sculpture under Professor Lanteri and graduating in 1910. A regular contributor to Royal Academy exhibitions for many years, she also showed her work in many other places, including the Paris Salons of 1914 and 1922. During the First World War she designed a special surgical dressing combined with a plaster cast, and worked in hospitals all over the country treating casualties. In 1919 she was awarded the CBE for her wartime service. In 1938 she won the Gleichen Memorial Award. Anne Acheson lived in Glenavy, Co. Antrim and also worked in London. Her earlier work was mostly in wood, but she later used stone, concrete and various metals. She specialized in garden figures and, on a smaller scale, portraits in pottery and porcelain. One of her finest works is a bronze architectural screen, executed in

Fig. 15. Left: shape 3161, Mermaid, modelled by Anne Acheson, white glazed sculpture, puce mark and title, dated 1937. Right: shape 2702, Nude Boy with Dolphin, modeller unknown, white Crownware body, brown mark, no date code. (Phillips)

1956 when she was well into her seventies. She died in 1962. Her work for Worcester, supplied as a freelance modeller in 1931, comprised Irish subjects (2920 and 2921) as well as Tangles (2919) and the popular figure of a girl (2930). In 1936 and 1937 she provided three further, rather strange models: Child with Butterfly (3157), Mermaid (3161) and Queen in the Parlour (3193).

Aumonier, Eric: A freelance sculptor who had a studio in Bloomsbury in the 1930s. He modelled animal and equestrian figures for Worcester in Art Deco style, produced by the factory in 1931. He devised his own colouring using small geometric shapes and sprigs, which were difficult for the factory workers to understand. His Young Horse (2877) proved reasonably popular, although the book-ends (2875 and 2876) and doe (2874) were unsuccessful.

Azori, A: A Frenchman working in Paris in the 1950s, specializing in terracotta. He provided one series for Worcester in 1956 (3585-3588) in Chinoiserie style. They were made in biscuit porcelain with a similar texture to terracotta and enhancing the sculptural style. At the same time Azori provided four models of cockerels (3581-3584).

Baker, Ethelwyn: A freelance sculptress who had a studio in St. John's Wood, London. She provided a small number of models for Worcester in 1931, although they had probably been modelled much earlier in the stylized Art Deco fashion. Her models have her monogram (EB in a circle) moulded on the bases and she requested that the paintresses picked her mark out in colour. (*see* also page 51).

Bargas, Henri: Born in Paris, he studied under Vermare. He exhibited a group

Fig. 16. Chinoiserie figures by A. Azori. Left: shape 3588, La Miroir. Right: shape 3586, La Fleur. Black marks, dated after 1960.

entitled *'Les Ailes Oriser'* (Broken Wings) at the *Salon des Artistes Français* in 1932. He supplied five models for Worcester (3124-3127 and 3155) in 1936, none of which was successful.

Blake, Geraldine: A freelance modeller who provided six equestrian figures for Worcester (3165-3170) in 1936. Strongly modelled, her figures resemble the historical style of Gwendoline Parnell, and deserved better success. Unfortuantely, the public preferred Doris Lindner's contemporary equestrian studies and very few of Geraldine Blake's models were made.

Bray, Jessamine S: A freelance sculptress who provided in 1931 the successful pair of figures June and Noel (2905 and 2906), modelled in conjunction with Sybil Williams. In a different style, the two lady modellers were also responsible for Bluebeard and Fatima (2903 and 2904).

Cane, Margaret: A freelance modeller who provided three figures of children produced in 1931 (2916-2918). Her work was reasonably successful and it is surprising that she was not asked for any further models.

Charol, Dorothea: Born on 22nd March 1889 in Odessa, Dorothea Charol was a German national and studied in Brussels, Dresden and Munich before settling in Berlin. She married a painter, A. Koglsperger, but they were divorced in 1930, and she emigrated to Paris and then London. While in Berlin, she modelled presentation figures and portrait busts, and she provided figure models for Max Pfeiffer's workshop in Schwarzburg and for the Volkstedt factory in Thuringia. She worked as a freelance for Rosenthal in the 1920s, modelling a particularly fine Pierrot in 1925. After her arrival in England in the 1930s, Miss Charol again worked as a freelance and is believed to have modelled for Wedgwood. Her reputation as a portrait modeller led to Worcester's asking her for a portrait plaque of King Edward VIII to commemorate his coronation, which never took place. Later in 1937, she modelled a portrait plaque of the Prime Minister, the Rt. Hon. Stanley Baldwin. She provided six figures for Worcester between 1937 and 1939, and it must be said that none was successful. The continental German styles of the 1920s were somewhat old-fashioned by 1937, and her ballet dancers (3186 and 3192) and bathing girls (3288 and 3289) are rather stiff and lifeless. Her best models were the Pierrot Group (3202) and the exotic figure Repose (3272), but perhaps this was felt to be a bit 'naughty' by the factory and not given the chance it deserved. Miss Charol frequently visited the

works during the late 1930s and was remembered by the paintresses for the quantity of vaseline which she put on her eyebrows. She remained in London until her death in March 1963.

Clemencin, François André: Born at Lyons, 7th October 1878, he studied under Coutan and exhibited at the *Salon des Artistes Français* from the 1900s until the late 1930s. He was awarded a second-class medal in 1921 and a gold medal in 1930, and was also made *Chevalier de Legion d'Honeur*. His freelance work for Worcester comprised four figures in 1922 (2798-2801). Few appear to have been made.

Crofts, Stella Rebecca: Born in Nottingham on 9th January 1898, her family moved to Ilford, Essex, in about 1900. From an early age she was crippled by tuberculosis of the bones and was educated at home by her sister. In spite of her disability, she was accepted by the Central School of Arts and Crafts in 1916, and studied there until 1922. She then joined the Royal College of Art for one year as a student of sculpture and pottery. She exhibited at the Royal Academy nine times between 1925 and 1962, and also exhibited at Venice, Toronto, Milan and Paris, where she was awarded a silver medal at the *Exposition des Arts Décoratifs* in 1925. She established a pottery in about 1925 in Ilford, moving later to Worsey Wood, Billericay, where she also had her own kiln, making and decorating all of her own groups. Her father acted as business manager and pottery assistant until he grew too old to carry the clay. Stella had made a particular study of animals and their movement at London Zoo, and most of her work is of groups of animals in a stylish sculptural fashion picked out in coloured glazes. She experimented with other bodies and her work has been seen in pottery, porcelain, semi-stoneware and terracotta. At Billericay she did quite a lot of commission work and would go and stay at people's houses to model family pets. Her models of animals were acquired by many museums including the Victoria & Albert Museum, Manchester Art Gallery and the Decorative Arts Museum in Milan. Stella Crofts was an accomplished paintress of animals in oil and water-colour, also working in bronze, and she even tried her hand at leatherwork and book illustrations. In ceramics, she also made wall plaques and tiles, small jewellery in pottery and some pots thrown on a wheel, but the disability which affected her hands resulted in her achieving very little success as a thrower. A few portrait figures by Stella Crofts are known, including a fine study of the Royal Princesses, Elizabeth and Margaret, with a dog, modelled in 1937 and now in the possession of the Queen. A figure of a lady with a deer is belived to be a self-portrait of Miss Crofts. This is owned by the Essex Naturalists Trust, of which she was a founder member. She died at Billericay in 1964, aged 66.

Stella Crofts' work for Worcester comprised seven models introduced in 1931, although these had mostly been modelled earlier in pottery. A group of a boy on a donkey is known, dated 1929, and a pelican ashtray has been seen from her own kiln at Ilford. A number of giraffe groups are known, dated between 1931 and 1948, and these were the most successful of her models used at Worcester. At the time of writing a group of Giraffes (2895) holds the record for a Royal Worcester figure (excluding Limited Editions), an example selling for £1,430 at Phillips in London in 1983.

Doughty, Dorothy: Born in San Remo, Italy, in 1892, a daughter of Charles Doughty and elder sister of Freda. Their father was a celebrated writer and explorer and their mother an accomplished water-colourist. Dorothy studied at the Eastbourne School of Art and became a keen naturalist and bird lover. All of her models for Royal Worcester were produced as Limited Editions and so do not come within the scope of this book, but her importance in the history and development of Worcester figure modelling cannot be too

strongly stressed. She died in October 1962. Her work is fully documented in *The American Birds of Dorothy Doughty*, published by Royal Worcester in 1962, and also in *Royal Worcester Porcelain*, by Henry Sandon.

Doughty, Freda G.: The younger sister of Dorothy, Freda first came to the notice of the Worcester factory in 1930, when the works were in a bad way and needed new figure models. Col. Clive, one of the directors of the factory, was staying with Miss Doughty's cousin and saw some figures which Freda had made and fired in her own kiln. He asked her to make something to submit to Worcester, and she modelled four small figures which were accepted (2912-2915). They were an immediate success and led to what Freda described as 'many happy years working for the company'. In all, one hundred figures by Freda Doughty were made by the factory and, with few exceptions, most were tremendously successful. Her best-known works, the Days of the Week and Months of the Year, have been made continuously since the 1950s. Some, indeed, have been in production since the 1930s, and still are being sold in china shops all over the world fifty years later. Her most successful figures were Grandmother's Dress (3081) and Boy with Parakeet (3087). Some of the factory workers joke that there were times in the late 1950s and early 1960s when these figures were virtually the only items the factory could sell, and that Miss Doughty's work kept the factory going. It is certainly true that she was able consistently to model figures which captured the playful innocence of children in a way which appealed to the buying public again and again. The 'Worcester Children', as they were called, were modelled from actual children, who were always welcome to visit the garden of her home in Goudhurst, Kent, which she shared with her sister, Dorothy. They were never asked to sit, but played naturally, making it easy for Freda to get a feeling of movement. A few figures were imaginary, whilst a very few were modelled with the help of photographs. She ran classes of modelling for children in her own home, and her models in clay were either taken to Worcester for moulding or were fired in the Doughtys' own kiln.

One visitor who saw some of the children happily playing commented, 'How many happy grandchildren you have!', a remark which greatly pleased Miss Doughty, who had never married. We have met some of the children who sat for Freda Doughty, now grown up with children of their own. All have fond memories of their visits to the Doughtys' garden. In a few cases a little boy would serve as the model for a figure of a girl, Miss Doughty noting that at a young age there is little physical difference between boys and girls. This causes slight embarrassment to the grown-up boys who recall that they were the models for figures such as Joan (2915).

Unlike her sister, Freda Doughty was not keen on the idea of Limited Editions, preferring her little figures to be available to anyone who wanted one. Some of her later, more ambitious models probably suffered for this, being unable to compete with the Limited Edition Victorian Ladies of Ruth Van Ruyckevelt, and the last eight models which she worked on for Worcester from 1958 to 1961 were all doomed to failure, whilst her earlier work still sold easily. By this time she had more or less retired to her home near Falmouth, having moved from Goudhurst. She remained there to nurse her elderly sister, Dorothy, who died in 1962. Freda, always a most private person, disliked publicity and strove to avoid it and enjoy a quiet retirement. She died in 1972.

Ellis, Aline R.: A sculptress who, with her husband, ran the Edbury Pottery in Pimlico, London in the early 1920s. Mrs. Ellis was the principal modeller of the partnership and two models by her, of a mare and a foal, were acquired by the Victoria & Albert Museum in 1920 through the National Art Collection Fund. A dog in unglazed pottery in the authors' collection shows great attention to detail,

and the same quality of modelling is seen in the dog models supplied to Worcester between 1940 and 1942. Toto (3331) shows tremendous movement and, like all of Aline Ellis' models made at the factory, was given a matt finish resembling closely the production of Mrs. Ellis' own pottery. All her models for Worcester seem to have been made exclusively for Alex Dickens and the American market.

Evans, Eric: Employed by the factory after 1915, working alongside Frederick Gertner as works modeller. No models have been identified as his work. He is belived to have come from the Potteries. Three animal models of 1935 (3096, 3100 and 3101) attributed to E. Evans are by either Eric or Ernest Evans.

Evans, Ernest A.: Son of George Evans, who had been the works modeller until 1906. Possibly responsible for most of the figure modelling until the arrival of Frederick Gertner in 1915, he is believed to have modelled the Netsuke animals (*see* page 11). His only signed figures are Jester (2213) and Pierrot (2393), originally issued in unglazed biscuit porcelain.

Evans, George: Born in 1850, he joined the factory as a modeller in 1862 and was responsible for many large vase shapes and possibly some of the figures attributed to James Hadley. It is likely that he modelled the series of Boer War soldiers in 1900 (2106-2111). He left the factory in 1906.

Evans, Sydney: Another son of George Evans, he was employed by the factory as a modeller, although it is not known in what capacity.

Foy, Peggy: A freelance modeller who is credited with seven models in 1955 (3552-3559). It is possible that the models were never delivered to Worcester, and no photographs or moulds exist at the factory.

French, Neal: Born in 1933, he began his training at Mid-Essex Technical College and School of Art, winning the Sidney Taylor silver medal as the outstanding student of the year. He developed a special talent for modelling under Huxley-Jones. In 1953 Neal entered the Ceramic School of the Royal College of Art where he studied under Professor R. W. Baker, graduating with a first-class diploma in design in 1958 and a silver medal for ceramic modelling. He was granted a travelling scholarship which took him to Italy, where he studied the work of the Renaissance sculptors. He joined the design staff of Royal Worcester under Professor Baker and succeeded Frederick Gertner in completing the series of Papal Guard officers, a task which once again took him to Italy. He remained at the Worcester factory until 1972 and was responsible for modelling tableware and designing patterns, as well as modelling the 'Playtime' series of children's figures (3747, 3748 and 3754-3757), two figures of ladies (3607 and 3620) and the Fontainebleau series for table decoration in hard porcelain. Neal French is a lecturer in three-dimensional design at Middlesex Polytechnic and his recent commissions include a bust of the Prime Minister for her constituency in North Finchley. He has a keen interest in ceramic history and collects early teapots. His published work includes a guide to industrial tableware, and he is joint author of a book on eighteenth-century blue and white Worcester porcelain. A life-long cricket enthusiast, and, in his own words, 'a persistent though mediocre amateur cricketer', he is a member of the MCC and was, whilst working for Royal Worcester, responsible for the design and much of the execution of the bowl presented to the MCC by Worcestershire County Cricket Club to mark the 150th anniversary of the establishment of Lords Cricket Ground. Whilst at the Royal College of Art and captain of its somewhat eccentric cricket team, Neal modelled a pair of cricketing figures intended as a parody of the Victorian flatback sporting figures. Since leaving Royal Worcester, Neal has produced these immensely humorous figures, usually in MCC and Worcestershire County Cricket Club colours.

Although we have not included shape numbers 3729 and 3730 (a right and a left hand) in this book, these are occasionally seen and were produced in limited numbers as a result of a misunderstanding. Neal designed a place setting for the tableware pattern 'Delecta' to promote the new pattern at an exhibition in 1961. Having himself modelled a right hand as a serviette holder, he had one made as a part of the display. The staff, however, took orders by mistake and the factory produced about fifty pairs just to satisfy the customers. These white glazed hands are occasionally seen and are worth looking out for.

Gertner, Frederick Martin: Born in Worcester in 1886, he was the son of a local carpenter and began his training working alongside his father as a wood carver, ornamenting some of the elaborate heavy furniture popular in Edwardian England. While attending evening classes in art and sculpture at the Victoria Institute in Worcester he met many of the workers from the porcelain works and became interested in modelling ceramics. His work won him a bronze medal and he was awarded a scholarship to the Royal College of Art, School of Sculpture. He became an associate of the R.C.A. and, in about 1913, took up a teaching post in Llanelli as an Assistant Art Master.

During the First World War the Worcester factory needed a skilled modeller to design several major new sets of figures and they remembered Frederick Gertner. Fred's heart had always remained at Worcester and he didn't need much tempting to give up his teaching and return to his birth-place, joining Royal Worcester in 1915 as principal Works Modeller. His first major work for the factory was to be his most important, two sets of figures in historical costumes issued in 1916, most of which were still in production sixty years later. His Military series, while largely direct copies of imported Dresden models, showed the same meticulous attention to detail which made his series of Kings and Queens of England such a success. Gertner's work at this time reflects his complete versatility. In 1917, as well as his large historical figures, he modelled a set of birds on simple stumps in a stylized format intended for mass-production. He is also likely to have modelled many of the nude child studies in 1917-1919, and a great many ornamental vase and tableware shapes were either modelled or adapted for production by Frederick Gertner.

When in 1931 and 1932 the factory set about revitalising its figure production, they turned to their resident modeller to design some new figures to complement the work of the many freelance sculptors. Gertner's series of Red Indians (2907-2910) were powerful studies but failed to appeal to the public who were more interested in pretty child studies. Dutch Boy and Girl (2922-2923) were just what was needed and these sold in great numbers, although his other models of children (3009-3010) did not fare so well, probably because they had to compete with the much more life-like work of Freda Doughty. Quite a number of Frederick Gertner's figures have been seen incorrectly titled by the paintress as the work of Miss Doughty, evidence of the latter's popularity while Gertner's work remains unknown. Yet his importance cannot be stressed too strongly. Working at the factory, his job was to adapt the figures by some of the freelance sculptors whose models had to be altered to suit methods of production. He was responsible for "cutting-up" many of the figures while Bob Bradley made the moulds, and in 1949 Fred was filmed cutting-up Miss Lindner's equestrian study of Princess Elizabeth for a publicity film called 'The Doctor Ordered Clay'. The years of experience showed in the old man's face as he cut precisely through the horse's head at just the right angle.

In 1956 Frederick Gertner began what was to be his last work for Worcester, a series of officers of the Papal Guards, their uniform showing the same finely researched detail as his historical figures of forty years earlier. Sadly only two figures were completed before ill health forced Fred reluctantly to retire, passing the responsibility for the Modelling Department on to his son, Paul, who had joined the works in 1950. Frederick Gertner died in 1960, leaving Neal French to complete the Papal Guards series which was issued in Limited Editions.

Greaves, Rachel: Born in 1908, she was the daughter of Dr Robert Bond Greaves MD, who, as well as being a physician, wrote poetry and published two volumes, *Lays by the Way* and *Lays and Lyrics*. She taught at Sheffield College of Art from 1924 to 1932 and then did freelance modelling until 1950, when she joined the staff at Birkdale Preparatory School, remaining there until her retirement in 1970. She first came to the attention of Royal Worcester when she visited the British Industries Fair and showed a photograph of a small seated ballet dancer to Joseph Gimson, who gave her an order for a set of dancers, seven in all (3171-3177), based upon well-known dancers of the period. These were originally intended to be depicted on water-lily bases, but the latter were removed because of subsequent supporting difficulties. Miss Greaves was called to the factory to assist in alternative arrangements and was later commissioned to model two busts of Seasons (3246 and 3247). Apparently none of these was sold and the moulds were returned to Miss Greaves.

After the war she assisted in the factory in the making of the Dorothy Doughty orange blossom sprays following a period of six weeks at Falmouth working with Miss Doughty. Many years later Henry Sandon met Miss Greaves and discovered the moulds for the dancers in the garage of her home in Sheffield, where she still lives. The Company reissued five of the ballet dancers in 1982 and a number were made. They were not, however, terribly successful, perhaps because Miss Greaves' original idea of pale grey colouring was not used, the figures being left with a hard white glaze and a gilded line around the base. These revived figures were given new names, such as 'Blithe Spirit' and will, of course, have the modern black mark and copyright date of 1982 under the bases.

Guero: This name appears in factory lists against shape no. 3121, a model of a tiger. We have been unable to trace any further information.

Lindner, Doris Lexey Margaret: Born in Llanyre, Radnorshire, on 8th July 1896, she studied sculpture at St Martin's School of Art and Frank Calderon's school of animal painting in London, and also at the British School in Rome. She worked in London as a freelance sculptress and became very skilled in the structure of animals, especially horses and dogs. Her work also encompassed more abstract sculpture and her human figures in Art Deco style received much praise in the late 1920s. She worked in many media, particularly stone, concrete and plaster, with occasional bronzes, but she was never a potter. Her work was exhibited at the Royal Academy and the Royal Society of British Sculpture, as well as at many other galleries, including the Glasgow Institute and the Leicester Gallery. She designed a few figures for Minton in the late 1920s and in 1930 was commissioned by Ambrose Heal to produce pairs of book-ends in brightly painted plaster, depicting Harlequin and Columbine and a rejected Pierrot. These sold in Heal's store for 3 guineas and were noticed by Joseph Gimson, who bought the copyright to make the book-ends in porcelain. These were produced in 1931 (2866 and 2867), together with three single figures and a small number of dog models. The figures were greeted with only moderate success, but the dogs were instantly best sellers and led to a whole series of small dog studies issued in the following two years. Doris herself still preferred to model figures and provided Naiad (3030) in 1933,

and dancing ladies (3086 and 3088) in 1935, in addition to her fine group of dancers (2949) of 1931. None of these was successful, and Joseph Gimson only wanted her animals. Doris always felt that her figures were not given a chance, and were not decorated as she wanted, in plain matt white or marbled to look like stone. She submitted a powerful figure of a reclining girl to Wedgwood in about 1934, issued as bookends in matt white glaze, but these also failed and she was never again asked to model single figures. Her talent lay in realistic depiction of animals and the occasional lifelike figure of a rider mounted on a horse. Her first series of equestrian studies for Worcester, modelled in 1935, (3114-3117) was instantly successful, and led the way towards ever more ambitious horse models.

Doris Lindner always modelled from life and would go to great lengths to study and sketch her subject before attempting any modelling. In 1936 she joined a tenting tour with Bertram Mills' Circus, following many performances from the ringside. During one show she realized just before the start that she had left some important tools outside and hurried to get them, to be met by a line of stallions charging towards her. She remembered that if a lion charges at you, you are supposed to stand your ground and stare him out, and so she did just that, not moving a muscle as the horses rushed past her. Her experiences led to her early groups of circus horses (3179 and 3180), which at the time proved very difficult to make. The factory preferred smaller models and in 1938 her series of sporting dogs (3228-3233) and Zoo Babies (3263-3266 and 3273-3274) were introduced. The latter were charmingly modelled from life, Doris paying many visits to London Zoo to record accurately in sketches the movement of playful baby wild animals. Both these sets were modelled on rectangular bases, which perhaps made them seem a little stiff. Reluctantly Miss Lindner agreed to the factory's wishes and they were all reissued in 1940 without bases. Sadly, the Zoo Babies were still not a success, although the Sporting Dogs, like her small dog series, became tremendously popular during the 1950s.

While Bogskar (3330) of 1940 was a failure, it showed Miss Lindner's ability to model portraiture. When, in 1948, a figure of Princess Elizabeth on horseback was proposed, Doris was the natural choice, and the Princess sat for her several times at Buckingham Palace. Doris remembered that when the model was completed it had to pass the careful scrutiny of King George VI, who asked his daughter to change back into her uniform of Colonel-in-Chief of the Grenadier Guards so that he could check every small detail. The King was satisfied, much to the relief of Doris Lindner, and the statuette was made as an Edition of 100. It was still rather stiff, but the increased technology and daring skill of the factory craftsmen meant that when Doris Linder modelled Queen Elizabeth's own daughter, Princess Anne, as an equestrian figure in 1970, the Princess' mount, Doublet, leaped over a fence with amazing movement.

Between 1947 and 1950 Doris Lindner modelled eight bird studies, but all were failures, the factory preferring the work of Dorothy Doughty. Doris did model a small number of birds for the Crown Staffordshire factory, but at Worcester she showed that she was foremost an animal sculptress. Her equestrian figures of champion showjumpers, begun in 1959, and her other major series of champion bulls and horses, all produced in Limited Editions, exhibit the attention to detail which places Doris Lindner amongst the top ceramic sculptors of this century. Her last major commission outside the factory was for a figure of the great racehorse Arkle, cast in bronze half life-size, to stand on Cheltenham racecourse, the scene of Arkle's greatest triumphs. Royal Worcester produced some of her later models, also in bronze, and Miss Lindner also modelled a series of small animals and dogs which were produced in cold-cast bronze by Heredities. Doris Lindner's last thirty years were spent

living in the delightful Cotswold village of Broad Campden. Here she had her studio, where she displayed some of her very modernistic stone and bronze sculpture in the style of Barbara Hepworth and Henry Moore, sculptors whom Miss Lindner much admired. We well remember many very pleasant visits to her studio to talk about her life and work. Her death in 1979 at the age of 82 was deeply felt by everyone in the factory at Worcester who had known her.

Mitchell-Smith: Shapes 3538 and 3557 are listed as Isobella and Philip, modelled by Miss Mitchell-Smith. No other details are known, and it is unlikely that her models were proceeded with.

Parnell, Gwendoline M: Came from an artistic family of Irish descent, her grandmother being a Lady-in-Waiting to Queen Victoria and her sister, Edith Farmiloe, a book illustrator. Gwendoline was a portrait painter until the First World War, when she was tempted by a request from the Board of Trade to produce crafts at home to compete with the traditional products of Germany. A visit to the 'Enemy Crafts' exhibition in 1914 at the Goldsmiths' Hall is described in her own words:

> Portrait painter went to the secretary of the exhibition and said 'What would you like me to do? Toys? Right!' Passing a table on which were some pretty bad German pottery figures, the portrait painter remarked 'We ought to beat that sort of thing standing on our heads.' Secretary: 'Then will you try, standing on your head?' Exit portrait painter, who stands on her head for three years in a tub of clay, learning the trade.

Her first effort was attempted with modelling clay, a paper knife and a hairpin. She next made a pottery figure which she took to a cousin who had a small enamelling furnace, and put it in very wet. In a few moments a terrific explosion took place which flattened them against the wall with fright, so she decided her amateur attempts were at fault. She went to the Camberwell School of Craft and became a student under Professor Lunn, former manager of the Royal Crown Derby factory. While at Camberwell she exhibited, at the British Industries Fair in 1917, a statuette of Henry VIII, and this was purchased by Queen Mary, giving Miss Parnell great confidence. She started her own pottery in 1918 in Upper Cheyne Row, Chelsea, and engaged several assistants. They moved to larger premises in Paradise Walk, Chelsea in 1921. She wrote that: 'to be a good potter one must be an efficient cook, an excellent dressmaker, and an artistic designer, have a considerable knowledge of chemistry and be something of a navvy to undertake the waging of clay.'

Her early work was freehand modelled; later, as she became more successful, moulds were used and the assistants played a much greater part in the production. Her 'Cheyne Figures' were influenced by Chelsea porcelain of the eighteenth century and by seventeenth and eighteenth-century British theatre. Her best-known figures were a series of humorous Ladies of the Russian Ballet, shown at the Women's International Art Club exhibition, 1919; a series of figures from the *Beggar's Opera* (1920-21); and sixteen characters from *School For Scandal* (1925). These were shown at the Paris Exhibition in 1925, winning a Grand Prix. In 1927 Miss Parnell was elected as the first president of the Guild of Pottery, and exhibitions of her work were held regularly in Chelsea as well as at Walker's Gallery in 1932 and Colnaghi's in 1933. These exhibitions included a set of figures of London Cries.

Some of Gwendoline Parnell's work was bought by Alex Dickens, and it is possible that he encouraged her to close her pottery in London and move to Worcester in 1935, beginning a period of seven years' modelling for the porcelain works. Her fame as a portrait modeller made her the ideal choice to model the Jubilee Statuettes of King George V and Queen Mary in 1935 (3089 and 3090), and these were followed by six further figures in the same year and eight models in 1936, including

her most impressive groups, The Planter's Daughter and The Powdering Mask (3138 and 3140), continuing the 'Cheyne-Chelsea' style of modelling which she had originated. Many of her figures were large and ambitious and consequently expensive, often selling in only small numbers. Her smaller figures, such as The Thief and Magnolia Bud (3145 and 3144), and the Chinoiserie Children (3354, 3362 and 3348) proved much more popular and sold in great quantities.

Gwendoline Parnell lived in Edgar Street, near to the factory, and was well-remembered at Worcester. The workers in the factory nicknamed her 'The Duchess' because she was always well dressed, rather in the Victorian style, and carried a parasol. Daisy Rea remembers travelling with Miss Parnell to Birmingham in 1938 to see George Robey's collection of oriental costume for ideas on how her large chinoiserie figures should be coloured. In the end she decided that the dress Miss Rea was wearing was the most suitable colour she had seen, and this became the colouring for the pair of Chinese Dancers (3194 and 3195) and all the subsequent chinoiseries. For her help over this and her other figures Gwendoline gave Daisy Rea an egg, finely gift-wrapped, a great rarity during the early years of the war.

Daisy Rea always fondly remembered her friendship with Gwendoline Parnell. Daisy was often invited to tea at Gwendoline's house, and there would always be a special cake made for the occasion. They often journeyed to Birmingham together and Gwendoline delighted in taking Daisy to a rather expensive hotel for tea. On one occasion, however, she was embarrassed to find she had no money and Daisy took her to a very cheap café. Gwendoline told Daisy afterwards that she had never enjoyed a tea so much.

Gwendoline Parnell returned to her Chelsea style for a series of London Cries, similar in style to figures made earlier in her own pottery. Six figures were modelled between 1938 and 1940, but all were failures

Fig. 17. Original factory photographs of the Chinoiserie Sayings Series modelled by Agnes Pinder-Davis. Top: shapes 3491, 3501, 3494. Bottom: shapes 3498, 3500, 3502.

and did not continue after the war. Her last figures were the Chinoiserie Children modelled in 1941. She moved from Worcester to The Old Rectory. Grafton Flyford, a village near Worcester. Two volumes of press-cuttings kept by Miss Parnell between 1919 and 1933 are preserved in the library of the Victoria and Albert Museum and throw considerable light on her work during this period.

Pinder-Davis, Agnes: Joined the Worcester factory during the Second World War, replacing Gwendoline Parnell as modeller of Chinoiserie subjects. An accomplished sculptress, her work is dramatic as well as curious. Her first models, Southwind and Westwind (3388 and 3396), issued in 1943 and 1944, were in a much earlier Art Deco style and very few were made. They were followed by four Chinoiserie figures

(3397-3400), which were initially sold just in white porcelain and were selected for the 'Britain Can Make It' exhibition held at the Victoria and Albert Museum in 1948. They were subsequently issued in colours and were very successful. Mrs. Pinder-Davis was at her best in Chinese style, and her work in other styles, such as the Watteau Figures (3402-3405) and Regency Figures (3414 and 3415), is very strange and did not sell well. Her finest figures were the large pair of Balinese and Siamese Dancers (3473 and 3474) modelled in 1951. They were the largest figures attempted by the factory and the graceful fingers and rich gilding caused endless problems for the workers. Kiln losses were heavy and it eventually took more than twenty years to make the twenty-five pairs in the Limited Edition.

In 1953 Agnes Pinder-Davis began a set of twelve small figures of chinoiserie children and animals, each representing a well-known saying. It was hoped that these would become as popular as the Days of the Week series, but, although of good quality and finely decorated, they were too strange and lacked the universal charm of Miss Doughty's children. Few of the Chinoiserie Sayings series sold well, and most were failures. Her last models for the factory were three London Cries in 1955 (3541-3543), but these did not seem to appeal and the factory did not put them into production. Mrs. Pinder-Davis retired to Worthing, Sussex, and in her last years in the 1960s she took up painting in oils. Her still lifes and garden scenes painted for local exhibitions are very fine, and well worth looking out for.

Pointon, William: Born in about 1860, he joined the factory in the 1880s as a staff modeller, and was responsible for some very fine Pâte-sur-pâte decoration of animals and landscapes in coloured clay, occasionally signing his work. He did some figure modelling for the factory and in 1916 was asked to model two figures of soldiers (2645 and 2646). His figures reflected the realities of life at the Front with a spirit which is lacking in previous figures of soldiers made at Worcester. No other figures are identified as his work.

Rea, Daisy: Although she was not, of course, a modeller, this book is dedicated to Daisy Rea. There are references to her throughout the book and so we have decided to include a brief biography.

Daisy was born in 1894 and started at the factory in September 1909, painting flowers, usually roses, in the traditional Worcester style of Hadley, sometimes on the famous 'stained ivory' ware. She began to paint the figure subjects, identifying her work with a mark number of 33, and she became forewoman of the paintresses, a position she held for the large part of the period covered by this book. Sadly, Daisy died in her 91st year in 1984, but she was able in her last years to provide us with a considerable amount of information about the figure subjects and modellers. The various modellers would usually indicate their choice of colours, but often had little idea of how the different colours work together on china. Daisy, therefore, invariably had to make changes, sometimes even suggesting a new name to go with a particular colour scheme. She would usually try any new ideas for colours on a plate to see how they appeared after firing in the kiln. Red was the least popular colour, and is not often seen on figures unless combined with another shade. Daisy would decide how long a particular figure should take to decorate, and a payment for the paintresses would be fixed, usually between 3d. and 6d. Daisy Rea was very proud when she revealed that she worked at the factory for a considerable length of time, outliving many of the great men painters. She met very few of the twentieth-century modellers but formed close friendships with Gwendoline Parnell and Freda Doughty. When guests were staying with Daisy, Freda and Dorothy Doughty always insisted that she took them to tea at the Doughty home, where Daisy often appeared as an 'exhibit', painting in the garden.

Ruyckevelt, Ronald Van: Born in 1928, he studied painting in Wimbledon and then spent three years at the Royal College of Art School of Ceramics, where he specialized in modelling. He became an Associate, and after one year of industrial practice was awarded the Diploma Des. RCA. He joined the design staff of Royal Worcester in August 1953 and the following year won the British Pottery Manufacturers' Federation Travelling Scholarship. He worked closely with the manufacture of the American Doughty bird models and in 1955 he was sent by the factory to Bermuda to study at first hand the tropical fish in their natural surroundings of coral-floored lagoons. He produced numerous sketches and paintings at an aquarium and local inhabitants helped him by bringing him fresh specimens which they had caught. Back in his studio in Worcester he produced seven large tropical fish models, made in Limited Editions, as well as six smaller models to be made in greater numbers (3572-3576 and 3579) and these proved a surprising success for the factory. In 1958 Ronald Van Ruyckevelt was asked to model six small models of American birds in the style of Eva Soper's popular series (3645-3650) and these were the last models of his that Worcester made in unlimited numbers. A visit to Florida led to a series of models of tropical flowers and dramatic models of big game fish, aimed at wealthy American sportsmen. Van Ruyckevelt caught specimens himself and rushed his fish back to the hotel, where he put them in his bath while making drawings at great speed. The hotel was most helpful and provided a refrigerator so he could keep his fish fresh, although there was not much room left after a dolphin had been squeezed in.

In 1965 a further visit to America led to a major series of North American game-birds. His skill as a modeller and experience in the manufacturing side resulted in finished models which were technically much further advanced than the Doughty birds had been. His finest model for Worcester was the group of two white doves made in 1970 to celebrate the Silver Wedding of the Queen and the Duke of Edinburgh. Ronald Van Ruyckevelt's wife Ruth began the important series of Victorian Ladies for Royal Worcester from 1958, and the couple ran their own factory in Malvern producing porcelain flowers mounted on ormolu stems, which were distributed by Royal Worcester. Ronald was responsible for completing the Victorian Ladies series and his last work for Worcester was the Queens Regnant series, an impressive set of five figures from Elizabeth I to Elizabeth II issued in Limited Editions in the 1970s. He left the factory in 1974 and moved to the United States.

Soper Eva L: Daughter of George Soper, a fellow of the Royal Society of Painters, Etchers and Engravers who founded a wildlife sanctuary. Eva and her sister continued the sanctuary and Eva had her own studio there, giving her plenty of opportunity to study the wild birds, which became tame, frequently entering the studio to eat from Eva's hand. In the 1930s she had an electric kiln installed in her studio and her glazed pottery models of birds were sold by Alex Dickens. Dickens introduced her to the Worcester factory in 1937 and she modelled four single birds that year, with a further eight models in 1938, all modelled to scale. Intended to be inexpensive, and aimed at the British market, they were quite unlike the larger Doughty birds. The series was an instant success, and in 1941 Miss Soper was asked for seven further single birds followed by six groups, each of two birds on a stump, introduced in 1942. Eva Soper's small birds were at first issued fully glazed, and it was not until the late 1950s that a matt finish was used to give the birds greater realism. The bird models are still popular forty years later.

Soper, Eileen: Born in 1905, she studied art under her father George Soper and became an accomplished engraver from an early age, exhibiting an etching at the Royal Academy in 1921 while still only 15.

Altogether she had eight etchings accepted by the Academy during the 1920s. Subsequently painting became more important, particularly book illustrating, and Eileen's friendship with Enid Blyton led to her providing illustrations for thirty five of Miss Blyton's childrens books between 1943 and 1968. She illustrated many other books with wildlife subjects inspired by the nature reserve which she ran with her sister Eva Soper, but it was her innocent happy children which brought her widespread acclaim. Eva had provided bird models for Royal Worcester and she probably introduced her sister to the company when a series of children studies was commissioned in 1941. Eileen Soper's series of seven figure groups (3346-3382) captures, through the innocent eyes of children, the realities of war at a time when the British public was experiencing these events. Nobody bought the figures and sadly neither Eileen nor Eva were asked for any further models. Shape 3332, a miniature teaset, is attributed in the archives to E. Soper. This is probably the work of Eileen rather than Eva.

Stabler, Phoebe (nee McLeish): A student at the Royal College of Art who was elected FRBS in1923 and worked in stone, bronze and terracotta. She came from an artistic family, her sister Minne McLeish being a textile and poster designer, and married Harold Stabler, an eminent sculptor and designer. They founded their own pottery with a kiln in their house at The Mall, Hammersmith, in about 1910, making gla-zed faience figures and garden sculptures. Phoebe Stabler was a shrewd business-woman and marketed her work widely. She sold many of her models to Doulton & Co. in 1913, and some of the same models were subsequently produced by the Poole Pottery of Carter, Stabler & Adams in the early 1920s, and in 1931 by Royal Worcester. Several of her models were also made by the Ashtead Potters Guild, a char-itable pottery established to give employ-ment to disabled veterans of the First World War. Between 1914 and 1922 the Stablers made a number of modelled panels for use in the garden, and one particular figure, 'Shy', a naked girl seated among flowers, was much acclaimed. In 1919 the Women's Art Club displayed the work of female designers. A group of little wax figures by Phoebe Stabler was described as 'the most desirable things in the show'. After she joined Carter, Stabler & Adams in 1921, her figures and special architectural commissions, modelled in conjunction with Harold Stabler, were shown at many international exhibitions, including the British Industries Fair at Olympia (1921), the British Empire Exhibi-tion at Wembley (1924), the International Exhibition of Modern Decorative and In-dustrial Art in Paris (1925), the Ideal Home Exhibition (1927) and the Inter-national Exhibition of Industrial Art in Leipzig (1927). The most important works by the Stablers were a war memorial for Rugby School (1922), a massive war memo-rial for Durban, South Africa, designed by H. L. C. Pilkington (1925), and a group of decorative panels for the mortuary at the Kensington Infirmary (1926). In the early 1930s, Phoebe Stabler no longer modelled for Poole and her work was gradually drop-ped. Phoebe was approached by Royal Worcester in 1930-31 and asked for models suitable for porcelain. She provided nine figures which were introduced in 1931 although all seem to have been modelled much earlier. The Old Goat Woman (2886) and Flower Girl (2880) had both been made by Doulton eighteen years before in 1913. They were no longer in production and Mrs. Stabler felt free to resell the models and reproduction rights to Royal Worcester. Doulton's figure of 'Sleep', issued in 1913, is very similar to Phoebe Stabler's figure Dreaming (2879) and was probably modelled at the same time. Many of these figures were nearly twenty years old and somewhat out of date before their introduction at Worcester. It is not sur-prising, therefore, that most were pro-duced in very limited numbers at Worcester, although the Old Goat Woman was still in production in 1955. A few bronzes by Phoebe Stabler are known, including a version of 'Sauce' (2881), and these may date from the 1930s. No further models were supplied to Worcester after 1931, and Mrs. Stabler seems to have retired from modelling. She died in 1955.

Stevens, Miss: A freelance modeller who provided three figures for Worcester, a very strange Jester (3483) in 1952, and in 1954 Red Riding Hood and the Wolf dressed up as her Grandmother (3510 and 3511). These were considered frightening by the public at the time and very few sold.

Stewart, Miss: A freelance modeller who is credited with only one figure for Worcester, a Flower Girl (3099), in 1935.

Williams, Sybil V: A freelance sculptress who modelled two pairs of figures in 1931 in conjunction with Jessamine Bray. June and Noel (2905 and 2906) were an immediate success and were the only figures introduced in the 1930s made in more than one size. Their large figures of Bluebeard and Fatima (2903 and 2904) were in a very different style.

The following letter was received by the authors after this book had gone to press, but we felt because of its importance we should reproduce it here in full. It is from *Ethelwyn Baker* who still lives near Saffron Walden in Essex.

"Dear Mr Sandon

Please forgive me for not having answered your letter before now-

Studied at the Slade School under Tonks and under Thomas doing sculpture for some time— and later went to the Academy where we were taught drawing, sculpture & painting but to my disgust not carving as the Academicians said carving was for stone masons — we were to do modelling.

An incident may amuse you — The eight men from Worcester came to view my Musicians & when I asked them to sit down — they did so and each chair broke up with a loud report — amidst roars of laughter — Everyone found the others funny — Not I. I was overcome —

Yes, the Polar Bears — that was the name given by the zoo. I modelled them in the zoo each day. The Musicians — I was introduced to Royal Worcester by Mr Harry Trethowan, head of the china department at Heals. Afterwards, Ambrose Heal refused to allow Heals to sell my Musicians, no doubt a commercial decision but a heavy blow to me as Mr Trethowan had calculated they would be sold by the firm—

I was assistant to Charles Sargeant for some years and modelled many works for him — but the Musicians and the Polar Bears were my only works for Worcester. Yes, I did have a studio near Lords Cricket Ground for many years —

Many thanks for your letter

Sincerely Yours

Ethelwyn Baker."

Chapter Five
Collecting

This chapter is intended to give advice and ideas to readers who are thinking of building up a collection of Royal Worcester figures.

In recent years twentieth-century Royal Worcester figures have started to become 'collectable', a word often misused nowadays but undoubtedly appropriate in this case. It is very easy, in fact, to build up a collection of these figures without the specialized knowledge required, for instance, by collectors of eighteenth-century porcelains. Such enthusiasts must rely on many years of experience in recognizing the many different ceramic bodies and glazes merely to try and identify the maker of a particular piece.

From the middle of the Victorian period Royal Worcester has proudly and clearly marked virtually everything made, and nearly every piece has its shape number clearly printed next to the mark along with a code which tells us the exact year of production. It is possible, therefore, to pick up almost any Royal Worcester figure and discover not only the date it left the factory but also, in many cases, the name of the figure and the modeller responsible for it.

Most collections begin with just one or two figures, perhaps received as a gift or possibly an inheritance. Their appeal is easy to see and it seems natural to want to add to them. How do you go about it? There is tremendous scope, although sadly not the degree of availability that one would like, as we cannot expect to pop into any antique shop and find Royal Worcester figures. They have to be hunted, and maybe this challenge is the most exciting part of any collection, there being always the possibility of discovering a great rarity.

When reading through the list of figures given in this book one will immediately realise that it is quite impossible to collect an example of every figure. Even with unlimited funds such a project would be impossible because so many of the figures fall into the 'extremely rare, possibly not produced' category. Some of these turn up from time to time and cause considerable excitement when collectors get to hear of them, but even a lifetime's searching could not possibly turn up all of these figures. There is certainly no need to be disheartened, however, as there were many figures which enjoyed such popularity that they were made in very great numbers, over a considerable period of years, and these can be found without too much trouble.

One obvious way to collect is to buy any Royal Worcester figure which you see at a price that you consider to be fair and reasonable. By this method a collection representative of the wide range of figures made by the factory will be assembled, and such an approach can be a very good way of starting to collect. Only by handling and living with different figures will you discover the sort of model you like best. It is then possible to specialize and look for those figures which appeal to you and which fit into your collection, whilst always having the option to sell off figures which no longer seem to belong with the others. A personal collection should comprise primarily figures which a collector finds attractive and wants to have around. In addition we have selected five other approaches a collector can consider when building up a collection with a theme.

1. Collecting by modeller

In Chapter Four we list biographies of more than thirty modellers who provided figures or animal studies made by Royal Worcester. Each modeller's work had its own distinctive style and, even if they are entirely different subjects, figures by the same modeller seem to live comfortably side by side. Some modellers offer tremendous scope, and with over a hundred figures to choose from it is not difficult to collect the work of Freda Doughty. All of her little children played happily together in the Doughty home and garden, and by grouping her Worcester children you can feel something of the atmosphere that she so obviously enjoyed when she modelled the originals from life. Doris Lindner's work covers a wide range of styles and sizes, from Art Deco figures to charming small dog models and magnificent equestrian studies, presenting the collector with great scope. The works of Gwendoline Parnell, Agnes Pinder-Davis or Stella Crofts can make interesting displays and can be added to by seeking the independent work from Miss Parnell's own Chelsea pottery, Stella Crofts' own animal sculptures, or oil paintings by Mrs. Pinder-Davis. Phoebe Stabler's work for Doulton, Poole and Ashtead can form an interesting collection alongside her Worcester figures.

2. Collecting sets

In addition to those figures which seem to go together naturally in pairs, the factory produced many models forming sets ranging in number from three or four up to as many as sixteen small dogs and eighteen English birds. Once two or three figures from a larger series are owned it is a natural aim to want to add to them and try to collect the whole set. This is particularly interesting when, as is often the case, some models within a set are rarer than others: collectors can be faced with an exciting challenge and often friendly rivalry will develop between two or more collectors looking for the same figure. The Children of the Nations, Nursery Rhyme series and Netsuke Animals offer endless opportunities to build up a collection, just as the Worcester candle extinguishers have been collected for many years. Whilst mostly introduced before the period covered by this book, the huge range of extinguishers, many of which were still being made in the 1950s, make the set the most collected of all Worcester figure subjects.

3. Collecting by style

The Art Deco models of Aumonier, Baker and Lindner, or the Chinoiserie figures of Parnell, Pinder-Davis and Azori can be grouped together in collections representing the taste of a particular period. Such a collection can be used very effectively in interior decoration.

4. Collecting different colourings

Some popular figures can be found in a variety of different colour schemes, and this offers an interesting sideline to collecting. Examples are Sleepy Boy (2918), known to have been painted in seven different colourings, and the very popular models Grandmother's Dress and Boy with Parakeet, each found in a great many different colourings.

5. *Collecting white figures*

A great many Royal Worcester figures can be found in an undecorated white glazed state. Usually these models developed some minor fault during the glost firing, and instead of being smashed up were committed to the 'Lump' sale, a special offer to the staff at the factory where the worst rejects and unfinished items were sold off particularly cheaply. These are frequently found in the Worcester area and can be collected relatively inexpensively. Most are unmarked and detective work is often needed to identify them as Royal Worcester figures. A number of rarely seen figures which proved unpopular when introduced were left in an unfinished white state when the series was withdrawn. These were often sent to the 'Lump' room, and in many cases the only examples of a model known to us are just white. Some of the more sculpture-like figures and groups look particularly striking in highly-glazed pure white porcelain, and a collection of these can produce an extremely effective display.

Once a collection of any sort has been started some thought is needed to develop it successfully, and certain things have to be considered carefully. Unless you are buying purely for investment, which is not really collecting in the true sense, one of the most important considerations is personal taste. Any collector gains satisfaction from owning a very rare item and it is the scarce and unusual which are particularly worth looking out for. It should be remembered, however, that the rarest figures today are generally the ones which did not sell well when introduced. Often they were not particularly good models, and one must surely question the motives behind the purchasing of a figure for reasons of rarity alone when it may, perhaps, have little to commend it aesthetically unless, of course, it fills a vital gap in a representative collection. At the other extreme, some of the rarest figures are also amongst the most charming and stunning

of all, and these are especially worth searching for.

When buying any figure it is essential to consider whether or not it is a good example, and it is always worth looking for the better painted early pieces. With few exceptions the standard of painting declined generally after the 1930s, largely because of ever-increasing production costs. The expenses involved in the running of a factory increase all the time and, as prices went up, fewer figures were sold. It became uneconomical to spend too much time colouring one small figure as the cost meant that few people would be able to afford to buy a finely painted and enamelled model. In order to produce the figures at a competitive price it became essential to spend less and less time on decorating. Many of the figures made in the 1960s and 1970s were rather sketchily painted, and this is an inevitable result of rising costs, and the days have long passed when a paintress could happily spend considerable time perfecting one small model.

At the end of this chapter we list the marks and date-codes found on most Royal Worcester figures. Where possible it is always worth trying to buy a figure with a date-code not too many years from its date of introduction. Whilst 1950s examples of a 1930s figure are perfectly acceptable, they should ideally, if possible, be replaced in a collection by an earlier example if one can be found at a fair price. Do not turn down the chance of buying a rare figure just because of a late date unless, of course, you know the whereabouts of an earlier example. A collection can always be upgraded when the opportunity arises.

The same considerations apply where damage is seen. Always, where possible, buy a figure in perfect condition, not only with investment in mind, but for personal satisfaction. Having said this, it would be most unwise to dismiss the opportunity of acquiring a figure which has a little damage. The only opportunity to complete some of the rarer sets, such as Doris Lindner's Zoo Babies, may involve accepting some degree of damage, and providing the price paid takes the damage into account it would be foolish to miss the chance. A damaged figure should cost a great deal less than a perfect one, and if the damage is a mere crack, it can often be scarcely noticeable. Where, of course, a figure is so badly damaged that it is disfigured, it might perhaps be left alone. Nothing looks worse than a figure missing an arm or a leg and even the best of restoration is unlikely to restore a very damaged piece to its former glory.

Modern repair and restoration has its supporters and opponents. In our view there is nothing wrong with restoration as long as it is well done, and the owner *knows* that it has been done. Certain damage can be very offputting but if this can be disguised so that the figure appears to be visually perfect, then the repair is worthwhile. What should be avoided is restoration just for its own sake, and we have seen many examples where the restored piece looks considerably worse than the damaged original. Restoration can be very expensive, and we would recommend serious consideration before embarking on it.

Sadly, restored figures are often passed off as perfect. The finest modern repairs can be virtually undetectable, and so, when buying a Royal Worcester figure from a dealer or an auction room, it is important to know exactly what you are buying. It is always safer and advisable to buy from a reputable dealer who is prepared to give a receipt which states that the figure is perfect, or lists exactly the damage or repair present when the piece is purchased. Some auctioneers mention damage in their catalogue and this can be a guarantee. If nothing is stated, always ask a member of the staff if any restoration is known to exist. The auctioneers may not know, but if they have suspicions they will probably say so. Never be afraid to ask such a question as it could prevent an expensive mistake.

Restoration is not the only pitfall for the unwary collector. It is alarming but we have seen just a few fakes on the market. These are not difficult to detect, but have caught one or two people off their guard. As far as we know, no copies exist of actual Royal Worcester figures. We have seen rather inferior figures, or perhaps unmarked Worcester ones, to which a Worcester mark has been added, and we have also seen one Continental figure in Kate Greenaway style which has had a genuine Worcester mark cut from a broken cup or saucer. This had been let into the base and sprayed over to hide the join. Other unmarked figures have had a crude copy of a Worcester mark or simply the words 'Royal Worcester' added in black paint on the base. As the figures themselves become more and more collectable the temptation for forgers is bound to grow, so watch out! Happily at present this problem is a very minor one.

More commonly found are redecorated white figures and these can sometimes be difficult to detect. A great many figures were sold off in the white in Worcester, and it was natural for the original owners to want them coloured. Most 'clobbered' figures, as these are called, were painted by untrained amateur hands at home, using tins of enamel paints designed for model aeroplanes and the like. These were not painted to deceive and were coloured for the enjoyment of the original owner. This clobbering is soft and can be easily scratched, although a few are more so-phisticated, being painted in ceramic colours and fired in small muffle kilns. In these latter cases the paint does not flake off and is fired into the glaze in the same way as the factory-decorated models. The usual giveaway is the absence of a factory mark, as the Royal Worcester white figures were almost always sold unmarked. When a marked, white figure has been refired, it is only the amateur quality of the colour-ing which gives it away; indeed, it is just possible that some of the very strange col-our schemes that we have seen and record-ed could be the work of outsiders.

Such clobbered figures were usually white glazed factory seconds. Very occasionally, however, an overpainted 'biscuit' figure is seen. 'Biscuit' refers to a piece which has been fired once but not glazed. These were not sold by Royal Worcester. Usually rejects at this early stage were smashed, but it was not unusual to see them given to children who toured the Worcester factory, and they do occasionally turn up on the market, perhaps rescued from a skip by the workmen. We know of a garden in Worcester which has a concrete birdbath set with 'biscuit' models of three of the Netsuke animals and one of Eva Soper's birds. Apart from the very few figures sold in 'biscuit' form and bearing Worcester marks, the Pierrots (2393) and the Azori Chinoiseries (3585-3588) for instance, it would be very unusual to find Royal Worcester figures in this form. Any seen do make an interesting addition to a collection.

There is one final word of warning to collectors. As we have mentioned, a number of figures were reissued at a much later date, cast from the original moulds which were often retained in store following the withdrawal of a model. Since the 1970s there have been new series of Sporting Dogs, candle extinguishers and Rachel Greaves ballet dancers. All have modern colouring and factory marks, often including the date of reintroduction. In the case of the ballet dancers they have been reissued in white glazed china or redesigned circular bases, and given new names. None of these should be confused with the more valuable originals and particular care should be exercised, as we have seen examples of the modern candle extinguishers where part of the mark has been scratched off to try to give an earlier appearance. There will usually be an obvious scar on the base and the poorer quality of the painting is normally a give-away.

Care and display

Once you have started to build up a collection the opportunities for display are almost unlimited. Whether a figure is placed by itself on a table or sideboard, or a whole collection in a cabinet, is entirely up to the collector. Figures may be displayed museum-like in rows on glass shelves, or gathered together in tableaux or conversation groups. Some sets such as the Fontainebleau figures were designed in this way, to be placed on a table during a meal. Some of the Worcester Children and most of the animal models fit comfortably into almost any interior, from Georgian or colonial to modern. The more stylish figures of the 1930s, however, need to be displayed in a more up-to-date setting. There is considerable scope for ingenuity and we know of one collector who places his Chinoiserie figures by Mrs. Pinder-Davis amongst his Chinese porcelain vases. The Months of the Year figures which we illustrate in this book are displayed by their owner on a specially-designed stand which allows the model representing the current month to be shown prominently in the centre. All figures are seen to best advantage out in the open and lose something when put behind glass, so it is inevitable that they will attract dust. This, however, is not a problem generally, as most Worcester figures seem to have been designed with easy cleaning in mind. With care, they will not come to any harm, but do not use strong chemicals or detergents for cleaning. A little soft soap or washing-up liquid is quite sufficient with the help of an old soft toothbrush or paint brush. Rinse the figure well and leave it to dry thoroughly before returning it to any piece of polished furniture. During washing, water will seep through the tiny blowholes used during firing, and this can leak through the same holes to leave unsightly marks on cloth or wood.

It only remains for us to wish you luck with your collecting, hoping that you will get as much pleasure from Royal Worcester figures as we have had in writing this book.

Chapter Six
Marks and Date Codes

We are fortunate that the Royal Worcester factory carefully marked virtually everything it made from the middle of the Victorian period to the present day. With very few exceptions, every figure which we have photographed for this book was marked; and, by referring to a simple code, it has been possible to work out the exact year of manufacture.

Since 1862 the factory has used the mark of a crown over a circle. Inside the circle are four cursive letter 'W's and a crescent, marks used by the factory in the eighteenth century; in the centre of the circle is the number 51 referring to 1751, the year in which the first Worcester factory was established. In 1891 the mark was changed by the addition of the words 'Royal Worcester England' around the circle, and a system of dots replaced the letters previously used to indicate the date. All the codes are listed at the end of this chapter. In almost every case the shape number is printed underneath or alongside the factory mark.

A lot of weight is placed by collectors on the colour of the mark, or 'backstamp', to give it its factory name. The workmen were reasonably consistent in the colour which they used for the mark, but we have seen many exceptions to the general rules. Normally, the colour used for the backstamp was as follows:

1880s up until about 1910	brown or black
about 1910 to about 1925	green
about 1925 to about 1940	puce
about 1940 onwards	black

Occasionally other colours are seen, such as blue, and often brown or black marks were used during the 1910s and 1920s. Some puce marks were used before 1925, and sometimes green was used in the 1940s or 1950s for larger printed marks such as those on the farm animal series.

From 1931 it became standard to record the modeller's name and the title of the figure. This was usually written in puce by the paintress, normally in the distinctive hands of Daisy or Grace Rea. This handwritten title was used on most figures until about 1940 and, although time-consuming, did give the figure a hand-made quality which helped sales. It must be stressed, however, that these details were always added by the paintress and the modeller did not sign the individual piece and played no part in the actual decoration of the figures. Occasionally we have seen examples where the paintress has written the wrong title or modeller on the base of the figures, and this naturally causes confusion. After the war it was usual to include the title and the name of the modeller in a special printed mark for each figure, almost always printed in black.

In about 1960 it was decided that the considerable task of adding a dot to each copper plate backstamp, every year, was no longer worthwhile and a mark with no individual date code was used on most figures. There are many exceptions. Figures with complicated marks, such as the larger equestrian studies by Doris Lindner, were still marked from the same copper plates and these were brought up to date each year. Some marks have been seen with an ® and twenty-four dots for

Year mark codes				
1891		Royal Worcester England added to mark	1925	★	and 9 dots
1892	•	1 dot to left of crown	1926	★	and 10 dots
1893	••	2 dots, one each side of crown	1927	★	and 11 dots
1894	•••	3 dots	1928	□	a small square below the mark
1895		4 dots	1929	◇	a small diamond below the mark
1896		5 dots	1930	☰	below the mark
1897		6 dots	1931	∞	below the mark
1898		7 dots	1932	∞∞	below the mark
1899		8 dots	1933	∞∞•	1 dot added
1900		9 dots	1934	•∞∞•	2 dots added
1901		10 dots	1935	•∞∞••	3 dots added
1902		11 dots	1936	∞∞	4 dots added
1903		12 dots (six each side of crown)	1937	∞∞	5 dots added
1904		13 dots (twelve dots at top and one underneath mark)	1938	∞∞	6 dots added
1905		14 dots (12 at top and 2 underneath)	1939	∞∞	7 dots added
1906		15 dots	1940	∞∞	8 dots added
1907		16 dots	1941	∞∞	and nine dots
1908		17 dots	1942	∞∞	and 10 dots
1909		18 dots	1943		No date code used
1910		19 dots	1944		No date code used
1911		20 dots (12 at top, 8 underneath)	1945		No date code used
1912		21 dots	1946		No date code used
1913		22 dots	1947		No date code used
1914		23 dots	1948		No date code used
1915		24 dots	1949	V	below the mark
1916		25 dots or replaced by new system	1950	W	below the mark
1916	★	star or asterisk below mark	1951	W•	1 dot added
1917	★•	star and one dot	1952	•W•	2 dots added
1918	•★•	star and two dots	1953	•W••	3 dots added
1919	•★••	star and 3 dots	1954	••W••	4 dots added
1920	★	and 4 dots	1955	••W•••	5 dots added
1921	★	and 5 dots	1956 W or ®		with six dots
1922	★	and 6 dots	1957 W or ®		with 7 dots
1923	★	and 7 dots	1958 W or ®		with 8 dots
1924	★	and 8 dots	1959 W or ®		with 9 dots
			1960 W or ®		with 10 dots

Generally speaking, no date code was used after 1960. In some cases, however, the system of dots continued until:

1974 W or ® with 24 dots

1974 and it is possible some could be dated even later. Generally, though, no date code was used after 1960. From about 1962 it became standard for new models to have on the bottom the word 'Copyright' and the date when the figure was registered; for instance, Mayflower (3656), has © Copyright 1962 associated with the mark. This is merely the date when the figure was registered, and this same date will appear on later copies of the same figure. Any earlier figure still in production will not usually record the copyright. All marks used after 1960 will have either an ® or © to indicate that the design is registered and cannot be copied. This takes the place of the registered number which is some-times recorded on the base of a figure.

The backstamp occasionally will record the retailer for whom the figure was made. Sometimes this will be written in full, such as 'designed especially for Aspreys', but normally an emblem was used, for instance a sailing ship on items made for Heals, and a Tudor rose above the cypher AD on pieces made for Alex Dickens, the London and New York fine art publisher. Occasionally a piece was marked with the name of the retailer and then not supplied for one reason or another. The name of the store had to be removed before the factory could resell the piece, and some-times a rough patch on the base of a figure will indicate where such a mark has been taken away. A number of powder bowls have been seen with the name of *Dubarry*

Fig. 18. A typical backstamp.

et Cie. ground away from the bases. Some figures still retain the original factory price labels which were attached to their bases. These small gummed labels had the price written in code, subsituting a letter for each number. The key word Worcester used was CHELMSFORD, with C = 1, H = 2, and so on. For example, the code CH/S meant that the item originally sold for 12s. 6d.

Chapter Seven
A Catalogue of Royal Worcester Figures, 1900 – 1970

This chapter consists of a list, in numerical order, of all Royal Worcester figures produced, or intended to be produced, in unlimited editions from the year 1900 until 1970. This is the result of many years of research culminating in an extensive search through records and archives preserved at the factory. We have tried to be as comprehensive as possible and must stress once again our eternal gratitude to the directors and staff of the Worcester Royal Porcelain Company for allowing us full access to all the material which survives in their possession. Without their help no book on Worcester figures could have been conceived. It is probably helpful to try and explain the reasoning behind the classifications we have used in this list.

1. Shape number: We have listed every figure which was ever given a shape number. The system of numbering began in this form in 1862, and by 1900 shape 2100 had been reached. The shape list also included all of the vases and other ornamental shapes made by the factory, and so, although this list runs numerically, many gaps exist where we have ignored anything that cannot even loosely be classed as a figure. Where a number of figures comprised a

set, these have been grouped together with appropriate cross-references inserted in the list. Additionally, where two or three figures obviously go together to form a pair or group, these have been treated likewise. Some figures listed here were probably not put into production. Where we believe this to be the case, we have still included the number and name in our lists, in case a completed or trial example ever turns up.

2. Name: Each figure was probably given a name right from the start, either by the modeller alone, or by the modeller and the Art Director. Where this name has been listed in the photograph books or other archives, we have recorded it here. Often a figure has subsequently been given a different name, possibly to improve sales, and where this is the case, we have listed both names. Many figures had no actual name which appeared under the base or in a catalogue. Some of these are listed in the records with descriptive names, such as 2632: 'Gentleman in Evening Dress with Cigar'. These names we have retained, even though sometimes they might seem strange, or indeed positively misleading. Only a very few figures have no recorded name at all. For the sake of clarification we have given these a brief descriptive title which identifies the model. In certain cases the name is the only detail we have for some figures which probably did not go into full production.

3. Height: As a guide we have listed the height of each model. These have been collected from several sources. The factory photograph books give a height for most figures up until about 1950. Other factory retail catalogues give the heights for the more popular figures. In many cases, sizes are not recorded. Where possible we have measured an actual example, and found that many of the heights listed in the photograph books are inaccurate, sometimes by as much as an inch either way. It should be remembered that the process of casting can result in some figures varying quite appreciably in height, and in certain cases where no records exist we have had to approximate the height based on our memories of examples which we have seen in the past. Therefore we must ask you to exercise caution where size is concerned, and we accept that some of the heights which we list may well be a little inaccurate.

4. Modeller: From about 1930 the factory lists tended to record not only the name of the figure, but also the original modeller. These names frequently appear on the figures themselves, and we are pleased to be able to record them here. Earlier this century, details of the modeller were rarely noted, and a certain amount of detective work has been needed to identify the modellers. In many cases we simply do not know who was responsible for the original model, and in a few other instances there is doubt, which we have noted. Our record is as complete as we have been able to make it.

5. Date of introduction: When each model was delivered to the factory it was given a shape number. The date which we record is the year in which this number was allocated. It would usually be many months before the mould-making, casting and final decorating was approved and the figure went on sale. To find a figure date-coded for the year of introduction is difficult in some cases, and these are well worth looking out for. Many figures which were given a shape number were, for one reason or another, not proceeded with, or withdrawn before full production started. These are still listed and we have noted a 'date of introduction' in all cases. We realise that the terminology is not satisfactory, but list the dates anyway with this note of caution.

6. Rarity: This category has presented us with the greatest difficulty. Whilst our researches in the factory have given us many clues, any indication of rarity has to rely largely on our own personal experience. After much deliberation we have divided the figures into seven categories, our own degrees of rarity. We have assigned a letter to each figure to record our estimate of its rarity. The length of time a figure was in production and notes in factory price lists have obviously helped, but our decision has largely been governed by the number of examples of each figure which we have seen or have known to exist in our twenty years of working at the factory or collecting Royal Worcester figures. We have had to make some difficult choices. In those cases where we have never seen an actual example, we have had to decide if the model was ever put into production at all: and, if so, whether it has just been by chance that it has never to our knowledge come on the market, or been seen by us in the many collections we have been fortunate enough to inspect. Most of the figures could probably fit quite comfortably into the rarity category either side of the one we have assigned to it, and it is likely that, in a few instances, as more examples become known to us, we will wish that we had used a different rarity grade here. We do feel, however, that although this is going to be a controversial area, it is important to record our experiences as a guide to other collectors. Finally, we must stress that rarity alone does not necessarily determine value. A rare figure from a collectable series or a particularly fine large group will be worth a great deal more than an equally rare small single figure, particularly if the latter is rare because it was unattractive or bad. Many of the common figures are by far the most charming and beautiful, and their popularity should not be held against them.

Rarity categories

A. *Extremely rare, possibly not produced*
   The figure was designed by the modeller but may never have progressed as far as the production of a finished figure. This category includes also models which were made, but in very small numbers, and of which we do not know of more than a single example.

B. *Very rare*
   Whilst we have seen only one or two examples it is probable that more were produced.

C. *Rare*
D. Two categories covering those figures which, although not often seen by us, must have been made in reasonable numbers.

E. *Less common*
F. Two categories covering certain figures no longer in production but made in fairly large numbers.

G. *Common*
   Figures which remained in production for many years and sold in very large numbers, some of them still being in production at the time of writing.

7. Description and other information: We have set out to include as much information as possible relating to each figure. As a result of successful research, some entries are much larger than others for which we have been able to find only very little information, and the length of the commentary does not necessarily reflect the importance of the particular model. In this section we have included a description of the figure and any other details we feel are relevant. We have recorded those colour schemes which are known to us. These are mostly taken from drawings preserved at the factory and are usually the original colourings suggested or approved by the modeller. Some of the colourings listed may never actually have been used, and there will be very many instances where figures have been coloured in different ways to those recorded here. Where prices are recorded, they are generally taken from factory books, and although the books are unclear, we suspect that in most cases the price is wholesale rather than retail. We feel that the prices are worth including as they indicate the relative cost of one model compared to others on sale at the same time.

2101 and 2102
Name   Hebe and Psyche
Height   29 ¼ in. and 30in.
Modeller   Unknown
Introduced 1900
Rarity   C
A pair of female standing figures in classical style wearing diaphanous robes; Hebe holds an oil lamp by her side, her other hand raised to her face; Psyche holds a slender amphora in both hands. Both stand on circular bases. We have seen a pair in white glazed parian, the original cost being 8 guineas. The pair was also sold coloured at a cost of 12 guineas.

2103 and 2104
Name   Cupid with Bow and Cupid
              with Sheaf
Height   19 ¾ in.
Modeller   Unknown
Introduced 1900
Rarity   B
A pair of figures, each depicting Cupid

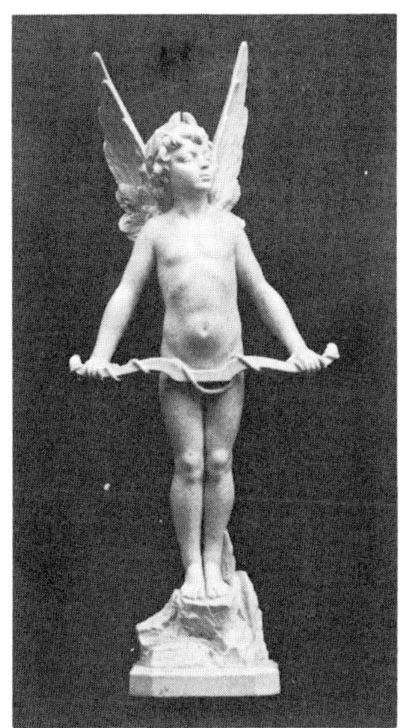

2103

standing naked on a rock; 2103 holds a bow horizontally across his middle, his face slightly raised, whilst 2104 looks down and holds an arrow taken from the quiver hung across his front. This pair is raised on chamfered square bases.

2105

Name	Flemish Man and Woman
Height	12in.
Modeller	Unknown
Introduced	1900
Rarity	B

A pair of figures of a youthful man and woman in elaborate costumes, both standing with baskets by their feet. The woman holds fruit in the folds of her robe and her partner holds flowers. They stand on stepped square bases.

2106 - 2111

Name	Boer War Soldiers of the City Imperial Volunteers
Height	7in.
Modeller	Unknown, probably George Evans
Introduced	1900
Rarity	C
2106:	Soldier of the Imperial Forces
2107:	Imperial Yeoman
2108:	Colonial Trooper
2109:	Soldier of the Black Watch
2110:	Handy Man
2111:	Guardsman

All are standing with a rifle on natural textured bases and were introduced when patriotic fervour was sweeping across the country. The figures were produced in various colourings, the most usual being shades of matt khaki, developed from the blush-ivory and shot-silk effects used on most of James Hadley's models. In rare instances full naturalistic colours were used with slight shot-gold. See also page 10. *(Colour plate 127).*

2161 and 2162

Name	Wandering Minstrels
Height	14½in.
Modeller	Unknown
Introduced	1901
Rarity	B

A pair of classical figures seated on rocky stumps. 2161 is a young man playing a flute, a water bottle hanging from his shoulders, and 2162 is a maiden in a diaphanous sleeveless dress, plucking at a lyre. The bases are roughly circular.

2213 and 2214

Name	Jester (first version) and Shepherdess
Height	7in.
Modeller	Ernest Evans
Introduced	1902
Rarity	Jester C, Shepherdess B

A pair of figures, a mediaeval jester poised gracefully with legs crossed and one arm on his hip, a fool's wand by his feet; his companion, a demure lady, stands with her arms behind her back. Both figures stand on textured square bases, and were probably issued in biscuit unglazed porcelain showing to full effect the fine quality of the modelling. A white glazed example in the Dyson Perrins Museum is signed on the back of the base EAE. The Jester was reissued in 1930 selling for 12s. 6d. fully coloured, but the Shepherdess is not known to have been reintroduced. Two colour schemes are recorded in respect of the reissued model:

1. yellow and orange with blue added to cap;

2. black, yellow and red with mauve and green shaded base.

(2213 Colour plate 77)

2322

Name	The Beadle
Height	6 ¾ in.
Modeller	Unknown, probably Ernest Evans
Introduced	1904
Rarity	B

2322

A figure of a portly gentleman dressed in the traditional uniform of a Parish Constable, a mace by his side, his right hand touching his lapel and standing on a textured rectangular base. The character of the Beadle was a popular figure in smaller English towns and immortalized by Dickens as Mr Bumble in *Oliver Twist*. The model was reissued in white in 1927 selling for 9s. and a coloured version sold in 1930 for 15s.

2374

Name	English Costume Figures
Height	12 ½ in.
Modeller	Unknown
Introduced	1905
Rarity	B

A pair of figures wearing seventeenth-century costume. The man wears a feather in his hat, with a cloak draped over one arm, the other arm being on his hip. His lady companion wears a long layered skirt with flounced sleeves and holds a fan. Both stand at the top of steps.

2375-2380

Name	Greek Figures on Plinths
Height	6 ½ in. and 6 ¾ in.
Modeller	Unknown
Introduced	1905
Rarity	A

2378

A peculiar set of three pairs of child studies, each of a boy and a girl standing on a square, sharply-moulded raised base. 2375 and 2376 wear long capes with hoods; 2377 and 2378 hold flowers in both arms, the boy with a pointed hat; 2379 and 2380 hold a dog and a kitten in their arms. The models combine elements of Hadley's Kate Greenaway styles and Japanesque bases. The significance of the 'Greek' title is not known.

2387

Name	Baby in Dressing Gown.
Height	5 ½ in.
Modeller	Unknown
Introduced	1905
Rarity	B

A figure of a young girl with wavy hair, dressed in a long gown with hood and long loose sleeves. A cord is loosely tied around her waist and she holds a purse in her right hand.

2388

Name	Weighed Out
Height	9in.
Modeller	Unknown
Introduced	1905
Rarity	A

A jockey dressed in racing colours, his head slightly raised, holding a whip with his saddle at his side. He stands on a high base applied with a shield inscribed 'Weighed Out'. The fine modelling suggests that this is a portrait of a particular jockey, but the subject has not been identified.

2389

Name	Early English Lady and Gentleman
Height	8 ¼ in.
Modeller	Unknown
Introduced	1905
Rarity	B

A pair of figures elegantly dressed in the fashions of Regency England. The gentleman sports a top hat and holds a whip and glove, whilst his lady wears a pointed bonnet, her left hand hitching up her long skirt and her right carrying a folded parasol. They stand on textured circular bases and are updated versions of James Hadley's costume figures of the 1880s.

2391

Name	Music and Song
Height	15 ½ in.
Modeller	Unknown
Introduced	1905
Rarity	B

A pair of figures of a mediaeval minstrel and his lady. He wears a short tunic and holds a lute, whilst she wears a long dress tied by ribbons and holds a song-sheet by her side. Both have their mouths open in song and they stand on shaped plinths applied with a scroll bearing the titles and foliage.

2393

Name	Pierrot with Ruff and Companion
Height	8in.
Modeller	Ernest Evans
Introduced	1905
Rarity	B

A pair of figures from the Italian Comedy. Pierrot wears a traditional costume with a ruff and pointed hat, a sweeping cloak behind. His female companion, carefully posed with legs crossed, has one hand raised to her face, and both stand on textured bases with moulded signature 'E. Evans.' Intended to be produced in unglazed biscuit porcelain, the modelling is particularly sharp. *(Colour plate 11)*

2468

Name	Clown's Head
Height	3 ¼ in.
Modeller	Unknown, possibly Ernest Evans
Introduced	1908
Rarity	C

A bust of a clown with a ruffled collar terminating in a hollow circular base, the hair shaped into three points and a grin on his face. The traditional hairstyle is possibly inspired by the early nineteenth-century clown Joseph Grimaldi. Although hollow, it is unlikely that the clown's head was made as a candle extinguisher.

2484

Name	Fish Ashtray
Length	5in.
Modeller	Unknown
Introduced	1909
Rarity	C

A model of a grotesque fish with curled stumpy tail, its mouth agape. Intended as an ashtray, but included here as it is probably more ornamental than functional. We have seen an example in Sabrina Ware, Worcester's high-fired Art porcelain, with mottled underglaze colours. The model was still available in white in 1927, priced at 2s. 3d.

2489

Name	Motorist
Height	5in.
Modeller	Unknown
Introduced	1909
Rarity	A

A candle extinguisher of a lady dressed for a car ride through the Edwardian country-side, her hands in the pockets of her long coat. Her cap is secured by a scarf tied at the neck and goggles protect her eyes. This was the first candle extinguisher to be introduced since 1882 and ought to have been popular, but it never seems to have gone into full production. One example is known in an experimental lustre finish. The moulds survived in the 1970s and a small number were cast at that time.

2514

Name   Rabbit Flower Holder
Height   4 ¾ in.
Modeller   Unknown
Introduced 1911
Rarity   D

A flower holder modelled as a rabbit seated upright, its ears raised alertly. An ovoid wicker basket hangs on the back and the rabbit stands on an irregular base. Usually seen decorated in blush-ivory with shot-gold, although a naturalistically coloured example has been noted. Still listed in 1927, the model was priced at 2s. 3d. white and 6s. 6d. in 'new silk' colouring, but was withdrawn by 1930. It was issued in 1927 without the basket and on a new plain base as shape 2842.

2517

Name   Duck Ring Stand
Height   6 ½ in.
Modeller   Unknown
Introduced 1911
Rarity   B

2517

A duck, realistically modelled with its neck and beak pointed upwards standing on a rock base. An example has been noted in blush ivory. Rings were placed over the duck's head when taken off the fingers.

2523

Name   Lady and Gentleman on
              Rococo Bases
Height   7in.
Modeller   Unknown
Introduced 1911
Rarity   A

A pair of figures of a lady in a crinoline dress holding a fan and a gentleman in fashionable eighteenth-century dress, a sash across his chest. Both stand on pierced rococo scroll bases.

2537

Name   Peacock Menu-Holder
Height   3 ¼ in.
Modeller   Unknown
Introduced 1912
Rarity   B

A stylized model of a peacock on a rocky base, the tail proudly displayed. The back has a slit intended to hold a menu or place card.

2543

Name   Witch
Height   3 ¾ in.
Modeller   Unknown
Introduced 1912
Rarity   E

A candle extinguisher formed as a witch in traditional pointed hat and long cloak, holding her faithful besom in front of her. This popular model was still produced in the 1950s. In 1927 it was priced at 1s. 2d. white, 2s. 8d. in stained-ivory, and 2s. 6d. fully coloured with jet-black hat and bright red cloak. A 1940s example has been noted in softer colours, the flame-red not being available because of wartime restrictions. An example was recently found in the ruins of a house destroyed by a bush fire in Australia. Although blackened, it was the only ornament to survive the intense heat. *(Colour plate 111)*

2568

Name   Mandarin
Height   3 ¾ in.
Modeller   Unknown, but Daisy Rea
              remembers this model being
              designed by Mr Sharp, who

looked after the Museum at the time

Introduced 1914
Rarity D

A candle extinguisher of a portly Oriental Potentate holding a circular fan. Fully coloured, it sold in 1927 for 2s.6d. Probably withdrawn by 1940, it was reissued in 1977. The model is usually coloured yellow and red, his black and blue hat having a red pompom. The fan is blue.
(*Colour plate 111*)

2582, 2588 and 2591

Names French Soldier (2582)
Territorial Soldier (2588)
Soldier of the Worcestershire Regiment (2591)
Height 7 ½ in., 7 ½ in. and 6in.
Modeller Unknown
Introduced 1914, 1914, 1915
Rarity B

2591

Three soldiers realistically and accurately modelled in uniform. Following the success of the Boer War soldiers, these models were once again brought out early in the First World War when patriotism was at its height. The French and Territorial soldiers stand with rifles by their sides. The Worcestershire soldier kneels on one leg, his gun held diagonally across his chest. Like the Boer War models, the khaki of the uniforms was represented by blush-ivory and shot colours, although fully coloured examples have been noted.
(*2582 colour plate 21*)

2604-2613, 2622-2624 and 2636

Name The Netsuke Animals
Modeller Unknown
Introduced 1916

A set of fourteen models of animals copied from Japanese ivory carvings and netsuke. All follow so closely the originals that it is a possibility that the moulds were taken directly from the ivory carvings. Like the originals, they are not to scale. Some proved unpopular and were discontinued, whilst others were still made in the 1950s. The modeller or modellers are unknown. All are modelled 'in the round' and were intended to be held and touched. See also page 11.

2604
Name Tortoise
Length 4 ½ in.
Rarity B

The model is a turtle, although it is called a tortoise in the Company records. It is normally seen in white with tinted head, feet and tail, but was also made in shot colours, selling for 3s. 6d. in 1930. It should not be confused with a smaller model of a tortoise issued *circa* 1913 in blush-ivory but not given a shape number. This smaller tortoise was made in large numbers and was taken from an earlier Worcester model of a large birdcage, modelled by George Evans, of which it formed a detail.
(*Colour plate 103, earlier model plate 104*)

2605
Name Snail
Length 1 ¾ in.
Rarity C

A snail, actual size, its head extended back over its shell. White and tinted and blush-ivory examples are known, whilst occasionally it is seen in other strong shot colours. It sold for 2s. in 1930.
(*Colour plate 58*)

2606
Name Cheetah
Length 3in.
Rarity C

Actually modelled after a Japanese carving of a tiger, the Worcester version is faintly moulded with stripes, but the archives list the name 'Cheetah'. Seen in white and tinted colouring as well as blush-ivory and a variety of strong shot colours, including jet-black. Sold in 1930 for 3s. 6d. (*Colour plates 58 and 103*)

2607
Name   Rabbit
Length   2in.
Rarity   E

A model of a rabbit at lodge proved to be the most popular of the series and was not withdrawn until about 1960. Early examples are white and tinted, and blush-ivory. Sold in 1930 for 1s. 6d. tinted and 2s. coloured, and produced in many different matt and gloss colours. This model was also made as a menu-holder with a slit cut in the back. (*Colour plates 103 and 104*)

2608
Name   Snake
Length   4in.
Rarity   A

A coiled snake, its head raised alertly. Although still listed in 1930, priced at 3s. 6d. coloured, we have not seen an original example. The model illustrated was recast from the moulds in 1975. Very difficult to make and rather vulnerable to damage. (*Colour plate 103*)

2609
Name   Cow
Length   6in.
Rarity   B

Modelled after a carving of a sacred buffalo, a rope draped over its back, it stands on four very slender legs. The cow and the fish are the only models from the series not listed in 1930. The example illustrated is the only one known to us. (*Colour plate 58*)

2610
Name   Mouse
Length   2in.
Rarity   E

A mouse nibbling at a nut held in its paws, its tail curled underneath. Like the rabbit, this model proved very popular, only being withdrawn in about 1960. It was selling in 1927 for 1s. 6d. or 1s. 9d. tinted and

2s. in a variety of colours including naturalistic mouse colour. The model was also used on ashtrays, as shape numbers 2827 and 2828, selling for 11s 6d. each in 1927. (*Colour plate 103*)

2611
Name   Fish
Length   4in.
Rarity   B

Copied from a Japanese ivory carving of a carp, its body strongly curved. Examples are known in blush-ivory and white and tinted. The model was not listed in 1930, although all others in the series apart from the cow were still in production at this time. (*Colour plate 104*)

2612
Name   Ape
Height   2 ¾ in.
Rarity   C

A monkey seated with feet crossed, scratching its nose with right forepaw. Photographs of the model unglazed show tremendous detail, mostly lost in glazed and enamelled versions. Most successful in blush-ivory and tinted colourings, it was also issued in a number of bright enamel colours, selling for 3s. 6d. in 1930. (*Colour plates 58 and 103*)

2613
Name   Ram
Length   2 ¼ in.
Rarity   C

A stylized model lying with head turned inwards, its coat strongly incised. Originally issued in white and tinted and blush-ivory colourings, it was also made in bright shot colours, selling for 3s. 6d. in 1930. (*Colour plates 103 and 104*)

2622
Name   Blackcock
Height   3in.
Rarity   B

Probably copied from a carving of a vulture, this is the only model in the series which has a flat base. It was issued in the same white and tinted and blush-ivory effects, and shot colours were also used. Sold for 3s. 6d. in 1930. (*Colour plate 103*)

2623
Name   Quail
Length   3in.
Rarity   C
This model closely follows a Japanese netsuke and was almost certainly cast directly from an original. Produced in a wide range of colours, various green glazes in particular being used to good effect. The raised single leaf is very susceptible to damage and is frequently seen restored. (*Colour plates 58, 103 and 104*)

2624
Name   Toad
Length   3in.
Rarity   C
Realistically modelled with legs folded close to its body. Most successful in a matt shot-bronze effect, as well as blush-ivory and white and tinted. Also made in bright enamels, it sold in 1927 for 3s. coloured, rising to 3s. 6d. in 1930.
(*Colour plates 57 and 103*)

2636
Name   Double Mouse
Height   2 ½ in.
Rarity   B
An addition to the Netsuke animal series, this is the only model depicting a pair. A smaller mouse sits on the back of another, the latter holding its paws to its face. We have seen examples in fine matt shot-bronze and ivory colours, as well as white and tinted. (*Colour plate 57*)

2614
Name   Unknown
Introduced 1916
Other details unknown
Rarity   A
Listed in a written archive list as 'figure', but we have been unable to find any further information. It is possible that 2614 never went into full production. The moulds were destroyed in March 1920.

2615
Name   Family Group, Mother and
               Two Children

2615

Height   5in.
Modeller   Unknown
Introduced 1916
Rarity   B
The first in a series of figures in a distinctive style of costume, probably inspired by contemporary continental porcelain. Mother and older daughter wear mob caps, the younger girl holding her mother's hand. All wear long skirts slightly crimped at the hem. The moulds were destroyed in March 1920.

2616
Name   Ladies in Mob Caps
Height   3 ¾ in.
Modeller   Unknown
Introduced 1916
Rarity   B
A group of two young ladies seated side by side, the older girl reading from a book, and both wearing mob caps, smart capes and long skirts. It was decorated in distinctive strong colours similar to others in the series (2615, 2617, 2620 and 2621). The moulds were destroyed in March 1920.

2617
Name   Wind
Height   5 ¾ in.
Modeller   Unknown
Introduced 1916
Rarity   C
A figure of a young lady in a similar style to 2615 and 2616, in this case a single figure in a mob cap, her arms below her cape and her long skirt blown from behind by the wind. She stands on a simple

mound base. Three colour schemes are recorded:

1. black chequered shawl, black dress and hat;
2. black shawl, black bottom to dress with blue spots just above;
3. same as 2, but with turquoise-green hat.

The moulds were destroyed in March 1920.

2618

Name   Boy and Rabbit
Height   3 ¼ in.
Modeller Unknown
Introduced 1916
Rarity   B

A figure of a young boy seated with legs apart on a circular mound, a pet rabbit cradled in his arms, looking down at a mouse. His smart dress is in similar style to 2615-2617 and 2620 and 2621. The moulds were destroyed in March 1920.

2619

Name   Crucifix
Height   7 ¾ in. × 7 ¼ in.
Modeller Unknown
Introduced 1916
Rarity   A

2619

A traditional figure of Christ on the Cross, his head slumped and a cloth around his middle. Intended to be mounted on a wooden cross with a separate - scroll

inscribed INRI, it sold in 1927 for 15s. in white. Mounted with a cross and plinth it cost £1. 3s. 6d.

2620 and 2621

Name   Crinoline Figure with Cap and with Book
Height   4 ½ in.
Modeller Unknown
Introduced 1916
Rarity   B

Two figures of ladies in bell-like crinoline skirts, one wearing a mob cap and the other bareheaded, a book held in her left hand. They are decorated in strong colours in similar style to other models in this series (2615-2618). it is possible these figures were intended to be used as bells with a clapper attached inside with plaster. Three colour schemes are recorded for 2620:

1. black cap, bag and details on dress;
2. same as 1, with rose sprigs on cap and dark and pale mauve dress;
3. mauve cap, black bag, purple-rose on dress.

Two colour schemes are recorded for 2621:

1. black and green dress with pink roses, black book;
2. dark green top and pale green bodice, red book.

The moulds were destroyed in March 1920. (*Colour plate 83*)

2622-2624

Name   Blackcock, Quail and Toad
(*See* 2604 for descriptions.)

2625 and 2626

Name   The Immaculate and St. Joseph
Height   14 ½ in. and 13 ¾ in.
Modeller Unknown
Introduced 1916
Rarity   B

A pair of statues of The Virgin Mary and St. Joseph in conventional style standing on textured circular bases, St. Joseph holding a lily in his right hand. Introduced in time of war and sold in white at actual cost only so that no profit was made from religious figures. In 1927 The Immaculate was selling for £2. 8s. 0d. in white, a coloured version costing 6 guineas. A pair has been seen richly coloured with shot-gold and raised on black and gold plinths.

2629, 2635, 2657 and 2658
The first four in a series of historical military figures modelled by Frederick Gertner, introduced in 1916. All are in accurate uniforms of the Napoleonic period and were issued fully painted and gilded. Similar historical military figures were being made in Germany at this time for sale in England to commemorate the centenary of the battle of Waterloo. Worcester's models seem to have been copied almost exactly from a series sold by Thomas Goode and Co. in London. The first four models were on grassy mound bases, later replaced by more formal ones. Some figures were short-lived, whilst others remained in production for a considerable number of years.

2629
Name   French Marine Officer
Height   10 ¾ in.
Introduced 1916
Rarity   B
Standing with one arm raised and painted in full colours. Withdrawn by 1930.

2635
Name   Coldstream Guards Officer,
              AD 1815 (First version)
Height   10 ½ in.
Introduced 1916
Rarity   B
Issued in full colours on a grassy base, this version was withdrawn shortly after introduction. A new version with minor variations was reintroduced the following year in 1917, shape number 2676.

2657
Name   Seaforth Highlander Officer,
              AD 1815
Height   11 ¼ in.
Modeller   1916
Rarity   E
In full uniform with kilt and standing on a grassy base, the model proved popular

2657

and was continued into the 1950s, although at some time the base was remodelled in line with others in the series. Fully coloured, it sold for £3. 7s. 6d. in 1927, rising to 16 guineas in 1955. In 1959 it was slightly remodelled as shape 3677 and was renamed Scots Guards Officer.

2658
Name   Royal Artillery Officer,
              AD 1815
Height   10 ¾ in.
Introduced 1916
Rarity   F

2658

Standing with both hands holding the hilt of his sword, on a grassy base. Like 2657, the model proved very popular, selling for £3 in 1927 and increasing to 15 guineas in 1955. It was still made in the 1980s.

2632 and 2633

Name   Gentleman in Evening Dress
           with Cigar and Gentleman
           with Cloak and Opera Hat
Height   5in. and 5 ¼ in.
Modeller   Unknown
Introduced 1916
Rarity   B

Two elegant figures, possibly in the same series as 2615-2618 and 2620 and 2621. Both depict young men in 'Turn of the Century' costume. One is standing propped up against a cloth-covered table, a cigar in his left hand and holding a book in the right. His companion wears a greatcoat beneath a long cloak which he pulls about him, a top hat held in his right hand. These have been seen painted in strong colours, including jet-black for the cloak. The figures were conceived without bases and, while ingenious, are somewhat top-heavy and susceptible to damage. The moulds were destroyed in March 1920. (*2633 Colour plate 120*)

2634, 2637, 2643, 2648, 2651, 2652, 2668 and 2672

A series of eight historical figures modelled by Frederick Gertner after paintings by Holbein, Van Dyke and others, the costumes accurate to the last detail. Introduced in 1916 and 1917, the figures reflect the mock-Tudor styles very popular in architecture and interior design both in England and, particularly, in the United States at the time. Whilst a small amount of transfer-printing was used in the colours, the extensive use of gold and concentration on detail made these the most costly Worcester figures of their size to date. Henry VIII and Mary Queen of Scots continued in production throughout the 1930s, whilst the remainder were withdrawn by 1927, only to be revived after the war. They remained popular into the 1970s and are still available at the time of writing. See also page 11.

Name   Mary Queen of Scots
Height   8in.
Rarity   G

2634

The most popular figure in this series, Mary was particularly popular during the early 1930s and was one of the figures represented by debutantes at the 'Porcelain Ball' (*see* page 16). Sold for £5. in 1927, the price rising to £22 in 1955.

2637
Name   Henry VIII
Height   9in.
Rarity   G

2637

Modelled after Holbein's famous portrait, the rich use of gold makes this an expensive figure. Despite the cost the model remained popular for over sixty years. The listed cost price rose steadily, from £4. 10s. in 1927 to £30 in 1955.

2643
Name   Edward VI
Height   8 ⅜ in.
Rarity   G

2643

The son of Henry VIII: the model was not so popular and was withdrawn by 1927. It was, however, reintroduced in the 1950s and remained popular after this time.

2648
Name   Elizabeth I
Height   9 ½ in.
Rarity   G

2648

Surprisingly, not as popular as her father Henry VIII, again withdrawn by 1927 yet reissued in the 1950s.

2651
Name   Charles I
Height   9 ½ in.
Rarity   G

2651

A fine model after Van Dyke, the figure was fitted with a metal cane. Withdrawn by 1927, but reintroduced in the 1950s.

2652
Name   Anne Boleyn
Height   8 ¼ in.
Rarity   G

2652

Henry VIII's tragic wife: the figure was withdrawn by 1927 but reintroduced in the 1950s.

2668
Name   Sir Walter Raleigh
Height   9 ¾ in.
Rarity   G

2668

Issued in 1917 as a pair to Elizabeth I. Withdrawn by 1927, but reintroduced in the 1950s. The figure was fitted with a painted metal sword in its left hand.

2672

2672
Name   Charles II
Height   9 ¾ in.
Rarity   G
The last figure in the series, issued in 1917. Fitted with a metal cane. Withdrawn by 1927, it was reintroduced in the 1950s.

2635
Name   Coldstream Guards Officer
(*See* 2629 for description.)

2636
Name   Double Mouse
(*See* 2604 for description.)

2637
Name   Henry VIII
(*See* 2634 for description.)

2643
Name   Edward VI
(*See* 2634 for description.)

2645 and 2646
Name   First World War Soldiers,
             Standing and Sitting
Height   10 ¼ in. and 5 ½ in.
Modeller   William Pointon
Introduced 1916
Rarity   B
Two figures on a different scale; 2645 is a standing soldier in a greatcoat with his kit-bag under his arm, whilst 2646 sits with his gun diagonally between his legs and is lighting a lucifer for his cigarette. By 1916 the reality of war in the trenches had been reported home and these figures are therefore much more true to life than the series issued at the outbreak of the war. (2582, 2588 and 2591). Produced in matt khaki and brown colours derived from the Boer War series, both were still in production in 1927, selling for £1. 10s and 17s. 6d. respectively. The standing soldier is very similar to the figure 'Blighty' produced by Royal Doulton in 1918.
(*2645 Colour plate 29*)

2648
Name   Elizabeth I
(*See* 2634 for description.)

2649 and 2650

Name   Lady with Mirror and Lady
          with Mask
Height   11 ½ in.
Modeller   Unknown
Introduced   1916
Rarity   A

A pair of female figures in classical style, both wearing a clinging dress revealing their left breasts. One is holding a mirror, her other hand on her head. Her companion lifts her carnival mask over her head with one hand, her other arm by her side. Both stand on circular bases. Still listed in 1927, they were available only in white at £1. 7s. each, and were withdrawn by 1930.

2651

Name   Charles I
(*See 2634* for description.)

2652

Name   Anne Boleyn
(*See 2634 for description.*)

2654 and 2655

Name   Female Dancing Figures
Height   11in.
Modeller   Unknown
Introduced   1916
Rarity   B

A pair of figures of young ladies in 'off the shoulder' long dresses, with bare arms and feet, standing on circular bases in dancing poses with arms outstretched.

2657

Name   Seaforth Highlander Officer
(*See 2629 for description.*)

2658

Name   Royal Artillery Officer
(*See 2629 for description.*)

2659 and 2660

Name   Classical Ladies with Lyre and
          Tambourine
Height   14 ¼ in.
Modeller   Unknown
Introduced   1916
Rarity   B

A pair of figures of maidens reverting back to the classical styles of twenty years previously. Both wear long sleeveless dresses and stand barefoot on shaped plinths. One maiden plucks at a lyre held in her left hand and the other beats a tambourine held in her right hand. The pair has been seen decorated both in traditional shot colours and in gold with heads and arms coloured in old ivory.

2661

Name   The Admiral or Admiral of
          the Blue, *circa* AD 1780
Height   10 ¾ in.
Modeller   Frederick Gertner
Introduced   1916
Rarity   G

2661

A figure from the historical military series by Frederick Gertner, this being the only naval officer represented. He wears full uniform predominantly in deep underglaze blue with gold trim, a telescope in one hand, the other hand on his hip. A sword hangs by his side and he stands on a black stepped base. Produced for more than sixty years, the figure cost £4 in 1927, rising to £22 in 1955, and it is still available at the time of writing.

2662-2667

Name   Birds on Stumps
Height   5 ½ in. to 7in.
Modeller   Frederick Gertner
Introduced   1917
Rarity   G

A set of six models of birds on stumps. These figures were originally intended to be made in the Crownware body, but were changed to china in 1918 on remodelled stumps, remaining in production until the 1960s. The birds were painted in bright naturalistic colours, the stumps being left white with small painted flowers and gilt flecks. They sold for between 3s. 6d. and 4s. each in 1931, rising to between £2. 5s. and £2. 15s in 1955. See also page 12.

2662 Bullfinch on Stump

2663 Budgerigar on Stump (female) (Originally called Parroquet)

2664 Budgerigar on Stump (male) (Originally called Parroquet or Parrot)

2665 Canary on Stump

2666 Kingfisher on Stump

2667 Goldfinch on Stump
(2662 and 2667 *Colour plate 89*, 2663 and 2664 *Colour plate 112*)

2668
Name　　Sir Walter Raleigh
(*See* 2634 for description.)

2672
Name　　Charles II
(*See* 2634 for description.)

2673 and 2674
Name　　　　Ball Players
Height　　　12in.
Modeller　　Possibly Frederick Gertner
Introduced　1917
Rarity　　　A
A pair of figures of maidens in diaphanous dresses. One is holding a ball in her right hand, her other arm outstretched, while her companion holds both arms out to catch the ball. Both stand on circular bases. Possibly inspired by Atalanta, a character from classical mythology who threw a golden apple to fend off her pursuers, a Meissen figure of whom was very popular from about 1910. This pair was available in white only, in 1927, costing £1. 17s. 6d. each.

2675-2677
Three further figures by Frederick Gertner in the historical military series, this time mounted on shaped stepped bases which were painted jet-black. All were withdrawn by 1930, although they were reintroduced in the 1950s.

2675

2675
Name　　　　3rd Dragoon Guards Officer, AD 1806
Height　　　11½ in.
Introduced　1917
Rarity　　　G
An officer in full uniform with cocked hat, his left hand on the hilt of his sword and his gloves in the other hand. Withdrawn by 1930, but reintroduced with reasonable success in the 1950s.

2676
Name　　　　Coldstream Guards Officer, AD 1815 (second version)
Height　　　11¾ in.
Introduced　1917
Rarity　　　D
An improved version of 2635 on a stepped base. It was withdrawn by 1930, possibly reintroduced in the 1950s, but replaced by a new version in 1959, shape 3675, with minor alterations to costume detail.

2677
Name　　　　17th Dragoon Guards Officer, A.D. 1814

2677

Height   11 ¾ in.
Introduced 1917
Rarity   G

A young officer standing on stepped black base, his left hand on his sword hilt. Gilt metal wire was added to the cap on later models. Withdrawn by 1930, but reintroduced in the 1950s to continue for more than twenty years.

2679 and 2680

Name   Columbine and Harlequin
                 (first versions)
Height   9 ½ in.
Modeller   Unknown
Introduced 1917
Rarity   B

A pair of figures in stylish theatrical poses, Columbine modelled as a ballet dancer in a short tutu, standing on tip-toe beside a gnarled tree stump support. Harlequin wears a skin-tight costume and poses with one finger raised, also on tip-toe by a tree stump. Both have tapering circular bases. Originally intended for the Crownware body, they were issued in ivory colourings with powder-blue costumes and plinths, and also in bone china with lighter colours. Withdrawn by 1930.
(Colour plate 101)

2681 and 2682

Name   Columbine (second version)
                 and Pierrot (first version)

Height   9 ½ in.
Modeller   Unknown
Introduced 1917
Rarity   B

A companion pair to 2679 and 2680, Columbine differing only in the position of her outstretched hands. Pierrot is fully clothed in a jacket, belted shirt and long stockings with pointed shoes, playing pan-pipes, his right leg raised. Both have tree stump supports on circular plinths. Originally issued in Crownware and coloured as 2679 and 2680. *(Colour plate 101)*

2683 and 2684

Name   Seated Nude Girl and Boy
                 with Flowers
Height   4 ½ in.
Modeller   Unknown
Introduced 1917
Rarity   B

The first in a series of nude figures inspired by Continental originals. Both young children sit with legs crossed on circular plinths, a bunch of flowers or leaves held in their arms. Inspired by a series of nude figures made by the Wächtersbach factory in Germany for the marriage of the Grand Duke of Hess in 1910. Like the originals they were made in the earthenware Crownware body with matt green bases and ivory finish. Also made with powder-blue bases but withdrawn by 1927.

2685 and 2686

Name   Standing Nude Boy and Girl
                 with Flowers
Height   6 ¼ in. and 6in.
Modeller   Unknown
Introduced 1917
Rarity   B

A pair of figures of nude children holding bunches of flowers across their chests and standing on simple conical bases. Like 2683 and 2684 these were inspired by German figures of 1910. Produced in Crownware and reissued in porcelain, selling in 1927 for 2s. 3d. each white and 7s. 6d. with powder-blue bases. They were also made in matt green and ivory. Withdrawn by 1930.

2687

Name	Nude Child seated on Plinth
Height	5 in.
Modeller	Unknown
Introduced	1917
Rarity	B

A single nude child seated sideways on a square plinth, one arm raised to the face. Like 2683-2686 made in Crownware in powder-blue or matt green with ivory.

2688

Name	Nude Female Leaning on a Pedestal
Height	6in.
Modeller	Unknown
Introduced	1917
Rarity	B

A figure of a young woman standing with her arms resting on top of a tapering square pedestal embossed with a mask, her face raised and looking forward. Produced in Crownware in powder-blue or matt green and ivory. Withdrawn by 1927.

2689 and 2693

Name	Nude Females with Slippers
Height	5¾ in.
Modeller	Unknown
Introduced	1917 and 1918
Rarity	D

The two most popular in this extensive series of nude figures, both modelled as young ladies seated on tapering square plinths. 2689 places a slipper on her foot whilst 2693 holds the slipper in her right hand by her side, her legs crossed. Originally made in Crownware and re-issued in china, decorated in ivory with matt green plinths and yellow slippers and headbands. Also made in powder-blue or shagreen with gold details. Selling in 1927 for 2s. 9d. each white and 8s. 6d. in powder-blue or shagreen. Probably withdrawn by 1930. (*2689, Colour plate 44*)

2690 and 2697

Name	Nude Bathers Reclining and Seated on Plinth
Height	7½ in. and 7¾ in.
Modeller	Unknown
Introduced	1917 and 1918
Rarity	C

The most elaborate pair in the series of nudes, both resting on stepped plinths as if beside a swimming pool. Their modesty is protected by garlands of leafy foliage. Issued in Crownware strongly coloured as illustrated, or in ivory and powder-blue or matt green, and reissued in china. Usually seen in white glazed parian. Sold in 1927 for 18s. each white and 2 guineas each in powder-blue. Withdrawn by 1930 (*2697, Colour plate 16*)

2691 and 2692

Name	Female Nudes Standing
Height	7½ in. and 7¾ in.
Modeller	Unknown
Introduced	1918
Rarity	C

A pair of figures of young ladies standing naked on tapering square plinths. 2691 holds one hand by her side, while the other coyly covers her breasts. Her hair is edged with a plaited fringe. Her companion 2692 also holds one arm by her side, the other reaching behind the shoulder. Issued in Crownware in ivory and powder-blue or matt green and reissued in china, selling in 1927 for 2s 6d. white and 8s. 6d. in powder-blue or shagreen. Withdrawn by 1930.

2693

Name	Nude Female with Slipper

(*See* 2689 for description.)

2694, 2702 and 2703

Name	Nude Boys with Fruit, Dolphin and Seaweed
Height	7in., 5¾ in. and 7½ in.
Modeller	Unknown
Introduced	1918 and 1919
Rarity	B

The first three in a series of seven models on distinctive circular bases. 2694 stands with a cluster of fruit over his shoulder. 2702 sits amidst waves, a dolphin's head emerging in the front. 2703 stands with garlands of seaweed held in front of him. We have only seen these in creamy-glazed Crownware, but they were probably made also in powder-blue. Withdrawn by 1927. (*2702 See* illustration on page 37)

2695 and 2696

Name   Flamingoes
Height   Approx. 6in. mounted
Modeller   Unknown
Introduced 1918
Rarity   B

A pair of models of the ornamental birds, one with neck outstretched, intended to be mounted with bronze legs and feet. We have seen one example fitted with the bronze legs, the bird fully coloured in strong pink, the backstamp printed beneath the tail feathers.

2697

Name   Nude Bather Seated on Plinth
(*See* 2690 for description.)

2698

Name   Nude Bather Kneeling
Height   8 ½ in.
Modeller   Unknown
Introduced 1918
Rarity   C

The most impressive of the series, the nude maiden kneels on a tall angular plinth, her breasts covered by her plaited hair, and leans slightly forward to look into the pool. Originally issued in Crownware, although usually found in white glazed parian. Sold in 1927 for 18s. white, and for 2 guineas on powder-blue or shagreen bases. It was also available in ivory and matt green. Withdrawn by 1930. The bather herself was also used on the cover of a circular powder bowl, shape No. 2783, introduced in 1920 for Dubarry et Cie., Brompton Road, London and was adapted for another powder bowl, No. 2820, with lotus flowers placed below her hands. These were in matt ivory, the bowls either pink, powder-blue or shagreen, costing between £1. 10s and £2. 7s. 6d. in 1927 depending on the size of the bowl.
(*2698, Colour plate 44*)

2702 and 2703

Name   Nude Boys with Dolphin and Seaweed
(*See* 2694 for description.)

2704-2707

Name   Nude Boys with Cornucopias (first versions)
Height   8 ½ in. and 8 ¼ in.
Modeller   Unknown
Introduced 1919
Rarity   B

Two pairs of figures of nude boys in the same series as 2694, 2702 and 2703, all with curly hair and circular bases. 2704 and 2705 are standing, both holding a cornucopia, one full of vines, the other flowers. 2706 and 2707 are seated astride cornucopias overflowing with exotic fruit. Issued in Crownware, possibly decorated in powder-blue. Withdrawn by 1927.

2715 and 2716

Name   Nude Girls with Garlands
Height   6in. and 5 ¾ in.
Modeller   Unknown
Introduced 1919
Rarity   B

A pair of figures of young girls seated on tapering square plinths, one holding a bound garland of leaves, the other with fruit and leaves. Issued in Crownware.

2717 and 2718

Name   Nude Boy and Girl with Roses
Height   6 ¼ in.
Modeller   Unknown
Introduced 1919
Rarity   B

A pair of figures of a young boy and girl on tapering circular plinths, the boy holding a basket of roses and the girl holding a long garland of roses and leaves. Like 2683-2686, these figures were possibly inspired by Wächtersbach figures of 1910. Still made in 1927, selling for 7s 6d. each in powder-blue or 2s. 9d. white.

2719 and 2720

Name   Nude Girls Seated with Roses
Height   5 ¼ in.
Modeller   Unknown
Introduced 1919
Rarity   B

A pair of figures of young girls seated on tapering square plinths. One holding a basket of roses with further roses and leaves by her side, her companion holds a bunch of roses in her arms. Produced in Crownware.

2723 and 2724

Name Drummer Boy and Vivandière
Height 7 ½ in.
Modeller Unknown, possibly James Hadley
Introduced 1919
Rarity B

A pair of figures of a boy and a girl dressed as soldiers with wide hats and smart jackets, the boy beating a drum hung around his neck. The girl holds a small flagon under one arm and both stand by square posts. Possibly modelled by James Hadley in the 1880s and reissued with a new number.

2725 and 2726

Name Kate Greenaway Boy and Girl (First version)
Height 6 ½ in.
Modeller James Hadley
Introduced Originally 1880, reissued 1919
Rarity C

A pair of figures of a boy and girl in prim and proper dress inspired by the illustrations of Kate Greenaway. The boy wears a boater and holds his hands behind his back, whilst the girl wears a poke bonnet and holds her hands together in front of her. Why the original models were re-numbered is not clear. The pair has been seen in a wide range of different colourings, but the recorded versions are:

2725 boy in green suit and white buttons, his collar slightly tinted in silk, shoes brown;
2726 girl in pale green dress, her collar tinted grey in frills, shoes brown.

2727 and 2728

Name Kate Greenaway Boy and Girl (second version)
Height 6 ¾ in.
Modeller Probably James Hadley
Introduced 1919
Rarity B

A pair of figures of a smartly dressed boy and girl; she has her hands behind her back, he has one hand behind his back and one holding his lapel. Both stand in front of square plinths. Probably reissued from original 1880s models by James Hadley and given a new number.
(*2728, Colour plate 75*)

2732 and 2733

Name Country Girls
Height 6 ½ in.
Modeller Unknown
Introduced 1919
Rarity A

A pair of figures of young girls dressed in long smock coats and wide-brimmed hats. One holds a gnarled walking stick and the other stands with one hand in her pocket, the other holding gloves. Possibly earlier models by James Hadley reissued, or modelled in Hadley's style.

2734 and 2735

Name Young Huntsmen
Height 7 in.
Modeller Unknown
Introduced 1919
Rarity A

2734   2735

A pair of figures of boys, one dressed as a huntsman in a long coat with a whip in one hand and a horn in the other, his cap pulled over his face. The other boy is dressed as a gentleman with a top hat by his side. Details of colouring unknown.

2780

Name Tigers, Couchant (first version)

Height 3in.
Modeller Unknown
Introduced 1920
Rarity A
A pair of tigers lying facing to left and right, their bodies slightly curved and front paws outstretched. The original colour design survives and shows that they were made in full naturalistic colouring. They sold in 1930 for 17s. 6d. each fully coloured. Withdrawn by 1940.
(*Colour plate 136*)

2783
Name Bather Powder Bowl
(*See* 2698 for description.)

2798 and 2799
Name Roses and Grapes
Height 10 ¼ in.
Modeller François Clemencin
Introduced 1922
Rarity B
A pair of figures of young maidens, naked except for slight drapery around their waists. One holds above her head a spray of roses and the other holds aloft a bunch of grapes. Both stand on circular bases. Produced in Crownware with the drapery in powder-blue and also produced in full colours or in shot silk with gilding and matt ivory. They cost between £1. 10s and £1. 17s. 6d. in 1927 depending on the colouring, although a coloured version in 1930 cost only 17s 6d. Withdrawn by 1940.

2800 and 2801
Name Female Nude with Mirror and Seated Nude with Leaves
Height 9 ¾ in. and 7 ½ in.
Modeller François Clemencin,
Introduced 1922
Rarity B
A pair of figures on circular grooved bases, naked except for drapery around their waists. One stands with a mirror held in her right hand above the head to shade her eyes, her left knee bent. The other sits on a rock covered by drapery, her left arm seeming to rest on an invisible branch with a spray of leaves in her hand. Produced in the same range of colours as 2798 and

2799, costing £1. 15s and 2 guineas each in powder-blue in 1927. Withdrawn by 1930.

2805 and 2806
Name Female Nudes Seated
Height 4 ½ in.
Modeller Unknown, possibly François Clemencin
Introduced 1922
Rarity B
A pair of figures of naked women, both seated sideways on a roughly circular base, their legs tucked to one side and their weight supported by their hands. The hair is raised in a bun and the figures are modelled with a greater degree of realism than most nude figures produced by the Company at this time. Produced in Crownware, costing 8s. in white, 13s. 6d. in powder-blue and ivory and 15s. in shot-silk and ivory in 1927. Withdrawn by 1930.
(*2805, Colour plate 44*)

2807
Name Infant Faun and Putto Powder Bowl
Height 7in.
Modeller Unknown
Introduced 1922
Rarity B
A pair of young children used on the cover of a powder bowl, the naked boy reaching out his arm to comfort a young girl faun seated beside him, her goat's legs folded in front of her. Made for Dubarry et Cie., 81 Brompton Road, London, the figures in ivory, the bowl in pink or powder-blue. In most cases the figures used on powder bowls were also produced as single models, but there is no evidence that this is the case here. An example of the bowl is in the Dyson Perrins Museum.

2820
Name Bather Powder Bowl
(*See* 2698 for description.)

2821-2823
Name Kookaburra
Height About 2 ¼ in.
Modeller Unknown
Introduced 1923-24
Rarity B

A model of a Kookaburra, the national bird of Australia. The single realistically modelled bird was placed on the cover of a powder bowl (2821), on the side of an ashtray (2822) and in the centre of a circular ashtray (2823). It was also produced as a single model but not given its own shape number. Withdrawn by 1927.

2827 and 2828
Name   Mouse Ashtrays
(*See* 2610 for description.)

2831, 2832, 2840 and 2841
Name   Mr. and Mrs. Toby
Height   6in., 3 ½ in. and 1 ¾ in.
Modeller   Unknown
Introduced 1927
Rarity   Large B, medium E, miniature D

A pair of traditional Toby Jugs issued in three sizes. 2831 is Mr. Toby standing dressed in a greatcoat and tricorn hat. The large 6 in. size has a separate cover forming the centre of his hat and he holds a mug in his right hand, a pipe in his left. The middle and small sizes have no cover and Mr. Toby holds just a wine glass in his right hand, his left hand being in his pocket. The large size was soon afterwards remodelled as 2840 to match the smaller jugs, his left hand also in his pocket. 2841 is Mrs. Toby, wearing a wide bonnet, long dress and apron, a basket over her right arm and an umbrella held in her left hand. The large size has a cover, although in both cases they were sold without the cover if desired for 6d. less. Usually decorated in strong colours, particularly deep blue and red enamel for the coats and waistcoats, or for Mrs. Toby's dress, their hats in jet-black. All sizes were still in production in 1955 but withdrawn by 1957. A version was made in 'bisque' colouring in 1952. The medium size Mr. Toby was issued with a perforated EPNS top as a pepper and salt pot costing 2s. 6d. coloured in 1927. This version is possibly shape no. 2832, and was withdrawn by 1930.

The same models and colourings were also used by other factories. Marked Goss and Carlton Ware examples have been noted as well as crude copies in Continental porcelain. It is not known which factory produced the original. Four colour schemes are recorded for shape number 2831:
1. blue coat, red waistcoat, black hat and trousers;
2. green coat, red waistcoat;
3. red coat, blue waistcoat;
4. green coat, yellow waistcoat.
A note against the drawings reads: '2/9d per dozen', presumably the rate which the painters received.
(*2831 and 2841, Colour plate 82*)

2842
Name   Wilfred
Height   4 ¾ in.
Modeller   Unknown
Introduced 1927
Rarity   C

A model of a rabbit seated upright with his paws held in front, his ears raised alertly. The base is a simple circular one. Produced in natural colours with the base usually in jet-black, it cost 3s. 6d. in 1927 and was probably withdrawn by 1930. This model was originally issued with a basket on its back as shape 2514.

2843
Name   Duck (first version)
Height   3 ¾ in.
Modeller   Unknown
Introduced 1927
Rarity   B

A model of a duck standing upright, wings folded by its side. The head hangs to one side with beak open and it has a plain circular base. It cost 4s. coloured in 1927 and was withdrawn by 1930.

2844
Name   Hush
Height   3 ¼ in.
Modeller   Unknown
Introduced 1927
Rarity   C

A candle extinguisher modelled as a little girl, her hair in ringlets, wearing a fluted bell-like skirt. Her left hand is held behind her back concealing a secret, one finger of her right hand raised to her lips. Produced in a variety of colourings costing 3s. when introduced. Withdrawn probably by 1930, this was the last candle extinguisher to be introduced, although other earlier models remained in production subsequently. Hush was reissued in 1975 as part of a new series but incorrectly assembled with her left arm in front of her. Four colour schemes are recorded although several others have been seen:

1. pale yellow dress, turquoise-blue ribbons, blonde hair;
2. pale yellow dress, pale pink ribbons, blonde hair;
3. pale yellow dress, chrome-green ribbons, blonde hair;
4. pale yellow dress, dark pink ribbons, brown hair.

(*Colour plate 111*)

2848

Name	Chinese Family Group
Height	5 ½ in.
Modeller	Unknown
Introduced	1928
Rarity	A

2848

A group of a chinoiserie lady and two children standing together on a lobed base modelled with clouds, the central lady holding a fan above her head. The factory price book lists no costings or decoration against the number and it was probably never put into production, although a single white glazed group has been noted. It is probable that no colour scheme was ever proposed.

2850

Name	Mephistopheles
Height	7in., 3 ½ in. and a miniature
Modeller	Unknown
Introduced	1929
Rarity	Large B, medium C, miniature B

A Toby Jug modelled as the Devil dressed demonically in flame-red suit, his pointed tail forming the handle. Tail, hat, collar, pointed beard and moustache were painted in jet-black. The large 7in. version has a cover fitting inside his hat and in 1929 cost 8s. 6d., or 8s. without the cover. The smaller sizes cost 3s. and 1s. 8d. each, fully coloured. Withdrawn soon after introduction.

2851-2854

Name	Elephant Jug, Cockatoo Jug, Pelican Jug and Squirrel Jug
Height	3 ½ in., 3 ¼ in., 4 ¼ in. and 3 ¼ in.
Modeller	Unknown
Introduced	1929
Rarity	B

A series of four jugs formed as animals in the style of Toby Jugs. Each animal is seated upright with its tail forming the handle, the squirrel seated below an overhanging leafy branch. All were painted in bright colourings using thick enamels, including a flame-red and rich deep yellow. The bases were usually jet-black. All were additionally issued with pierced EPNS tops forming salt and pepper pots and 2851 was also made as a mustard pot.

2855

Name	Bonzo
Height	3in.
Modeller	Unknown
Introduced	1929
Rarity	B

A model of the famous cartoon dog created by George Study. Bonzo appeared in a comic strip and prompted all manner of manufacturers to produce Bonzo merchandise. The Royal Worcester model faithfully reproduces the grin which made Bonzo so appealing and he sits with one paw raised, his tongue extended. The model was available tinted in shades of

puce and pink, as well as fawn, or black with tinting; the cost in 1929 was 1s. 8d. each, or 2s. each with the top of the head pierced to form salt and pepper pots. Withdrawn soon afterwards.
(*Colour plate 55*)

2856

Name　　Jester Jug
Height　　6 ¾ in.
Modeller　Unknown
Introduced　1929
Rarity　　B

A Toby Jug and Cover in the form of a mediaeval jester holding his jester's wand, his costume in angular Art Deco style hung with bells. An elaborate model, it was expensive at 10s. 6d. fully coloured, whereas the Toby Jugs of this size cost only 8s. 6d. Withdrawn by 1940 and probably much earlier.

2857

Name　　Paddy
Height　　6 ¼ in.
Modeller　Unknown
Introduced　1929
Rarity　　A

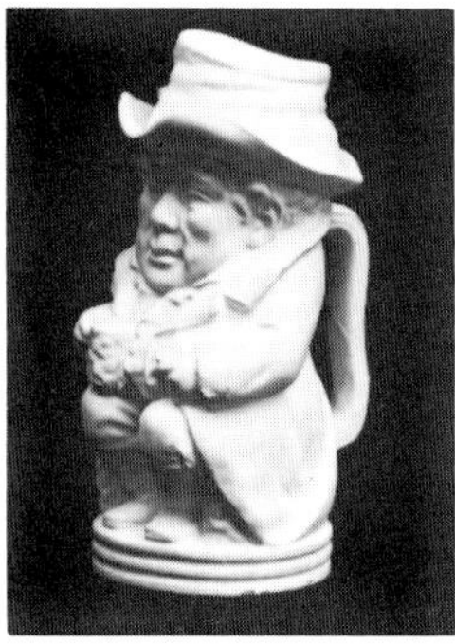

2857

A traditional Toby Jug and Cover modelled as an Irishman seated on a circular base, a mug held in his right hand. The model sold for 8s. 6d. in 1929. The jug was probably aimed at the Irish-American market following the success of Doulton's character jugs, but like most of Worcester's Toby Jugs it was not a success. Probably withdrawn by 1930. The recorded colour scheme has a green top coat, red jacket, green trousers, shamrocks on mug and a black hat.

2858

Name　　Brer Rabbit (first version)
Height　　3 ¼ in.
Modeller　Unknown
Introduced　1929
Rarity　　B

A model of the popular children's book character created by Joel Chandler Harris in his Uncle Remus stories. He stands fully dressed in jacket and waistcoat, his ears hanging down. The model was produced in bright colours selling for 3s. in 1929, but withdrawn shortly afterwards. Three colour schemes are recorded:
　　1. green coat, red waistcoat;
　　2. red coat, blue waistcoat;
　　3. blue coat, red waistcoat;

2865

Name　　Cora
Height　　6in.
Modeller　Doris Lindner
Introduced　1931
Rarity　　B

A figure of a nude lady seated on a rectangular base, turning to look at a pigeon, her long hair extending to the base. Also produced without a plinth or pigeon. Original price was 15s., or 12s. without the plinth. Very few were made, and it was withdrawn by 1940. Two colour schemes are recorded:
　　1. ivory-flesh coloured, pink surround and base;
　　2. same as 1, with green base.

2866 and 2867

Name　　Harlequin and Columbine
　　　　　Book-end and Pierrot
　　　　　Book-end
Height　　8in.
Modeller　Doris Lindner
Introduced　1931
Rarity　　A

A pair of models intended to be mounted as book-ends. 2866 depicts Harlequin holding Columbine in a loving kiss, his outstretched right arm pulling at a curtain. 2867 has Pierrot, the unsuccessful suitor, standing forlornly against a similar curtain. Harlequin wears a black mask and

| 2866 | 2867 |

bright chequered costume, Pierrot and Columbine dressed in white, the curtains strongly shaded in red. The cost in 1931 was 17s 6d. each coloured, or 25s. each mounted with black wood as book-ends. Doris Lindner, while working as a freelance modeller in London, had produced the book-ends herself in painted plaster for sale through Heal's Department Store. Joseph Gimson had seen these and asked for further models from Doris Lindner as a result.

2868 and 2869

Name Harlequin and Pierrot
(second versions)
Height 6 ½ in. and 6in.
Modeller Doris Lindner
Introduced 1931
Rarity C

A pair of figures of the characters from the Italian Comedy modelled in Art Deco style. 2868 stands with his legs crossed and one hand extended. 2869 leans slightly backwards with his hands together and both have octagonal bases. They cost 7s. 6d. each in 1931 and were subsequently issued in mottled grey to simulate stone. This colouring is extremely rare. Two colour schemes are recorded for 2868:

1. litho grey and orange squares with Persian red shoes, grey base;
2. persian red, apple green, black and orange squares with Persian red shoes and black base.

Three colour schemes are recorded for 2869:

1. crimson with black stand;

2. litho grey, black cap and buttons;
3. green with silver stand and buttons, silver cap.

See also 2999. *(Colour plate 40)*

2870

Name Terrier on Plinth
Height 3 ½ in.
Modeller Doris Lindner
Introduced 1931
Rarity C

A model of a terrier standing alertly with tail raised, on rectangular base. Decorated in white with red-brown patches, as a wire-haired terrier, the base in pale fawn or green. This and 2871 were the first animal models by Doris Lindner and their success inspired the great series of small dogs issued in the following year without plinths. 2870 was reissued without a plinth as 3026 and could also be coloured as an Airedale. The terrier on plinth sold for 5s. 6d. in 1931 and was withdrawn by 1940. It was also used on the cover of a powder bowl as 2927.

2871

Name Setter on Plinth
Height 3in.
Modeller Doris Lindner
Introduced 1931
Rarity B

A model of a red setter lying with front paws outstretched, on a chamfered rectangular base. Strongly coloured in chestnut-red, the base in pale fawn or green. Like 2870 the model was reissued two years later without a plinth as No. 2952. Both sold originally for 5s. 6d., and the latter version was still produced in 1940, costing 6s. Withdrawn by 1948.

2872 and 2873

Name Fox and Hound Ashtrays
Height 4in.
Modeller Doris Lindner
Introduced 1931
Rarity E

A pair of plain circular ashtrays applied at one side with a lying fox and a lying hound, their angular bodies curved to fit the shape of the trays, the fox's head raised alertly. These were always painted in naturalistic colours, the trays shaded in pale fawn or cream. The ashtrays were also used as the covers for tobacco jars made for the retailer Betzeman, Nos. 2925 and 2926, and the fox and hound themselves were issued alone on slight bases as 2950 and 2951, to be mounted in silver by Betzeman, or together on either side of a long pen tray, shape No. 2947.

The ashtrays sold for 5s. each in 1931, rising to 18s. 6d. in 1952. Withdrawn by 1955. The models were reissued in 1954 without ashtrays or bases as 3527 and 3528, but probably very few were made.

2874
Name   Sleeping Doe
Height   4 ¾ in.
Modeller   Eric Aumonier
Introduced 1931
Rarity   B

A model of a young deer in Art Deco style, its body curled tightly with its head turned inwards, on a rounded rectangular base. The modeller designed the piece to be coloured with small circles on a pale shaded fawn ground and a border of loops around the base to represent railings. The model was subsequently issued in mottled grey to simulate stone. It cost 12s. 6d. coloured in 1931 and was withdrawn by 1940. The workers at the factory found the model incomprehensible, and awarded it a rather crude nickname.

2875
Name   Horseman Book-end
Height   8 ¼ in.
Modeller   Eric Aumonier
Introduced 1931
Rarity   B

A single model of a man clinging to the reins of a rearing horse, modelled in curious Art Deco style, the rider facing to one side so that he would face the wall if placed at the right-hand end of a row of books. The colouring designed by Aumonier was a shaded fawn ground with painted coloured circles, the rider in colours with spots and sprigs on his jacket, the base edged with loops to represent

railings. The models cost 17s. 6d. each in 1931 or 25s. mounted on wooden book-ends. Withdrawn by 1940. The model was incorrectly ascribed to Doris Lindner on one publicity photograph, and it is possible this error could occur on actual models. (*Colour plate 94*)

2876
Name   Lion Book-end
Height   6 ¼ in.
Modeller   Eric Aumonier
Introduced 1931
Rarity   B

A single model of an heraldic lion rampant, intended to be mounted supporting a black wooden shield as a book-end. It was decorated in mottled grey to simulate carved stone, the lion's claws picked out in colour and with small painted circles. It sold for 17s. 6d. or 25s. fully fitted-up in 1931, and was withdrawn by 1940.

2877
Name   Young Horse
Height   6 ¼ in. with base
Modeller   Eric Aumonier
Introduced 1931
Rarity   D

A stylized Art Deco model of a foal standing squarely on a rectangular base. Intended by the modeller to be painted with tiny green or blue leaf sprigs or shapes on a white or fawn ground, the base edged with loops to represent railings. Subsequently the model was issued in mottled grey-blue to simulate stone. It was also made without a base, and then usually marked on the inside of the rear legs. It has also been seen mounted on a flat mirror base and as a blotter. It sold in 1931 for 10s. 6d. Although it was reasonably successful, the workers in the factory did not understand the model. They gave it the rather irreverent nickname of 'Peeing Horse' because one of the paintresses spilt some water on her bench one day beside the model and it looked as if the horse was responsible. The model was withdrawn by 1940. (*Colour plate 59*)

2879

Name Dreaming
Height 4in.
Modeller Phoebe Stabler
Introduced 1931
Rarity C

A small figure of a girl kneeling with her hands on her lap above a tall chamfered square base, wearing a long plain night-dress and shoulder-length blonde hair. It sold for 6s. 6d. in 1931 and was withdrawn by 1940. Seven colour schemes are recorded, the first five listed as having a smaller base than the final two:

1. ivory, indigo base;
2. yellow, indigo base;
3. light chrome-green, indigo base;
4. turquoise-blue, black base;
5. pink, indigo base;
6. pink, brown base;
7. turquoise-blue, brown base.

2880

Name Flower Girl (first version)
Height 8in.
Modeller Phoebe Stabler
Introduced 1931
Rarity B

A figure of a lady standing dressed in a long plain yellow dress, a basket of flowers on her left arm, her right hand holding a baby wrapped in her pink and blue striped shawl, standing on a stepped octagonal base. It sold for 22s. in 1931 and was withdrawn by 1940. The figure had earlier been supplied by Phoebe Stabler for Doulton, who made it between 1913 and 1938 under the title 'The Lavender Woman'.

2881

Name Sauce
Height 8 ¾ in. with plinth
Modeller Phoebe Stabler
Introduced 1931
Rarity C

A figure of a girl standing on a shaped base and leaning forward with a mischievous grin on her face, her hands held together in front and her short skirt revealing her tiered petticoat at the back. It was available with a tall black plinth or just a flat base

and was one of the models mounted as a lamp (illustrated in this form on page 17). Phoebe Stabler's original model was also cast in bronze. The Worcester figure sold in 1931 for 22s. or 15s. without plinth. It was still available in 1940 for £1.5s. increasing to £1.12s. 6d. in 1948. Withdrawn by 1952.

Several colour schemes are recorded, although the model has also been seen decorated with shot-silk effect and shaded gold:

1. green, yellow petticoat, black base, blonde hair;
2. yellow, pink petticoat, black base, light brown hair;
3. mauve, light brown petticoat, light brown hair;
4. turquoise-blue, golden-fawn and orange petticoat, orange-brown hair;
5. pink, white petticoat, black base, yellow hair;
6. emerald-green, green base;
7. sea-green, green base.

(*Colour plate 8*)

2882

Name Boy on Boar
Height 3 ¼ in.
Modeller Phoebe Stabler
Introduced 1931
Rarity B

2882

A model of a naked child seated on the back of a boar standing on an oval base. The animal was naturalistically coloured although the modelling of the boar shows Phoebe Stabler's weakness at animal modelling. Similar models were designed by Phoebe Stabler for Poole Pottery in the 1920s.

2883 and 2884

Name   Little Dancer and Coquette
Height   3 ¼ in.
Modeller   Phoebe Stabler
Introduced   1931
Rarity   C

Two small figures of young girls on square bases. Little Dancer sits with her legs crossed, her hands together in front of her, whilst Coquette kneels, her head turned coyly to one side. Both were issued in a number of colours, mostly sculptured with very little painted detail. Six colour schemes are recorded for Little Dancer:

1. ultramarine-blue dress, shaded pink, black base;
2. yellow dress, black base;
3. light chrome-green dress, black base;
4. turquoise-blue dress, black base;
5. pink dress, shaded stronger pink, black base;
6. light chrome-green dress, shaded in folds, brown base.

Nine colours are recorded for Coquette:

1. white dress and bonnet with mauve blobs, indigo base;
2. ivory-shaded pink dress, ivory bonnet black base with green top;
3. egg-yellow dress, black base with green top;
4. light chrome-green, highlights egg-yellow, black base with orange top;
5. turquoise-blue shaded ultramarine, black base with orange top;
6. pink dress, black base with green top;
7. flame dress, black base with green top;
8. turquoise-blue shaded ultramarine, brown base with orange top;
9. as 8 but with brown base.

Little Dancer was also issued on the cover of a powder bowl as shape No. 2938.
(*Colour plate 42*)

2885

Name   The Mother
Height   7 ¾ in.
Modeller   Phoebe Stabler
Introduced   1931
Rarity   B

A group typical of Miss Stabler's sculptural style depicts a mother sitting with a baby on her lap, another child standing naked by her side. The woman is dressed in peasant style and the model has a stepped octagonal base. The most expensive of Phoebe Stabler's models, it sold for £1. 15s. in 1931. The mother usually wears a green dress and the base is blue. Royal Doulton produced a somewhat similar figure, entitled 'Motherhood', also designed by Phoebe Stabler, between 1913 and 1938.

2886

Name   The Old Goat Woman
Height   5 ¾ in.
Modeller   Phoebe Stabler
Introduced   1931
Rarity   D

A model of an elderly Belgian peasant holding the reins of a goat by her side on a circular base, a pottery jar over one arm. The figure was the most successful of Phoebe Stabler's models, produced in bright colours and reasonably priced at £1. 5s. in 1931, rising to £4. 8s in 1955. It was withdrawn by 1957. Like 2880 the figure had previously been made by Doulton, under the title 'Milking Time', between 1913 and 1938. Three colour schemes are recorded:

1. bonnet white, blue squares on dress, apron white, slight grey in folds, ivory shoes, egg-yellow pot, fawn goat and green base;
2. flame bonnet and cloak, pale yellow apron with pink line, ivory pot, purple and white goat with brown base;
3. green bonnet, lavender and yellow shawl, green dress, white apron, black and white goat.

(*Colour plate 27; an original publicity photograph of the model mounted as a lamp is shown on page 17*).

2887

Name   Pick-a-Back
Height   8in.
Modeller   Phoebe Stabler
Introduced   1931
Rarity   B

A figure of a mother giving her child a pick-a-back ride on her shoulders, a charming family study although perhaps lacking the movement such a group needs to succeed. Costing £1. 5s. in 1931, the figure was withdrawn by 1940. Usual decoration comprises a yellow and grey striped coat, red and blue-grey shapes on dress, shaded in folds. The original drawing has written against the dress, 'consideration taken when the design lies in a fold'. The child has shot-shaded yellow coat and pale ultramarine-blue trousers. *(Colour plate 53)*

2891 and 2892

Name   Greyhounds and Hare
Height   3in.
Modeller   Stella R. Crofts
Introduced 1931
Rarity   B

A group of four greyhounds racing and a separate model of a running hare. The dogs run on a stylized green rectangular base, their coats naturalistically coloured and the hare leaping through the long grass. This is the only Worcester model conceived in two parts, although they were priced separately in 1931 at £1. 5s. and 3s. respectively. The difficulties presented by the complex colouring scheme account for the relatively high price for the time.

2893

Name   Pelican Ashtray
Height   3 ¾ in.
Modeller   Stella R. Crofts
Introduced 1931
Rarity   B

A model of a pelican, its beak raised, perched beside an octagonal pool forming an ashtray. The bird is tinted white with a coloured beak and cost 6s. 6d. in 1931. It was withdrawn by 1940. A pelican ashtray was made by Miss Crofts at her own pottery in Essex in about 1929.

2894

Name   Boy with Donkey
Height   6in.
Modeller   Stella R. Crofts
Introduced 1931
Rarity   B

An elaborate model of a child seated on the back of a donkey, a basket of fruit hung from both sides. The animal lowers its head to eat from a sack of carrots and the group is naturalistically coloured, on a pale rectangular base. This demonstrates Miss Crofts' ability to model figures as well as animals, although at 2 guineas in 1931 it was one of the most expensive figures of the period and is consequently very scarce. It was withdrawn by 1940. A similar group is known from Stella Crofts' own pottery, dated 1929 titled 'Donkey Eating Carrots'. *(Colour plate 125)*

2895

Name   Giraffes
Height   8in.
Modeller   Stella R. Crofts
Introduced 1931
Rarity   B

A group of three giraffes, standing on a roughly square base. Two adults stand upright, their necks crossed, whilst the third, younger, animal reaches down to nibble the long grass. The model is based on a similar composition in glazed pottery made by Miss Crofts in her own studio in Essex, several examples of which are known dated from 1931 onwards. The sculpture converts reasonably well to porcelain, but the fine detail of the colouring is really not suited to the stylized shape of the model. For some reason the figure is not listed in the factory costings book, possibly because the time-consuming painting made this such an expensive model that it was only available to special order. It is believed that the painting of this model was by George Evans. At the time of writing Giraffes holds the record for any single unlimited twentieth-century Worcester figure sold at auction, an example selling at Phillips in 1983 for £1,430. *(Colour plate 74)*

2896

Name   Calf
Height   2 ¼ in.
Modeller   Stella R. Crofts
Introduced 1931
Rarity   A

2896

A model of a young calf lying on a square base, its head turned back to lick its rear legs. Again typical of Miss Crofts' very stylized animal models, the calf is not successful in porcelain and production was very limited, despite the figure costing only 6s. 6d. in 1931.

2897

Name	Cat Eating
Height	3in.
Modeller	Stella R. Crofts
Introduced	1931
Rarity	B

A model of a cat licking from a saucer of milk, on a long rectangular base, its tail curved gracefully to one side. An impressive model technically, but costly to decorate, it sold for 12s. 6d., more than twice the price of other similarly sized animal models. Even so it is surprising that the model was not a success, as the subject has always been popular and the figure has considerable charm. The cat is recorded as having been available in either black or brown.

2898, 2899, 2901 and 2902

Name	Victorian Musicians
Height	8½ in. to 9¼ in.
Modeller	Ethelwyn Baker
Introduced	1931
Rarity	B

Four figures forming a series, although they were issued separately, and comprising:
2898 The Harpist.
A lady standing beside her harp, a letter held in her right hand.
2899 The Lute Player
A man standing with right foot raised on a plinth, his lute held with both hands in front of him.
2901 The Flute Player
A man standing with his legs crossed, his right elbow resting on a tall column and the narrow flute raised to his mouth.
2902 The Song
A lady in a long over-dress with a bustle back, her mouth open to sing and a song sheet held at arms length in front.

All are curiously modelled, with elongated limbs and features, and were known to the factory workers as 'The Longies'. The paintresses thought these models very strange and could not understand them. Although they are described as Victorian Musicians two of them, The Harpist and Flute Player, are dressed in costume of the early nineteenth century.

The colouring designed by Miss Baker was tones of grey to enhance the sculptural feel of the figures. When they failed to sell in this colouring Daisy Rea designed a new scheme for each, concentrating on naturalistic colours and patterns for the dresses, printed sprigs from a tableware pattern being used on the singer's dress. In an attempt to boost sales, the models were mounted by Charles Selz as table lamps, the shades decorated with a line of music, and 2901 is illustrated in this form on page 17. See also page 51.

Unmounted, they sold for 30s. each in 1931, and all had been withdrawn by 1940. The modeller's monogram of EB in a circle appears moulded and painted on the back of each base.

All four figures were issued in a grey ground colour, usually with indigo hair, but the following alternative colourings are recorded:
2898
1. Brown ivory dress with pale ultramarine spots and grey stand. The outer part of the harp is orange and the inner part Donville black and wood brown.
2. Same as 1 but with green dress.
2899
1. Claret coat with brown neck-tie.
2. Dark claret coat with blue neck-tie.

2901
1. Wood brown coat, ivory-shaded base, mauve waistcoat.
2. Blue coat, light brown base, yellow and mauve waistcoat.

2902
1. Rose du Barrie pink dress, with yellow collar.
2. Orange dress with turquoise-blue collar.

(*2898, 2899, 2902 Colour plate 19*)

2900

Name   Sam and Barbara
Height   6 ½ in.
Modeller   Ethelwyn Baker
Introduced   1931
Rarity   B

A pair of models of polar bears intended for mounting as book-ends. Sam is on the left and Barbara the right, both seated upright with their front paws raised on a block, their pointed heads looking away from each other. The polar bears were issued largely in white with slight pink tinting, costing 8s. 6d. each or 15s. each mounted as book-ends.

Sam was purchased by London Zoo from John Lund on 1st September 1920 and remained at the Zoo until 24th February 1938, when he was loaned to Sir Garrard T. Drake. Sam died at Maidstone Zoo in September 1939. Barbara was at London Zoo from 1904 until 1923, and Ethelwyn Baker would have modelled the pair in the early 1920s. It is quite likely that her models were spotted by Mr. Gimson in her studio, and the original names were retained. (*Barbara, Colour plate 18*)

2901

Name   The Flute Player
(*See* 2898 for description.)

2902

Name   The Song
(*See* 2898 for description.)

2903 and 2904

Name   Bluebeard and Fatima
Height   10 ¼ in. and 10in.
Modeller   Sybil Williams and Jessamine Bray

Introduced 1931
Rarity   B

A pair of fine large figures of the notorious Bluebeard and his final wife Fatima. Bluebeard wears a turban, his long robes tied with a sash. He pulls up his right sleeve in preparation for combat, a gilt sword in his hand. Fatima wears long robes and veil ornamented with raised enamel and gold. She holds a single key in her raised right hand, a bunch of keys hanging by a chain from her waist. Her expression is inquisitive, as she is curious to open the door forbidden to her by Bluebeard following their marriage. Fatima was to open the door and discover the bodies of Bluebeard's former wives only for her husband to return and order her to death. She was saved just in time by her brother, who killed Bluebeard.

A somewhat similar figure of Bluebeard was also produced by Royal Doulton between 1917 and 1938, and the figures were probably inspired by Diaghilev's Russian Ballet performance of *Scheherazade*, based on *The Arabian Nights*. Some of the Worcester figures were mounted as lamps, but both were withdrawn by 1940. The figures were not greatly popular and this may have been due to the fact that many people considered the characters on which they were based to be unlucky. These most impressive figures cost £2.5s. each when issued, and the recorded colourings are as follows:

Bluebeard: Deep cobalt-blue beard and moustache, dark eyebrows with a little blue on them. Sword hilt to be gilt – also earrings and buttons. Bright scarlet sash, yellow turban, black and green base. The records mention that the figure was also painted 'flame', and examples have been noted in green.

Fatima: 1. Light green shot dress; pencilled-ivory pantaloons; black and 'Paddy' green base with pink strawberry top; shot turquoise and pink cloak with green jewelling and white enamel spots;
2. Yellow dress with brown top; greyish-blue pantaloons and cloak.

(*Colour plate 35 and jacket*)

2905 and 2906

Name   Noel and June (first version)
Height   4 ½ in. small size and 7in.
              large size
Modeller   Sybil Williams and Jessamine
              Bray
Introduced   1931
Rarity   Small E., Large D

A pair of figures of young ladies dressed in elaborate crinoline skirts representing different times of the year. Noel wears a fur-lined coat and carries gaily coloured Christmas parcels and a Christmas tree. June holds a peaked bonnet by her side with a bunch of flowers in her right hand. The figures were both made in two sizes and were sold either as a pair or singly. The large figures sold for £1. 15s. each in 1931, rising to £4. 12s. in 1955. The small figures cost 7s. each in 1931, rising to £1. 17s. 6d.in 1955. June and Noel were the first really successful figures to be introduced in the 1930s. They sold in fair numbers and when the Porcelain Ball was held in London in November 1931 (*see* page 16), the two models were chosen as typical of the Worcester range. In view of the success of June and Noel it is perhaps surprising that Miss Bray and Miss Williams were not asked for any further models. One figure of June has been seen entitled 'Delphine'.

Three different colourings are recorded for Noel and ten for June, and one of the modellers has written 'please paint the faces rather deliberately'.

Noel:

1. Dress turquoise green with yellow and purple balloons, pale yellow and green bonnet;
2. Dress blue with pink balloons, turquoise-blue and green bonnet;
3. Dress shaded peacock, orange and red balloons, pink bonnet.

June:

1. Chintz.	6. Light blue
2. Pink.	and ultramarine.
3. Yellow chrome-green.	7. Clover.
	8. Yellow.
4. Pink with shaded frills.	9. Blue.
	10. Golden orange.
5. Turquoise and ultramarine.	

A note mentions that numbers 2, 3, 8, 9 and 10 were also done with shot-gold sheen.(*Colour plate 31*)

2907-2910

Name   Red Indian Series
Height   6in. – 7in.
Modeller   Frederick Gertner
Introduced   1931
Rarity   B

A series of four figures of North American Indians. All are wrapped in traditional blankets and stand on octagonal bases.

2907

Indian Chief, 7in., dressed in a long feather head-dress, his arms folded defiantly. Decorated with green, blue and red designs.

2908

Indian Brave, 7in., a younger warrior with a single feather in his hair, his blanket pulled tightly around him. Decorated with brown, black and red squares and designs.

2909

Indian Squaw with Child on Back, 6 ¼ in., a woman carrying an infant in a papoose on her back.

2910

Indian Squaw with Child on Shoulder, 6in., a similar figure of a woman, her child in a papoose looking out over her left shoulder.

The figures were designed as a set, with the whiteness of the porcelain allowed to contrast with strong enamel colours. The models are true to life and differ from the popular idea of Red Indians seen in Hollywood Westerns. Although not expensive at 10s. 6d. each in 1931, few seem to have been sold. All were withdrawn by 1940. 2909 is very similar to a Rosenthal figure of the same subject, and this may have inspired Worcester's version.
(*2907 Colour plate 122*)

2911

Name	Lady with Fan
Height	7 ¼ in.
Modeller	Frederick Gertner
Introduced	1931
Rarity	B

2911

A figure of a young woman, in the style of the 1850s, her dark hair tied in ringlets, holding a partly open fan in front of her. A coloured fichu is held round her shoulders, her long tiered and pleated crinoline skirt painted with tiny floral sprigs. Similar in style to the popular Noel and June (2905 and 2906) this figure did not share the same success. Selling for £1. 5s. in 1931, it had been withdrawn by 1940. Two colourings are recorded:

1. yellow dress with pink ribbons and mauve fan;
2. blue, green and pink dress, purple ribbons and scarlet-red fan.

2912 – 2915

Name	Michael, Tommy, Mischief and Joan
Height	2 ½ in., 4 ½ in., 3 ¼ in. and 4 ¼ in.
Modeller	Freda Doughty
Introduced	1931
Rarity	E

The first models from Miss Doughty were an instant success. The figures were conceived as a set of four, but Tommy and Joan proved particularly popular as a pair.

Michael is a young child with curly hair, crawling with one arm raised in the air. Mischief is a girl seated by a clump of flowers, pulling the petals from a single flower in her hand. Tommy stands with hands behind his back, his face wearing a mischievous grin, whilst Joan holds the hem of her short skirt. The four figures illustrate Freda Doughty's ability to capture the naturalism of children, and sold in great numbers. Produced in a wide range of colourings, all sold for 6s. 6d. each in 1931, rising to 17s. 6d. in 1955. All were withdrawn by 1957. Mischief was also used on the cover of a powder bowl, as 2928.

The recorded colourings are as follows:

2912 - Michael:
1. blue;
2. yellow;
3. green;
4. flame with added yellow.

2913 - Tommy:
1. yellow, mauve shorts;
2. flame, mauve shorts;
3. white, with delicate blue and pink flowers, blue shorts.

The figure is also recorded as having been painted either pink, mauve or green with shot-gold sheen all with turquoise-blue shorts.

2914 - Mischief:
1. yellow, pink flowers;
2. white, pink and green flowers;
3. blue-green, violet and yellow flowers;
4. flame-red, spots picked out in brown;
5. shot jade-green with shot-gold sheen;
6. shot-mauve with shot-gold sheen;

2915 - Joan:
1. pale yellow dress, purple knickers.
2. flame dress with yellow spots, yellow knickers.
3. white dress with green touches, red knickers.

(2912 and 2914 Colour plate 66; 2913 and 2915 Colour plate 85)

2916

Name	The Mongrel Pup
Height	7 ½ in.
Modeller	Margaret Cane
Introduced	1931
Rarity	C

2916

A figure of a little girl with short straight hair and a plain, strongly coloured dress, kneeling on a flowering tree stump. She is lovingly hugging a puppy dog. An appealing model, it cost 16s. 6d. in 1931 but only 16s in 1942. It was not reintroduced after the war. Possibly the fact that the dog looks away from the viewer contributed to the apparent lack of popularity of the figure. Four colourings are recorded:

    1. shot sea-green and turquoise dress.
    2. yellow.
    3. blue and yellow.
    4. flame.

The dog can be either brown and white or black and white.

2917

Name	Sea Urchin
Height	6 ¼ in.
Modeller	Margaret Cane
Introduced	1931
Rarity	D

A simple figure of a young boy seated naked astride a post, his hands resting on the top of the post. The child is flesh-toned with straight brown hair, the base shaded in darker brown. Like most of Miss Cane's models, the child in not as lifelike as Freda Doughty's children, but he does have considerable charm and proved reasonably popular, costing 10s. 6d. in 1931 and 11s. in 1940. Withdrawn by 1948.
(Colour plate 62)

2918

Name	Sleepy Boy
Height	3in.
Modeller	Margaret Cane
Introduced	1931
Rarity	E

A little boy seated with his arms tightly around his legs, his head resting sleepily on his knees. He wears a plain jumper and shorts, on a plain oval base. A very simple figure, but modelled to convey considerable detail. The figure cost 6s. 6d. when introduced, increasing to 15s in 1955, and was withdrawn by 1957. The following colours are recorded:

    1. chrome-green sweater, indigo base;
    2. mauve sweater, shaded green base;
    3. yellow-shaded orange sweater, shaded green base;
    4. pink sweater, indigo base;
    5. ultramarine sweater, indigo base;
    6. ultramarine and pink sweater, golden-fawn base;
    7. flame sweater, golden-fawn base;

In all cases the shorts are "Toby Jug" brown and the shoes golden-fawn, except for no. 6 with brown shoes and no. 7 with ultramarine and pink shorts. *(Colour plate 68)*

2919

Name	Tangles
Height	9 ½ in.
Modeller	Anne Acheson
Introduced	1931
Rarity	B

A figure of a naked child holding above her head coloured ribbons attached to three balloons by her feet, the ribbons tangled around her left leg and in her hair, on a textured circular base. Miss Acheson's original pencil and water-colour design for the colouring still survives, and is illustrated on page 34. Here she has given specific instructions to the paintresses to try to imitate the effect of the twisted ribbons. The original price was £1. 2s. and few were sold. It was withdrawn by 1948 at the latest, probably much earlier. The child's body is ivory-coloured and the balloons are a mixture of blue, yellow, pink and green.

2920

2921

2920 and 2921

Name	Lough Neagh Mary and Dublin Flower Girl
Height	7in. and 6in.
Modeller	Anne Acheson
Introduced	1931
Rarity	B

Two models of women in traditional Irish costume. Lough Neagh Mary stands holding in her left arm a circular basket of fish; the Dublin Flower Girl is seated surrounded by her wares, a bouquet held in her hands. They cost £1. 2s. 6d. and £1. 2s. when introduced and were withdrawn by 1940.

2922 and 2923

Name	Dutch Girl and Dutch Boy
Height	5 ¼ in.
Modeller	Probably Frederick Gertner
Introduced	1931
Rarity	E

A pair of small figures in national costume, both holding two baskets of flowers, standing with clogs on their feet on textured circular bases. Issued in bright colours, most often a brilliant flame-red, this pair proved very popular. The price rose from 15s. each when introduced to £1. 1s. 6d. in 1955. They were withdrawn by 1957. Following the introduction of Freda Doughty's Children of the Nations series, there was some confusion within the factory regarding the modeller of these figures. Some examples occur bearing a

painted title 'modelled by F. G. Doughty'. We believe this pair to be the work of Frederick Gertner and most of the examples seen are attributed to him. The recorded colour schemes are as follows:

2922 - Dutch Boy:
1. Dutch-blue trousers, Dutch-green jacket.
2. toby-brown trousers, flame jacket.
3. flame trousers, purple jacket.

2923 - Dutch Girl:
1. turquoise-blue skirt, peacock-blue top.
2. flame dress, mauve top.
3. white dress with ultramarine-blue stripes, white top.

(Colour plate 86)

2924

Name	The Fortune Teller or Mother Machree
Height	5 ¾ in.
Modeller	Freda Doughty
Introduced	1931
Rarity	D

A finely modelled figure of an old lady seated on a bench, stooping forward and wagging her finger. A very unusual model from Miss Doughty, who proved that her ability to capture naturalism was not restricted to her child studies. Rumours in the factory suggest that Mother Machree was an old lady who lived in Severn Street near the factory and used to terrify some of the younger paintresses. When introduced the figure cost £1. 2s. 6d. or could be bought fitted as a lamp for £2. 12s. 6d. In spite of the somewhat haggard character of the old lady which caused the workforce to dislike the figure, it proved very popular, still selling in 1955 at £3. 6s. It was withdrawn by 1957, but while moulds of other models were destroyed a note records that the block moulds for this one were kept. The figure is recorded as having been issued in two colourings, although the first of these is the more usually seen:
1. flame colouring with ultramarine-shaded pink parts.
2. Green underglaze colours, white stockings visible at back of dress.

(Colour plate 23)

2925 and 2926
Name   Fox and Hound Tobacco Jars
(*See* 2872 and 2873 for description).

2927
Name   Terrier Powder Bowl
(*See* 2870 for description)

2928
Name   Mischief Powder Bowl
(*See* 2914 for description)

2930
Name   Betty, Buttercup, Marigold,
           Lavender, Pansy, Lily or Rose
           (first version)
Height   3 ½ in.
Modeller   Anne Acheson
Introduced 1931
Rarity   E

A figure of a girl seated on a circular mound strewn with flowers, a kitten cradled in her arms. This seems to be the only figure which was given a different name depending on its colouring, and Daisy Rea recalled that she herself suggested some of the names after trying out a new decoration.

The recorded colours are as follows, although others have been seen:

1. 'Buttercup', egg-yellow dress;
2. 'Pansy', violet dress;
3. 'Marigold', marigold-coloured dress;
4. 'Rose', red dress.

A few examples have been noted where the name of the modeller is incorrectly given as F. G. Doughty. The example of Lavender illustrated in this book, is confusingly inscribed on the base 'B. Bragg', although nobody named Bragg is listed in the factory archives. The figure cost 10s. when introduced for all colourings, rising to £3. 10s. in 1955. All were withdrawn by 1957. The model was also used on the cover of a powder bowl as 3001. (*Colour plate 99*)

2931
Name   Bill
Height   8in. and 4 ½ in.
Modeller   Doris Lindner
Introduced 1931
Rarity   C

A model of a bull terrier seated on a flat rectangular base. The model was made in two sizes, the larger having the name 'Bill' moulded into the base. Naturalistically coloured in pale colours with darker patches, the base normally shaded in very light green. Both sizes were still produced in 1955, the larger model having increased in price from 17s. 6d. in 1931 to £3. 10s., and the smaller one from 5s. 6d. to £1. 10s. Both were withdrawn by 1957. 'Bill' was modelled on an actual dog named Bill which belonged to Colonel Fortescue, a friend of Miss Lindner.

2932 and 2934
Name   Sealyham
Height   4in., with stand 4 ½ in.
Modeller   Doris Lindner
Introduced 1931
Rarity   C

A model of a Sealyham terrier standing with its tail raised and head turned slightly to one side, a simple collar round its neck. Issued on a rectangular plinth (2932) and without a base (2934). This dog was also placed on a rounded rectangular ashtray (2935). When introduced the models each cost 12s. 6d., or 17s. 6d. on an ashtray, and all were withdrawn by 1940.

2936
Name   Argentina or Spanish Lady
Height   8in.
Modeller   Anne Acheson
Introduced 1931
Rarity   C

A figure of a lady in traditional costume with long dress and shawl, her hands on her hips and a raised comb in her hair. She stands on a chamfered square base. The figure seems to have been named as Spanish lady for only a very short time before the change to Argentina. A large figure, always well-coloured, and originaly costing £1. 5s., it proved unpopular, and to try and boost sales some were mounted as lamps with a distinctive shade (*see* illustration on page 17). It was withdrawn by 1940. The following colours are recorded:

1. Egg-yellow shawl, delicate pearl effect on dress.
2. Yellow shawl, cerise skirt.
3. Pale lemon-yellow shawl, green dress.
4. Flame and yellow shawl, green dress.
5. Black shawl, flame and yellow dress.
6. Red shawl, green dress.
7. Blue shawl, orange skirt.

(*Colour plate 26*)

2937

Name   Girl and Rabbit
Height   4 ½ in
Modeller   Unknown
Introduced   1932
Rarity   A

A figure of a young woman seated with one rabbit on her lap and two others by her side. A further rabbit is by her feet on a circular concave base and the girl's head is turned to one side. For some reason the figure is unlisted in most factory records and was never costed for colouring. Production was probably very limited.

2938

Name   Little Dancer Powder Bowl
(*See* 2883 for description).

2941-2946, 3026-3029, 3033, 3034, 3243 and 3293-3295

Name   Small Dog Series
Height   Between 2in and 2 ¾ in
Modeller   Doris Lindner
Introduced   1932 (2941-2946), 1933 (3026-3034), 1938 (3243), 1939 (3293-3295)
Rarity   E

A series of sixteen miniature models of dogs sculpted from actual dogs by Doris Lindner. These followed the success of the same modeller's slightly larger dog models and were intended to appeal to a wide market, selling inexpensively. All cost the same price, 3s. 8d. in 1932, rising to 13s. 6d. in 1955. In addition, the Terrier, No. 2870, was reissued without a plinth as part of this series and given shape number 3026; it was a little larger and cost slightly more

after 1948. All were withdrawn by 1957. The series comprised the following:

2941 Pekinese standing.

2942 Terrier sitting, painted as a Wire-haired Terrier or as an Airedale.

2943 Dandie Dinmont.

2944 English Springer Spaniel or Black Cocker Spaniel.

2945 English Bulldog.

2946 Aberdeen Toy Terrier or Scottie, standing.

3026 Terrier standing, painted as Wire-haired or Airedale, the head slightly to the right.

3027 Terrier standing, head turned slightly to the left (also made as an ashtray as 3156).

3028 Sealyham Terrier.

3029 Scottie Terrier.

3033 Cocker Spaniel.

3034 Pekinese sitting.

3243 Welsh Corgi.

3293 Dalmatian.

3294 Dachsund (light or dark colouring).

3295 Alsatian (first version).

(*Colour plate 25; for 2943 see also Colour plate 137*)

2947

Name   Fox and Hound Pen Tray
(*See* 2872 for details).

2949

Name   The Dancers
Height   9 ¾ in
Modeller   Doris Lindner
Introduced   1932
Rarity   C

A group of a lady and gentleman dancing in smart evening dress, their bodies held closely together, modelled in graceful Art Deco style on a rectangular plinth. The figure was conceived by Miss Lindner as a sculpture, and she intended it to be coloured in mottled grey to simulate stone. A few were issued in this way, but the factory thought this too ambitious and

Daisy Rea designed a new colour scheme, giving the gentleman a blue-grey suit and bow tie and the lady a flame-coloured dress. It was also tried out in gold sheen colouring using the shot silk technique. It cost £1. 10s. coloured, or £1. 5s. in mottled grey, and was withdrawn by 1940. In a letter dated 17th August 1931, Miss Lindner writes 'I enclose a rough sketch for colouring, the same idea as in your 'Victorian figures' and the faces painted in the same delicate way. I should also like to see it done in the grey crackled effect, which I think would look best.' (*Colour plate 28*).

2950 and 2951

Name   Fox and Hound
(*See* 2872 for description.)

2952

Name   Setter (without plinth)
(*See* 2871 for description.)

2953-2956

Name   Fox and Hound Menu-
             Holders
Height   2 ¼ in to 2 ¾ in
Modeller   Unknown
Introduced 1932
Rarity   C

A set of four models fitted with slots to support menu cards. The three hounds and one fox are modelled in low relief with filled-in bases and all were naturalistically coloured, the bases in bright green. They were sold as sets of four in fitted boxes, although they are more often found singly. They do not seem to have sold in any great numbers. Doris Lindner, who modelled most of the fox and hound studies at this time, told us that the menu-holders were not her work.

2957-2967, 2969-2974, 2975-2992, 2995, 2996, 3002-3005 and 3007

Name   Brooches, mainly in the form
             of dogs, birds and fish,
             intended for mounting on
             hats. Some were also tried as
             menu-holders.
Modeller   Unknown

2993 and 2994

Name   Fox and Hound Sitting
Height   7in. and 6 ¾ in.
Modeller   Doris Lindner
Introduced 1932
Rarity   F

A pair of large models of a fox and a foxhound both sitting alertly, naturalistically coloured. They were originally intended as book-ends but it is not clear whether they were to be mounted on wood angles as they do not seem heavy enough to support the books by themselves. They proved very popular, originally costing 10s. 6d. each and they remained in production until the 1970's. In 1933 the factory tried out the heads only mounted as wall models (3024 and 3025). They never went into full production but a few were made and are occasionally found in the Worcester area. Doris Lindner, on seeing an example of one of the heads, said she had not realized they had gone into production.
(*2993, Colour plate 5*)

2997 and 2998

Name   Fox and Hound Lying
             Straight
Height   4 ½ in.
Modeller   Unknown, probably Doris
             Lindner
Introduced 1932
Rarity   B

A pair of models of a fox and a foxhound lying on long rectangular plinths. They were produced specially for Betzeman to mount, probably as menu or place markers. The somewhat stylized modelling resembles closely Miss Lindner's Fox and Hound ashtray, although records cannot confirm these are her work. They sold for 5s. each and production was very short-lived. Both were reissued in 1956 without bases as shapes 3570 and 3571, selling for 18s. each.

2999

Name   Columbine (third version)
Height   6 ½ in.
Modeller   Doris Lindner
Introduced 1932
Rarity   B

2999

A figure of Columbine in somewhat stylized Art Deco style, standing with one hand pulling up her sleeve, on an octagonal base. The figure was intended to match Harlequin and Pierrot (2868 and 2869) which Miss Lindner had modelled the previous year. It cost 12s. but proved very unpopular, and is much rarer than the companion models. Four colourings are recorded:

1. white, shawl coloured green with yellow and pink flowers, grey base.
2. as 1 but with shot-silk coloured dress.
3. flame, green cloak, black base.
4. as 2 but green base.

3001
Name   Girl with Kitten Powder Bowl
(See 2930 for description.)

3002-3005
Name   Brooches
(See 2957 for description.)

3006
Name   Sweet Nell of Old Drury
Height   9in.
Modeller   Anne Acheson
Introduced 1932
Rarity   C

A large figure of Nell Gwynne, the notorious mistress of Charles II, dressed in a long, slightly ballooned skirt. An orange is held in her raised right hand with a basket of oranges over her other arm, and she stands on a chamfered square base. Expensive at £1. 10s., it was withdrawn by 1940. Seven colourings are recorded for the dress: turquoise, grey-green, flame,

green, primrose-yellow, shaded-pink and mauve, and it has also been seen in a shot-gold sheen. (*Colour plate 80*)

3007
Name   Brooches
(See 2957 for description.)

3008
Name   Sea Breeze
Height   8 ½ in.
Modeller   Freda Doughty
Introduced 1932
Rarity   F

A figure of a girl poised on tiptoe on a rock, her simple skirt blown by the wind, with a seagull by her feet on the wave-lapped base. This was the first of a great range of studies of children from Miss Doughty on a larger scale than that of her very first set of four small models (2912-2915), and many were to enjoy enormous success over a great many years. Sea Breeze originally cost 15s., or 2 guineas fitted as a lamp with shade, and the model without the lamp increased in price to £3. 10s. by 1955. It was withdrawn by 1957. Five colourings are recorded:

1. green and pink, base brown, blue and green;
2. blue and green, base as 1;
3. pink and blue, base green and blue;
4. yellow, green and brown, base multicoloured;
5. pink, base as 1.

(*Colour plate 17*)

3009
Name   Baby on Cushion or Sleeping Baby
Length   5in.
Modeller   Probably Frederick Gertner
Introduced 1932
Rarity   B

A figure of a young child asleep in the softness of a cushion, naked except for a thin drape across its middle. The figure is possibly inspired by a traditional sculpture of the same subject, often known as Somnus, reproduced by Wedgwood and others. It cost 10s. when introduced, rising to 12s. in 1940, and was withdrawn by 1948.

One example has been seen inscribed 'Sleeping Baby modelled by F. Doughty'. This is probably an error, but some doubt must exist over the attribution of the modeller. (*Colour plate 116*)

3010

Name   Happy Boy
Length   5in.
Modeller   Frederick Gertner
Introduced 1932
Rarity   C

A figure of a young boy lying on his back with knees raised, his head resting on his hands. He has blonde wavy hair and his simple tunic is usually coloured purple. Originally selling for 10s. it rose in price to 12s. in 1940, and was withdrawn by 1948. (*Colour plate 126*)

3011

Name   Peter Pan
Height   8in.
Modeller   Probably Frederick Gertner
Introduced 1932
Rarity   E

A young boy with short hair seated on a stump with pan pipes raised to his lips and a rabbit crouching on his lap. The figure has been seen in a flame colouring, but is more usually either brown, blue or green. A popular figure, it cost 15s. in 1932, rising to £3. 4s. 6d. in 1955. It was withdrawn by 1958. (*Colour plate 121*)

3012

Name   Spring (first version)
Height   9in.
Modeller   Freda Doughty
Introduced 1932
Rarity   E

A figure of a girl with long hair standing on a simple mound, a lamb held lovingly in her arms. The figure proved very popular and was still produced in 1955, when it cost 3 guineas. The following colours are listed:
1. mauve dress, fair hair, green base, purple flowers;
2. yellow dress, brown hair, green base, white flowers;
3. pink dress, golden hair, green base, pink flowers;
4. turquoise and blue dress, fair hair, green base, blue flowers.

(*Colour plate 63*)

3013

Name   Seal
Height   Unknown
Modeller   Unknown
Introduced 1932
Rarity   A

A model of a seal on a rock, its tail and nose raised. Records do not survive listing modeller or any cost price, and it is possible the model was withdrawn before full production commenced.

3014

Name   My Favourite
Height   5 ½ in.
Modeller   Freda Doughty
Introduced 1932
Rarity   F

A figure of a young girl with short curly hair kneeling on a grassy mound, lovingly hugging a rabbit chosen from a litter of baby rabbits with their mother on the base beside her. The colours recorded are blue, green, ultramarine, pink, flame, yellow, light chrome-green and chintzy-blue. My Favourite proved popular with the buying public and was in production until recently. (*Colour plate 110*)

3024 and 3025

Name   Fox and Hound Heads
(*See 2993 for description.*)

3026-3029

Name   Small Dogs Series
(*See 2941 for description.*)

3030

Name   Naiad
Height   4 ½ in.
Modeller   Doris Lindner
Introduced 1933
Rarity   B

A figure of a naked girl kneeling, her legs forming the base. Her body curves gracefully and her head is bowed, her arms held tightly against her side. The decoration was to be 'ivory for silks colouring all over' with yellow hair. Daisy Rea remembered that this figure was placed as a centrepiece in a bowl of water surrounded by floating flowers. It was made exclusively for Aspreys, selling for 12s. 6d. coloured. It was still made in 1940 but withdrawn by 1948. (*Colour plate 44*)

3031 and 3032

Name   Salmon and Trout
Height   about 4 ½ in.
Modeller   Unknown
Introduced 1933
Rarity   B

Two models of fish lying as if freshly caught, their tails and heads slightly raised. We have only seen white examples, but it is likely that they were to be painted by the men, possibly by W. H. Austin who specialized in fish. It is probable that very few were made.

3033 and 3034

Name   Small Dog Series
(*See* 2941 for description.)

3040

Name   The Kiss
Height   4 ¾ in.
Modeller   Unknown, possibly Doris
              Lindner
Introduced 1933
Rarity   A

A figure of a young lady kneeling, her tiered dress neatly gathered around her. She holds her left arm against her breast with her head slightly raised, her lips waiting to receive a kiss. Like Naiad (3030) it was issued in matt ivory colouring and was also available with a green dress. It failed to sell and was withdrawn by 1940. (*Colour plate 131*)

3062 and 3063

Name   Polar Bear Eating and Polar
              Bear Looking Up
Height   3 ¼ in. and 4 ¾ in.
Modeller   Doris Lindner
Introduced 1934
Rarity   B

A pair of models in an Art Deco style intended for mounting as book-ends and

sold by Grant of Torquay. We have seen several unmounted models and it is likely that they were also sold in this way. Mostly white with slight tinting in brown and purple tones, the models were not a success. They were also issued mounted on ashtrays as shapes 3184 and 3185, raised on rectangular bases representing pools. These were introduced in 1937, selling for £1. 5s. and again not many were made. (*3063, Colour plate 18*)

3066-3075, 3103, 3104 and 3178

Name   Children of the Nations
Modeller   Freda Doughty
Introduced 1934 (3066-3075), 1935 (3103
              and 3104), 1936 (3178)

A set of thirteen figures of children in costumes representing different Nations of the World. This first major series from Miss Doughty followed the success of her earlier child studies and these figures were to be extremely popular, some of them continuing in production into the 1970s. Wales, Scotland and Ireland were added to the original ten models, quite probably to meet public demand for the missing countries of the British Isles. Interestingly, from the numbers we have seen, Wales seems to have been more popular than England. The rarest models are Spain, Italy and Japan, while China and Burma were the most popular. There were, apparently, no colour variations.

3066
Name   Egypt
Height   5 ⅜ in.
Rarity   E

A boy wearing an orange djellaba or smock with mauve and chrome-green stripes. His Fez hat and shoes are flame-coloured and he stands on a light and dark brown mound, holding a simple mouth organ to his lips. (*Colour plate 34*)

3067
Name   Italy
Height   3 ¾ in.
Rarity   D

A girl selling flowers, a basket full of coloured blooms to her right-hand side and flowing on to her lap as she sits. A single flower is held above her head with her left hand. Her dress is mauve and she wears a jacket which is a mixture of light chrome-green, yellow and sea-green. The basket is golden-fawn and the flowers are ultramarine and pink. Her headscarf is yellow and pink.

3068
Name   Burmah
Height   5in.
Rarity   G

A dark-skinned boy, an ultramarine and blue garment around his waist, standing on a dark brown mound. He wears scarlet bracelets and beads around his neck. His left hand touches the top of his garment and his right strokes his chin as though he is deep in thought. The records show that his skin was to be painted 'brown for Indian features'. (*Colour plate 70*)

3069
Name   Greece
Height   5 ½ in.
Rarity   E

A boy dancing wearing an orange jacket and stockings shaded with mauve. He wears a black, green and scarlet jewelled bodice above a flame waistband and a white pleated skirt. His felt hat is flame and ultramarine and he stands on a light brown mound. Nearly all of Freda Doughty's figures were modelled from the children who visited her house and Daisy Rea recalled being there herself when this figure was conceived. Many children were present with their nannies and Daisy was painting in the garden. She remembers a little boy being coerced by his nanny into kissing a little girl goodbye. Rather reluctantly and shyly he eventually consented, and the face of the figure of Greece depicts the face of the boy as he kissed the little girl. (*Colour plate 34*)

3070
Name   Spain
Height   5 ¼ in.
Rarity   D

A girl standing on a small light-coloured mound on which pink, yellow and green

flowers grow. She wears a pink dress and white apron with pretty floral decoration. Her waistband is black and she wears a floral band on her hair which is coloured 'Austrian' brown. In her right hand she holds a small mauve and yellow parasol.

3071
Name   India
Height   3 ½ in.
Rarity   F

A dark-skinned boy seated and wearing a plain tunic and turban. He holds to his mouth a small grey pipe which he blows. The turban is painted turquoise-blue and peacock and the tunic is a mixture of mauve, yellow and golden-fawn. The boy's skin is to be 'brown for Indian features'. (*Colour plate 70*)

3072
Name   Japan
Height   3 ⅜ in.
Rarity   D

A girl seated and wearing a pink kimono with pretty flowers painted light chrome-green and mauve. She holds a yellow fan to her face and has 'Austrian' brown hair decked with mauve flowers.

3073
Name   China
Height   2 ⅜ in.
Rarity   G

A small boy seated and eating from a rice bowl held to his mouth, chopsticks in his right hand. He wears a sea-green, yellow and peacock jacket with peacock trim. His trousers are painted ultramarine and blue with mauve shadows. He wears pink shoes and his hair is 'Donville' black. (*Colour plate 70*)

3074
Name   Holland
Height   5 ½ in.
Rarity   E

A girl standing on a light grey mound, her hands held together at her waist. Her white dress is shaded pink and mauve with an ultramarine check design and she wears an ultramarine and blue bodice with scarlet beads around her neck. Her clogs are painted golden-fawn and her pointed hat is white. (*Colour plate 34*)

3075
Name   England
Height   5 ⅝ in.
Rarity   E
A golden-haired girl standing on a natural green and yellow mound base, holding a bouquet of daisies which she has picked. Her dress can be either pink or, more usually, ultramarine shaded pink, and the flowers are white and orange. Her hair is golden-fawn and yellow.

3103
Name   Wales
Height   5 ½ in.
Rarity   F
A girl standing on a natural-coloured green and yellow mound base. She wears a pink dress with white apron and a black Welsh hat over a white bonnet. She holds yellow and orange daffodils in her arms. (*Colour plate 38*)

3104
Name   Scotland
Height   5 ⅝ in.
Rarity   E
A girl standing on a roughly circular base strewn with purple heather. She wears a pink jacket, with green and yellow kilt and a white and brown sporran. The girl has golden hair and holds her hands on her hips. (*Colour plate 38*)

3178
Name   Ireland
Height   5 ¾ in.
Rarity   E
The final and just the tallest of the figures in the series. A girl standing on a natural coloured green and brown mound base. She wears a 'Paddy' green-striped dress and white apron, a red scarf around her neck. She is picking shamrock and a brown basket of shamrock hangs from her right arm. Her hair is shaded in golden-fawn and 'Austrian' brown. (*Colour plate 38*)

3076
Name   Woodland Dance
Height   4in.
Modeller   Freda Doughty
Introduced 1934
Rarity   G
A figure of a young girl kneeling on a grassy mound. She holds in her left hand a pipe, which she blows. An audience of rabbits listens attentively in front of her whilst a bird and a squirrel watch from her right-hand side. There are four colourings listed under the name 'A Woodland Dance':
   1. yellow;
   2. pink;
   3. blue;
   4. sea-greeen.
This immensely popular and charming group was made for a great many years, at least until the early 1970s. (*Colour plate 48*)

3078
Name   Rabbit Herald
Height   4 ¾ in.
Modeller   Unknown
Introduced 1934
Rarity   A

3078

A figure of the white rabbit from *Alice in Wonderland*, dressed as the Court Herald, his tunic decorated with hearts, a ruff around his neck. He holds a scroll in his left hand, a trumpet in his right. He stands barefoot on a textured base. The illustration shows the original plasticine model for a proposed figure which was probably not put into production. The shape number was subsequently reused for a vase and cover.

3081

Name   Grandmother's Dress
Height   6 ½ in.
Modeller   Freda Doughty
Introduced   1935
Rarity   G

A figure of a young girl trying on a long dress which reaches the ground to form the base, her head covered by a small cap and her hands by her side. Grandmother's Dress, together with Boy with Parakeet (3087), have undoubtedly proved to be the most popular of all twentieth-century Royal Worcester figures, and it is said that there were times when their high sales kept the factory going during the difficult 1950s. There are five recorded colourings for the dress, although others have been tried at various times:

1. pink shaded with ultramarine;
2. blue;
3. yellow;
4. green with yellow highlights;
5. purple.

All of these colours could be bought with added gold sheen. Daisy Rea remembered that pink was the first colour suggested by the modeller, whilst she herself created most of the other colourings. It was a very easy figure to decorate and, because it did not take long, the paintresses would not earn very much for each figure they worked on. (*Colour plate 78*)

3082

Name   The First Cuckoo
Height   6 ½ in.
Modeller   Freda Doughty
Introduced   1935
Rarity   F

A young girl stands on a woodland mound strewn with primroses, some of which she has gathered in the folds of her dress. She looks upwards as she hears the cuckoo. A delightful figure which enjoyed consider-

able success, continuing until the early 1960s. Four colourings are recorded for the dress, although others have been seen:

1. Mauve;
2. pink;
3. blue;
4. white with yellow shadows and turquoise-blue and ultramarine trim.

(*Colour plate 32*)

3083

Name   Sunshine
Height   5in.
Modeller   Freda Doughty
Introduced   1935
Rarity   E

A young girl sits on a wall, her legs crossed in front of her, flowers gathered in her lap. A popular figure which remained in production until the late 1950s, it is recorded in five colourings:

1. shaded-ivory and grey dress, mauve flowers;
2. turquoise-blue dress with shaded-yellow flowers;
3. yellow dress, mauve flowers;
4. pink dress, mauve flowers;
5. yellow dress, orange-brown flowers.

(*Colour plate 54*)

3084

Name   Dandelion
Height   4in.
Modeller   Freda Doughty
Introduced   1935
Rarity   C

A young boy sits on a roughly circular base decorated in greens and browns to represent a woodland mound. His legs are crossed in front of him and a white rabbit looks up from each side. He holds a dandelion flower in his raised hand. Two colourings are recorded for the boy's smock:

1. turquoise with blue and pink shadows;
2. yellow with egg-yellow in folds.

The figure is very similar to My Favourite (3014) which was already selling well, and although Dandelion was still made in 1955 it seems to have been much less popular.

3085

Name   Poodle, Champion Spriggan
           Bell
Height   8 ½ in.
Modeller   Doris Lindner
Introduced 1935
Rarity   A

Modelled from life, this champion show dog is well-groomed with a 'lion' cut. It stands alertly and is naturalistically coloured. It was modelled, we believe, to celebrate Spriggan Bell's victory in an important dog show, but the subject was soon forgotten and, at £1. 17s. 6d. each, very few were sold. (*Colour plate 56*)

3086 and 3088

Name   Dancing Lady and Dance
Height   8in. and 8 ½ in.
Modeller   Doris Lindner
Introduced 1935
Rarity   B

3086

A pair of figures of young ladies in closely-fitting diaphanous robes, both adopting a very stylish dancing pose. Dancing Lady holds the raised hem of her dress in her left hand, a rose held in her right. Dance stands with her arms outstretched, both holding the hem of her silk robe. Miss Lindner intended the dancers to be decorated in mottled grey to simulate stone, but the factory preferred matt ivory, with gold sheen for the robes. They sold for £1. 7s. 6d. each and were exhibited

prominently on Worcester's stand at the British Industries Fair in 1935. Both were withdrawn by 1940.
(*3088 colour plates 43 and 117*)

3087

Name   Boy with Parakeet, or
           Parakeet
Height   6 ½ in.
Modeller   Freda Doughty
Introduced 1935
Rarity   G

A young boy dressed in an elegant suit with open neck and cuffed at the hem, a parakeet perching on his folded right arm, his left arm by his side. Parakeet and Grandmother's Dress (3081) were the two most popular figures made at Worcester and are still available at the time of writing. Five colourings are recorded for the boy's suit, and all could be heightened with a gold sheen:

1. turquoise and ultramarine.
2. pink and ultramarine.
3. chrome-green and yellow.
4. yellow.
5. mauve with blue lining.

(*Colour plate 12*)

3088

Name   Dance
(See 3086 for description.)

3089 and 3090

Name   King George V and Queen
           Mary
Height   9in.
Modeller   Gwendoline Parnell
Introduced 1935
Rarity   C

The factory saw the Silver Jubilee of the King and Queen as an opportunity to produce a special commemorative issued as a Limited Edition. Gwendoline Parnell had not previously worked for Worcester but she had built up a reputation as a portrait modeller and produced these figures from photographs. The King is dressed in naval uniform and both wear garter robes. He holds an unrolled map of part of the British Empire, she a folded fan. They stand on square bases and were issued with black-painted wood plinths. The strong colouring by Daisy Rea contrasts with the whiteness of the porcelain, and the King's uniform is picked out in gold. Sold as a Limited Edition of 250 but abandoned after only seventy-two pairs had been sold following the death of the King. Although Limited and therefore outside the scope of this book, their importance made us decide that they should be included. For further details see Chapter 2, page 18. *(Colour plate 109)*

3091 and 3092

Name   King George V and Queen Mary, small busts
Height   2 ½ in. or 4 ½ in.
Modeller   Gwendoline Parnell
Introduced 1935
Rarity   B

Produced from the same models as the Jubilee Statuettes, the busts were intended to be less expensive souvenirs and were not part of a Limited Edition, although in fact very few seem to have been made. Fully coloured, and set on small wooden plinths, they retailed at 12s. 6d. each. It is possible that they were instantly withdrawn, at the time of the King's death, as we know of several white glazed examples which must have been sold off locally. Some were made with circular porcelain plinths, 4 ½ in. high overall. *(3091, colour plate 13)*

3093 and 3094

Name   Penguins
Height   4 ¾ in.
Modeller   Doris Lindner
Introduced 1935
Rarity   B

A pair of models of penguins, slightly comical in appearance. 3093 has its beak raised while its companion looks down. They stand on square bases and are naturalistically coloured. Probably modelled from life at London Zoo, they sold for 8s. each in 1939 and were withdrawn by 1940. *(3094, colour plate 92)*

3095 and 3105

Name   Good Luck To Your Fishing and Hit!
Height   5 ¼ in. and 7 ½ in.
Modeller   Gwendoline Parnell
Introduced 1935
Rarity   B

Two rather charming figures of Cupid. 3095 kneels on a square plinth, his hands held out in front and a pair of pink wings on his back. Around the base, which usually has a marbled effect printed on the lower part, are the words 'Good Luck to Your Fishing'. 3105 is a figure of Cupid standing wearing a white tunic and holding a bow and arrow, a mischievous grin on his face, pink wings on his back. The bow is purple and he wears pinks shoes. The records show that this figure could also be painted with a blue and brown bow. This pair does not appear to have sold well, which is a little surprising, although the models are certainly in a very different style from the popular Freda Doughty children. Both were sold with wooden plinths if desired and were still made in 1940, although withdrawn by 1948. See also page 19. *(3105, Colour plate 119)*

3096

Name   Elephant
Height   3 ⅜ in.
Modeller   Ernest or Eric Evans
Introduced 1935
Rarity   B

A small model of an elephant standing with its trunk curled low. The only example we have seen is enamelled in bright green, and it sold for 4s. 6d. coloured in 1935. A smaller version was also made in 1935, only 2 ⅝ in., given shape No. 3102. Both were withdrawn by 1940. *(Colour plate 24)*

3097

Name   Lady Bountiful
Height   7 ¾ in.
Modeller   Gwendoline Parnell
Introduced 1935
Rarity   D

A fine figure of a lady stepping over a low wall. She wears an elegant long dress with a *décolleté* neckline with a flower in the centre, and a wide straw hat; in her left hand she holds an evening bag, while her right hand hitches up her long skirt. It cost £1. 15s. 6d. in 1935, rising to £4. 5s. in 1957, being withdrawn soon after the latter date. Two colourings are recorded:

1. white dress with sprigs in Bordeaux red with a blue bodice;
2. letter-pink dress with sage-green bodice and turquoise-blue crosses on white blouse.

(Colour plate 87)

3099
Name Flower Girl (second version)
Height 7 ½ in.
Modeller Miss Stewart
Introduced 1935
Rarity A

3099

A figure of a lady flower seller holding a baby in her arms, dressed in a long dress and cloak with a hat and scarf round her neck; there is a basket of flowers by her side on a small octagonal base. No other details are known and this seems to have been Miss Stewart's only model for Worcester. It has an uncanny resemblance to Phoebe Stabler's Flower Girl (2880) of 1931 and may well have been inspired by the earlier figure.

3100 and 3101
Name Lion and Tiger (second version)
Height 3in. and 2 ⅝ in.
Modeller Ernest or Eric Evans
Introduced 1935
Rarity B

A pair of models both standing on all fours with heads raised, looking forward. The lion has a bushy mane while the tiger has a slight mane around its neck. They sold for 3s. each and were withdrawn by 1940. No details of colourings are recorded.

3102
Name Elephant
(See 3096 for description.)

3101 and 3104
Name Wales and Scotland
(See 3066 for description.)

3105
Name Hit!
(See 3095 for description.)

3106
Name The Duchess's Dress
Height 9 ½ in. and 5 ¾ in.
Modeller Freda Doughty
Introduced 1935
Rarity Large D, Small E

A figure of a girl in a wide party dress making a slight curtsy, one hand hitching up her skirt, the other holding a posy. The figure was made in two sizes and, whilst the large version is uncommon, the small size continued until at least 1957. Five colourings are recorded:

1. turquoise-blue and sea-green dress, with shot-gold sheen.
2. yellow dress, pink and green highlights.
3. pink, 'painted flowers on dress by men painters'.
4. sea-green dress.
5. shot-rose dress.

(Colour plate 41)

3107
Name Applause
Height 7 ¼ in.
Modeller Gwendoline Parnell
Introduced 1935
Rarity C

A figure of a young lady, her head bowed forward, accepting adulation from her audience. The usual colouring of the dress is 'shot temple' pink with 'old ivory' and turquoise-blue fringe, although it was also made in a strong yellow and green colour with sprig decoration and jet-black hair. (*Colour plate 114*)

3108
Name   Amaryllis
Height   9 ⅝ in.
Modeller   Gwendoline Parnell
Introduced   1935
Rarity   C
A figure of a lady in Miss Parnell's 'Cheyne Chelsea' style inspired by eighteenth-century figures. She wears a balloon-like dress flanked by flowering bocage on her shoulder. Her hands are crossed, lifting her apron. The base has floral rococo scrollwork. The usual colour of the dress is pink, with turquoise-blue edging to the scroll base. These colours could also be reversed. The figure remained in production into the 1950s. The following colourings are also recorded:
  1. 'Donville' black dress with yellow top, the bottom part being green with white flowers and embossments in 'regular' red.
  2. pale sea-green dress with yellow bottom part and embossments traced in 'old' gold.
(*Colour plate 39*)

3110
Name   Bear
Height   2 ¼ in.
Modeller   Unknown, probably Eric or Ernest Evans
Introduced   1935
Rarity   B
A figure of a bear staring ahead, all four feet on the ground.

3111
Name   Bal Masqué
Height   9 ⅝ in.
Modeller   Gwendoline Parnell
Introduced   1935
Rarity   D
A figure of a lady standing upright, her hands held together to the right of her neck, her face looking slightly to her left and a carnival mask hanging from her

arm. The base is either square or round. The figure is typical of Miss Parnell's 'Chelsea' style and resembles some of her figures of characters from Restoration comedies. Five decorations are recorded:
  1. dress blue and copper green with mauve and pink inner and sea-green shoes;
  2. dress shot pea-green with ivory and claret inner and sea-green shoes;
  3. dress pink with sea-green, mixed yellow and grey inner;
  4. dress turquoise-blue with mauve and yellow inner and sea-green shoes;
  5. dress pink with turquoise-blue, sea-green and yellow inner and yellow shoes.
Although production was somewhat limited, the figure did continue to be made surprisingly late, even into the early 1960s. (*Colour plate 95*)

3114-3117
A series of four equestrian models by Doris Lindner introduced in 1935. All were on pale green bases and were sold together with black-painted rectangular wooden plinths. While usually seen fully glazed, some were issued in matt colouring. All four remained in production until the 1970s, although they do not seem to have sold in great numbers. See also page 20.

3114
Name   At the Meet
Height   7 ¼ in.
Rarity   F
A figure of a lady riding side-saddle, her left hand holding the rein and her right her skirt. Her bay mount's head is lowered to scratch its leg. The model stands on a rectangular base shaded in green. The lady wears a long navy-blue habit and top hat. (*Colour plate 124*)

3115
Name   Huntsman and Hounds
Height   7 ½ in.
Rarity   F
A model of a huntsman riding his flecked grey horse at a walking pace, with two hounds standing on the rectangular

plinth, one either side of the horse. The rider wears bright hunting pinks and holds a painted metal whip and long rein.

3116
Name   Over the Sticks
Height   7in.
Rarity   F
A model of a chestnut racehorse jumping a fence, its jockey sitting well back. The study captures the moment when the front feet have landed on the ground whilst the back legs are just above the fence, the extended tail swishing. The base is rectangular. The jockey has been seen dressed in various racing silks which may have been painted to order. The reins were in painted metal. *(Colour plate 47)*

3117
Name   Cantering to the Post
Height   6 ⅜ in.
Rarity   F
A model of a bay horse cantering to the start of a race, the jockey holding on to a tight rein. The horse holds its head in rather majestic fashion, its tail fully extended in eager anticipation. A rail is to the right of the horse. The jockey's colours could be painted to order.

3118
Name   Pekinese Puppy Group
Height   2 ½ in.
Modeller   Doris Lindner
Introduced   1935
Rarity   C
A delightful group of four Pekinese huddled closely together and descending in height from left to right. Naturalistically coloured, they were the first of the small dog groups by Miss Lindner; despite their considerable charm, they do not seem to have sold well.

3119 and 3162
Name   Sealyham Cigarette Box and Scottie Cigarette Box
Name   3 ¼ in. and 3 ½ in.
Modeller   Doris Lindner
Introduced   1936
Rarity   A

3119

Two rectangular boxes and covers modelled as three Sealyham puppies and three Scotch terrier puppies looking out over the top of a wooden crate. Perhaps it was felt too sad to see the puppies in a crate, for very few examples seem to have been made. (3119 *Colour plate 137)*

3120
Name   Dog Calendar
Height   3 ½ in.
Modeller   Doris Lindner
Introduced   1936
Rarity   B
Two models of spaniels seated on a rectangular base flanking an adjustable calendar made of simulated ivory cards which slot into a metal holder. We have seen an example with the spaniels painted black, the base in pale green.

3121
Name   Tiger (third version)
Height   5 ⅛ in.
Modeller   Guero (?)
Introduced   1936
Rarity   A
A figure of a tiger prowling with head bent low, his mouth beside his front foot, on a rectangular base. A slightly stylized model on a large scale, unlike any other Worcester animal models of the time. The name 'Guero' appears against the model in one factory book, and we assume this to be the name of the modeller.

3122

Name   Fawn
Height   Unknown
Modeller   Unknown
Introduced 1936
Rarity   A

No photograph survives and the figure is not recorded except by name. It is probable that the piece never went into production.

3123

Name   Maytime
Height   3 ¾ in.
Modeller - Doris Lindner
Introduced 1936
Rarity   D

A model of two young lambs friskily playing together in May time, on a rectangular base. The lambs are creamy-white with black feet, the rectangular base in pale fawn or green. This is the first of four models by Miss Lindner of farmyard animals, and was reissued without a base in 1954 as number 3516. (*Colour plate 105*)

3124 and 3125

Name   Goats
Height   5in. and 5 ½ in.
Modeller   Henri Bargas
Introduced 1936
Rarity   B

Two models of young goats, one with its head turned round to lick a raised hind leg. The companion model stands on all four legs with its head raised. Both are on rectangular bases. They were painted naturalistically but, perhaps lacking the realism of Miss Lindner's animal models, do not seem to have been successful. Both were reintroduced in 1954, without bases, as shapes 3530 and 3531, but it is probable that few were made.

3126

Name   Pierrot Puff Bowl
Height   6 ½ in.
Modeller   Henri Bargas
Introduced 1936
Rarity   A

A powder bowl and cover curiously modelled in Art Deco style, with Pierrot lying on the base beside a circular bowl, looking up at Columbine, who sits on the cover, her legs crossed to one side. The illustration in Colour plate 133 shows the proposed colour scheme, and it is likely that some were made, although we have not seen an example.

3127

Name   Looking over Shoulder
Height   5in.
Modeller   Henri Bargas
Introduced 1936
Rarity   B

A small powder bowl and cover in complete contrast to Bargas' Art Deco Pierrot bowl. 3127 is naturalistically modelled as a naked boy seated on the lid of a rounded octagonal box embossed with fruit and leaves, the child in flesh tones, the box shaded in pale blue lustre. A charming model, but surprisingly very rarely seen. (*Colour plate 65*)

3130

Name   Spaniel Puppy Group
Modeller   Doris Lindner
Introduced 1936
Rarity   C

A group of three spaniel puppies huddled together, two with heads touching and the third with head lowered to its feet. Naturalistically coloured in black and brown, this is a charming model which, like 3118 and 3133, rather surprisingly does not seem to have sold well. (*Colour plate 50*)

3131 and 3132

Name   Young Foxes and Young Foxhounds
Height   2 ½ in.
Modeller   Doris Lindner
Introduced 1936
Rarity   3131 C, 3132 D,

A delightful study of three fox-cubs, one looking ahead alertly whilst the cubs to either side appear sleepy; and a companion model of three foxhound puppies resting drowsily together. Both models were aimed at the fox-hunting fraternity, and the hounds, rather expectedly, seem to have sold better than the foxes. The hounds were still in production in 1955, but were withdrawn shortly afterwards. (*Colour plate 88*)

3133
Name Puppy
Height 2in.
Modeller Doris Lindner
Introduced 1936
Rarity B

A model of two bulldog puppies, their heads together and an empty bowl to their left. On the bowl is painted the word 'Puppy'. A delightful model capturing the characters of the bulldogs in their expressions, surprisingly selling only in very small numbers. (*Colour plate 10*)

3138 and 3140
Name The Planter's Daughter and The Powdering Mask
Length 7 ¼ in. and 7in.
Modeller Gwendoline Parnell
Introduced 1936
Rarity 3138 D, 3140 C

Two large and impressive groups in Miss Parnell's 'Chelsea' style, inspired by eighteenth-century porcelain figures. The Planter's Daughter is dressed in an elegant crinoline gown adorned with ribbon, and sits reading from an open book. At her feet a coloured servant kneels holding a bowl of fruit. The companion lady, Powdering Mask, also sits in a large crinoline, a mirror held before her face, a servant girl at her feet attending to her long skirt. Both are seated on rectangular bases adorned with scrollwork at the corners. Planter's Daughter continued to be made into the 1950s, but Powdering Mask seems to have been withdrawn much earlier. The recorded colourings for each are as follows:
Planter's Daughter: Shot-pink dress with fawn added to top and marine and sea-green ribbons on the hat. The chair is painted with a 'dark brown mixture' and the servant has a green and shot-cloves coat and green shoes. The base is traced in 'old' gold, i.e. unburnished.
Powdering Mask: Shot-blue and copper-green dress, sea-green hat and pink

ribbon. The chair is painted with a 'dark brown mixture' and the servant has a petunia head piece and a yellow coat. The base is traced in 'old' gold and 'Persian' red. (*3138, Colour plate 102*)

3139
Name Recollections
Height 12in.
Modeller Gwendoline Parnell
Introduced 1936
Rarity B

3139

A figure of a gentleman in eighteenth-century costume with a tricorn hat; he stands supported by a pedestal, his expression deep in thought. The style resembles Miss Parnell's *Beggar's Opera* series modelled in the early 1920s in Chelsea, but fifteen years later the figure was perhaps a little old-fashioned and failed to sell in any numbers. Two colourings are recorded:
1. white coat with pink and brown designs and green cloak, black and gold hat and white plinth;
2. primrose-yellow coat, black and green hat and marbled plinth printed in Harrod's brown (copper plate).

The model was still listed in the 1950s but it is unlikely that many were sold.

3140
Name The Powdering Mask
(*See* 3138 for description.)

3141

Name   Kittens Group
Height   2 ¼ in.
Modeller   Doris Lindner
Introduced   1936
Rarity   B

A delightful study of three tiny kittens huddled together rather sleepily, coloured naturalistically in tones of brown, blue-grey and white. Undoubtedly the most appealing of Miss Lindner's small animal groups, this is surprisingly the rarest, and presumably made in very small numbers. The colouring was painted underglaze, which tends to give a smudged appearance. (*Colour plate 50*)

3142

Name   The Frog
Height   7 ½ in.
Modeller   Gwendoline Parnell
Introduced   1936
Rarity   C

A figure of a lady in Miss Parnell's 'Chelsea' style. She is seated in fancy skirts and holds a riding whip, a frog by her side on the rectangular base. The dress was painted primrose-yellow and she wears a black hat and shoes. The frog is green. (*Colour plates 123 and page 15*)

3143

Name   The Summit
Height   9in.
Modeller   Gwendoline Parnell
Introduced   1936
Rarity   A

A figure of a naked maiden seated on a tall rock, gazing down to the wave-lapped base, her legs draped in seaweed. This figure possibly did not go into full production.

3144 and 3145

Name   Magnolia Bud and The Thief
Height   4 ½ in.
Modeller   Gwendoline Parnell
Introduced   1936
Rarity   D

Two small figures in East Indian style. Magnolia Bud is an Oriental girl kneeling with a fan held by her side, a single flower bud raised in her right hand in front of her. The Thief is an Indian child with elaborate turban and jewelled rings on his fingers. Both are raised on square plinths, coloured either in simulated veined marble or white with a thin turquoise or pink line. The costumes are usually coloured pink with details in peacock-blue and sea-green, or in turqoise with pink edging. Small and inexpensive, the pair proved fairly popular and continued into the 1950s. (*Colour plate 52*)

3146

Name   Calves
Height   4in.
Modeller   Doris Lindner
Introduced   1936
Rarity   D

A model of two calves, the one looking over the shoulder of the other, standing on a rectangular base. The second of the farm animal groups, it was coloured naturalistically, usually white with red-brown patches. The original plasticine model was supplied by Miss Lindner and cut up by Len Morris ready for mould-making. Unfortunately the model of one calf's head was misplaced by the mould-maker, who made an extra cast of the other head, with no one realizing. The model remained, though, with two identical calves heads and was reissued without a base in 1954 as number 3515. Calves sold for £1. 17s. 6d. in 1937. (*Colour plate 105*)

3147 and 3148

Name   Children with Lambs
Height   Unknown
Modeller   Unknown
Introduced   1936
Rarity   A

Two figures of which no details are recorded other than the title 'Child with Lamb (flowers in arms)' and 'Child with Lamb in arms'. It is probable the figures never went into production.

3149

Name   Sister
Height   6 ¾ in.
Modeller   Freda Doughty
Introduced   1936
Rarity   E

A model of a young child, her left hand holding the fold of her dress, her right arm around the shoulder of her younger brother and both gazing upwards. They stand on a textured circular base. Three colourings are recorded:

1. boy's trousers blue, girl's dress pink with green flowers;
2. boy's trousers green/blue, girl's dress white with pink and green flowers;
3. boy's trousers yellow, girl's dress shot-pink with 'diaper pattern in 1163 pink by Miss Rea'.

Sister was fairly expensive, selling for £2. 10s. in 1937, but even so it proved reasonably popular, continuing into the 1950s. *(Colour plates 49 and 115)*

3150

Name　　Two Babies
Height　　3 ¾ in.
Modeller　　Freda Doughty
Introduced　1936
Rarity　　F

A group of a young boy crawling on a simple mound base, a puppy looking playfully up at him. This figure sold quite well, remaining popular into the 1950s. The boy's shirt could be either blue, white/grey or white/mauve, and the dog white or brown and white. *(Colour plate 48)*

3151

Name　　Water Baby
Height　　6 ⅛ in.
Modeller　　Freda Doughty
Introduced　1936
Rarity　　E

A figure of a naked youth seated on a rock, left hand on left knee and right hand on the rock, which stands on a textured circular base coloured to represent the blues and greens of the sea. It sold for 17s. 6d. in 1937 and was withdrawn by 1955.

3152

Name　　Foals
Height　　5 ½ in.
Modeller　　Doris Lindner
Introduced　1936
Rarity　　D

A study of two young foals, the one with head bent licking the front leg of the other, both standing on a rectangular base, naturalistically coloured, the base shaded in pale green. The third group in Miss Lindner's young farm animal series, it seems to lack the delicate modelling seen in her other horse models, but is still a charming study and was reissued without a base in 1954 as number 3514.

3153

Name　　Kids at Play
Height　　4 ¾ in.
Modeller　　Doris Lindner
Introduced　1936
Rarity　　D

A study of two playful young goats frolicking on a rectangular base. Naturalistically coloured in tones of grey-blue and white, the base in pale green. The last of the young farm animal groups by Miss Lindner and, surprisingly, the most popular of the series. It was reissued without a base in 1954 as number 3517. *(Colour plate 105)*

3154

Name　　The Drum or The Drummer
Height　　7in.
Modeller　　Gwendoline Parnell
Introduced　1936
Rarity　　D

A figure of a lady in elaborate eighteenth-century dress standing on a square base, beating a drum with two small drumsticks. Although typically in Gwendoline Parnell's 'Chelsea' style, it is interesting to note that the figure was often ascribed by the paintresses to Freda Doughty. This was probably just an error, but it does make one consider the possibility that it was felt that Miss Doughty's name might prove more popular than Miss Parnell's. Three colourings are recorded, and one initialled by Miss Parnell names the figure 'The Drummer' although more have been seen titled 'The Drum':

1. shot primrose-yellow dress with red and black decoration, yellow and chrome-green base.
2. red, black and ivory dress with pink around drum, 'Chinese sea-green' sleeves and chrome-green base.

3. imperial red, black and pink dress with dark brown sleeves.
(*Colour plate 87*)

3155

Name	Sheep
Height	5in.
Modeller	Henri Bargas
Introduced	1936
Rarity	B

A model of a young sheep standing on a rectangular base, its head turned to the right. Like Bargas' other animal studies (3124 and 3125) the model is stiff and lifeless compared to Miss Lindner's May-time Lambs, and was soon withdrawn.

3156

Name	Dog Ashtray

(*see* 3027 for description.)

3157

Name	Child with Butterfly
Height	4¾ in.
Modeller	Anne Acheson
Introduced	1936
Rarity	B

A figure of a winged nymph seated on a roughly circular leafy base, smiling upwards at a butterfly which has landed on her right hand, the left hand raised towards her head. The butterfly could be painted either pink or blue.
(*Colour plate 118*)

3160

Name	Bubbles
Height	6½ in.
Modeller	Freda Doughty
Introduced	1936
Rarity	F

A figure of a young girl blowing bubbles, her hands held high above her head, her left hand supporting a glass bubble. In a bowl beside her are more glass bubbles and a pipe, and she kneels on a circular base. Although certainly not a copy of the famous painting of the same name by Sir John Millais used by Messrs Pears for their soap advertisements, the popularity of the subject must surely have been in Miss Doughty's mind when she conceived the figure and gave it the name. The bubbles were supplied by a glass factory and were glued on to the figure at Worcester. The glue has rarely lasted and has often discoloured to a muddy brown. The dress is usually either pink or turquoise-blue.
(*Colour plate 3*)

3161

Name	Mermaid
Height	5¼ in.
Modeller	Anne Acheson
Introduced	1936
Rarity	C

A figure of a mermaid astride a fish. Her long hair blows behind her head towards the fish's tail, pointed upwards. The fish and the mermaid both look forward as they swim, raised on a wave forming a rectangular base. Although designed to be softly coloured with turquoise-green edging to the scales and blonde hair, we know of two examples just in white, but fully titled underneath and clearly sold by the factory as white sculptures. Three colourings are recorded:
1. shot sea-green all over.
2. pencilled sea-green with ivory flesh.
3. fish sea-blue, orange on mermaid's tail.

(*see* illustration on page 37).

3162

3162

Name	Scottie Cigarette Box

(*see* 3119 for description.)

3163

Name   Polo Player
Height   7in.
Modeller   Doris Lindner
Introduced 1936
Rarity   G

A study of a polo player dressed for the game, steering his galloping chestnut mount, whose head is leaning to the left. In his right hand he holds his polo stick and looks to the ground, following the ball. The horse stands on a rectangular base. Modelled with a great sense of movement, the group proved reasonably popular and remained in production until the late 1970s. This model is known with both glazed and matt finishes. The polo stick and reins are made of painted metal.

3164

Name   Hog Hunting
Height   7in.
Modeller   Doris Lindner
Introduced 1936
Rarity   G

An impressive study of a sportsman on horseback in pursuit of a wild boar. The bay horse canters carefully over the rough ground and the base is rectangular. The rider wears khaki-coloured clothes and a pith hat and holds a painted metal spear. The group captures well the movement of the subject and was still in production in 1979.

3165

Name   Banbury Cross
Height   8in.
Modeller   Geraldine Blake
Introduced 1936
Rarity   C

Inspired by the famous nursery rhyme 'Ride a cock horse to Banbury Cross to see a fine lady upon a white horse....' this is the first of five equestrian figures by Miss Blake and depicts a lady dressed in smart nineteenth-century riding costume, a feather in her cap. She rides side-saddle and holds painted metal reins. The figure did not continue after the war and probably only a small number were made.

3166

Name   Highwayman
Height   8½in.
Modeller   Geraldine Blake
Introduced 1936
Rarity   C

An equestrian group of a masked highwayman in tricorn hat, a pistol held in his hand, the horse with docked tail standing on a rectangular base and painted jet-black, reminiscent of Dick Turpin's mount Black Bess. Like Geraldine Blake's other work, the model is stiff, lacking the movement of Doris Lindner's equestrian studies, and production was very limited.

3167

Name   Yonder He Goes
Height   8in.
Modeller   Geraldine Blake
Introduced 1936
Rarity   C

A figure of a huntsman mounted on a standing horse. He wears hunting pink and raises his right hand to his mouth as he calls after the fox. The model is much stiffer than Doris Lindner's Huntsman and Hounds (3115) and, like all of Miss Blake's models, lacks the realism and sense of movement which Miss Lindner was able to capture. Production seems to have been very limited.

3168

Name   Bengal Lancer
Height   8½in.
Modeller   Geraldine Blake
Introduced 1936
Rarity   B

An equestrian figure of an Indian Officer in full uniform and turban, mounted on a standing horse. In spite of a certain amount of detail in the costume, the group is very stiff and lifeless and, since it was expensive to produce, it is not surprising that it was soon withdrawn.

3169

Name   Young Entry
Height   7in.
Modeller   Geraldine Blake
Introduced 1936
Rarity   B

A figure of a girl riding her pony at an equestrian event. It conveys a little more movement than Miss Blake's other models, but still looks 'wooden' compared to Doris Lindner's figures. Very few were made.

3170

Name	Mare and Foal
Height	8 ½ in.
Modeller	Geraldine Blake
Introduced	1936
Rarity	B

3170

A group of a young foal standing alertly beside its mother, on a long rectangular base. The model was not a success, in particular because of the rather lifeless modelling of the mare. The foal is captured much more realistically and, to try and make something of the model, was issued on its own the following year as shape 3187. A few were sold but both versions were withdrawn by 1940.

3171-3177

Name	Ballet Dancers Series
Modeller	Rachel Greaves
Introduced	1936
Rarity	A

A set of seven figures of ballerinas modelled on young stars of the Russian Ballet. Each is dressed in a simple tutu and adopts a graceful pose, on a strongly shaped base. We illustrate the original colour scheme, but it is not known if many were coloured, as the series was withdrawn almost immediately and the moulds returned to Miss Greaves. They were, however, listed in 1937 retailing at £1. 17s. 6d. each. The moulds were kept in her garage until 1970, when, with Henry Sandon's encouragement, they were brought back to Worcester and five of them were made in a new series glazed in matt white with gold line decoration. The new series was mounted on circular bases and was withdrawn in 1985. The original colour designs for 3171, 3174, 3175 and 3177 are illustrated in colour plate 135. See also pages 21 and 43.

3171

Name	Arita
Height	5 ¾ in.

3172

Name	Tamara
Height	5 ¾ in.

3173

Name	Tatiana
Height	5 ¾ in.

3174

Name	Anna
Height	6 ½ in.

3175

Name	Alicia
Height	Unknown

3176

Name	Natasha
Height	6 ½ in.

3177

Name	Irina
Height	5 ¾ in.

3178

Name	Ireland

(*see* 3066 for description.)

3179

Name	Circus Horses Rearing
Height	10 ⅞ in.
Modeller	Doris Lindner
Introduced	1937
Rarity	D

A large and impressive group of three stallions rearing as part of their act. The horse in the centre looks ahead whilst the other two turn towards the middle. The animals are flecked grey with bright red sircingle, side reins and breastplate. Miss

Lindner modelled the group from life at Bertram Mills' circus, and she has captured the horses so realistically that little imagination is required to enjoy the atmosphere of the circus. The hind legs and tails join to a large white rectangular base, and the group was sold with a deep black plinth. The model remained in production until the early 1970s, but its high cost and the many problems involved in its manufacture meant that relatively few examples were sold. The original plasticine models for this and its companion figure, 3180, are illustrated on page 29.

3180

Name Circus Horses with Rider or 'In the Ring'.
Height 10 ¼ in.
Modeller Doris Lindner
Introduced 1937
Rarity D

A companion group to 3179, and similarly impressive, three circus ponies with a single lady rider straddled over the middle horse and holding all three reins. The outer horses are flecked grey, as in 3179, but the central animal is steel grey. The girl wears a short yellow dress decorated with red stars and revealing a white slip. Her hair is golden brown with white plumes. The horses stand on a large white rectangular base and the model was sold with a black-painted wooden plinth. It remained in production until the early 1970s, but like 3179, the difficulties involved in making such a large group and consequent high cost meant that few were sold.

3184 and 3185

Name Polar Bear Ashtrays
(*see* 3062 for description.)

3186

Name Ballet Dancer (first version)
Height 11 ¼ in.
Modeller Dorothea Charol
Introduced 1937
Rarity A

A figure of a smiling ballerina standing upright, her hands crossed together in front of her, on a round plinth. The figure resembles the continental style of modelling which Dorothea Charol had used at Rosenthal in the 1920s. It was perhaps old-fashioned by 1937, and very few were sold. The dress was painted turquoise and the base powder-blue with gold tracing around. She wears a head band with gold, turquoise, green and scarlet beads. It retailed in 1937 for £4. 14s. 6d., a high price reflecting the large size of the figure, and few were sold. (*Colour plate 131*)

3187

Name Foal
(*See* 3170 for description.)

3188

Name Foxhound Calendar
Height 4 ¾ in.
Modeller Doris Lindner
Introduced 1937
Rarity C

A model of a hound on a rectangular base, facing from right to left, its tail curved upwards, modelled with long grass filling the space between the dog's legs and body. It was intended to be mounted with an adjustable calendar made of simulated ivory cards slotted into a metal holder on the base in front of the dog, but we have seen an example which has never been mounted.

3192

Name Ballet Dancer (second version)
Height 10 ¼ in.
Modeller Dorothea Charol
Introduced 1937
Rarity A

A figure of a female ballet dancer in performance, her head turned slightly to the right. She holds her right hand to her chest with her left arm extended and stands on an irregularly shaped base. The dress was decorated in shot-grey with pencilled blush-pink. She wears pale pink shoes and has 'shot-tan' skin and tinted features. Like Dorothea Charol's other large dancer (3186), the style was old-fashioned by 1937, and few were sold. (*Colour plate 131*)

3193

Name	The Queen in the Parlour
Height	6in.
Modeller	Anne Acheson
Introduced	1937
Rarity	B

A figure of a lady seated, a crown on her head and a long flowing robe extending from her head to the rectangular stepped base. The Queen is eating bread and honey and is taken from the nursery rhyme 'Sing a Song of Sixpence...'. The figure does not appear to have been popular and we have seen very few examples. Two colourings, however, are recorded:

1. ultramarine and pink cloak, ivory dress with red and green flowers, silver-grey base and 'best purple' carpet.
2. ultramarine, peacock and chrome-green cloak, pink designs on white dress, brown-ivory base and silvery-grey carpet.

(The original colour design is illustrated in Colour plate 133.)

3194 and 3195

Name	Chinese Dancers
Height	9 ½ in.
Modeller	Gwendoline Parnell
Introduced	1937
Rarity	B

A pair of fine large chinoiserie dancing figures of a man and woman with hands held at shoulder height. His hands are slightly apart whilst she holds one hand above the other, and they both stand with one leg raised in front of the other above small square bases. Miss Parnell's first attempt at chinoiserie, they appear to have been tried out in a variety of colour schemes. It is believed that the original intention was for the pair to be issued as a Limited Edition in fitted boxes, but this idea was abandoned, possibly following the failure as a Limited Edition of Miss Parnell's Jubilee Statuettes two years before. The Chinese Dancers were intended to be part of a garniture with two musicians and a group making a centre piece, but these were never modelled.

(Colour plate 36 and jacket)

3197-3200, 3234-3236, 3238-3240, 3248, 3249 and 3333-3338

Name	Small British Birds Series
Modeller	Eva Soper
Introduced	1937-1941
Rarity	G (3248 and 3249 F)

A series of eighteen models of popular British birds, all modelled by Eva Soper and each to scale, on a simple base moulded with leaves and foliage. Originally issued fully glazed, but subsequently painted in matt enamels to give a higher degree of realism. All were modelled by Miss Soper in her studio in a wildlife sanctuary run by her family. They proved very popular and, with the exception of the Jay and Woodpecker, which seemed over-sized, all are still in production at the time of writing.

3197
Name: Robin
Height: 2 ¾ in.
Introduced: 1937

3198
Name: Wren
Height: 2 ⅛ in.
Introduced: 1937

3199
Name: Blue Tit
Height: 2 ¼ in.
Introduced: 1937

3200
Name: Wood Warbler
Height: 2 ¾ in.
Introduced: 1937

3234
Name: Thrush
Height: 4 ¾ in.
Introduced: 1938

3235
Name: Kingfisher
Height: 3 ⅛ in.
Introduced: 1938

3236
Name: Sparrow
Height: 3 ⅜ in.
Introduced: 1938

3238
Name: Bullfinch
Height: 2 ⅞ in.
Introduced: 1938

3239
Name: Goldfinch
Height: 2 ¼ in.
Introduced: 1938

3240
Name: Chaffinch
Height: 3 ⅛ in.
Introduced: 1938

3248
Name: Jay
Height: 5in.
Introduced: 1938

3249
Name: Woodpecker
Height: 4 ½ in.
Introduced: 1938

3333
Name: Hedge Sparrow
Height: 2 ½ in.
Introduced: 1941

3334
Name: Nuthatch
Height: 2 ⅜ in.
Introduced: 1941

3335
Name: Great Tit
Height: 2 ½ in.
Introduced: 1941

3336
Name: Marsh Tit
Height: 2 ¼ in.
Introduced: 1941

3337
Name: Nightingale
Height: 3 ⅜ in.
Introduced: 1941

3338
Name: Goldcrest
Height: 2 ¼ in.
Introduced: 1941
(3197, 3238, 3336 Colour plate 100)

3202
Name   Pierrot Group
Height   10 ½ in.
Modeller   Dorothea Charol
Introduced   1937
Rarity   A
A large group, with Pierrot on bended knee before Columbine, looking up at her and offering a flower. He wears a loose smartly styled suit, she a long, layered dress and pointed high-heeled shoes. They are mounted on a wide cogged oval base. The continental style of Dorothea Charol is seen at its most elaborate in this large group, which, like her other figures for Worcester, proved unsuccessful, very few being made. The records show that Columbine has pale pink bows with painted roses on her dress and a beauty spot on her face. Pierrot wears a shot-grey suit and black shoes. *(The original colour design is illustrated in Colour plate 133.)*

3222
Name   The Candlestick
Height   10in.
Modeller   Gwendoline Parnell
Introduced   1937
Rarity   A
A figure in the 'Cheyne Chelsea' style, a lady wearing a balloon-like dress mounted with raised ribbons, and holding a chamber candlestick. She stands on a square base, looking back over her shoulder. Possibly made as a companion to 3111, but quickly withdrawn. Figures looking backward do not generally prove popular.

3224
Name   The Bridesmaid (or Rose Maiden)
Height   8 ¼ in.
Modeller   Freda Doughty
Introduced   1938
Rarity   D
A figure of a young bridesmaid descending the church steps which form the base. The girl carries a bouquet in her arms and wears a yellow dress. Her brown hair is adorned with a light green ribbon, and a

similarly-coloured shoe protrudes below the bottom of the dress, whilst petals from the flowers fall onto the dress and steps. One of Freda Doughty's few failures from the 1930s, it did not sell in any great numbers and was withdrawn by 1955. The records show that the dress was also painted in a mixture of white, green and grey. (*Colour plate 81*)

3225

Name	Dancing Waves
Height	8 ¾ in.
Modeller	Freda Doughty
Introduced	1938
Rarity	F

A figure of a young girl with arms outstretched. She dances bare-foot on waves, which form a roughly circular base. The usual colour of the dress is pink and the girl has blonde hair. The waves are naturalistically coloured. The records show that the dress could also be green. A popular model, it was withdrawn in 1958. (*Colour plate 17*)

3226

Name	Only Me
Height	5 ½ in.
Modeller	Freda Doughty
Introduced	1938
Rarity	G

A small figure of a young girl, her left hand holding her pretty dress and her right hand held to her face. Her bare feet stand on the roughly circular base. The dress is usually white with slight pink and blue patterns. Her blonde hair is adorned with green ribbons.

Freda Doughty had been asked by a friend to make a model of their young son teaching his little sister to walk. This painted plaster group was the prototype of two separate figures made by Worcester. With only minor alterations, the little girl became Only Me, whilst her brother, with the addition of some ducks, became the figure Johnnie or Farmer's Boy (3433). Only Me was a considerable success and was still made in the 1970s. (*Colour plate 76*)

3227, 3250, 3252, 3271, 3299 and 3300

Name	The London Cries
Height	6in. – 6 ½ in.
Modeller	Gwendoline Parnell
Introduced	1938-1940
Rarity	B

A series of six figures of lady street vendors who toured the streets of London in the seventeenth and eighteenth centuries. Each had her own distinctive call to sell her wares. The Worcester figures are all dressed in simple clothes and display a sample of their wares. They stand on plain square bases. Gwendoline Parnell had begun a series of London Cries while still in Chelsea. These were based on prints of 1711 and were exhibited at Walker's Gallery in July 1932. Her pottery figures included the cries 'Fair Lemons', 'Holand Socks' and 'Ripe Strawberries', but we do not know if any of the Worcester figures were based on the earlier Cheyne Chelsea series. Reproduction prints of Old London Cries were very popular in the 1930s, but we have been unable to trace which particular prints Miss Parnell's figures were based on. None of the Worcester set sold well, and all were withdrawn by 1948.

3227	
Name	'Delicate Cowcumbers to Pickle'
Introduced	1938

3227

'Cowcumber' was an early English spelling of cucumber. The lady holds one cucumber in her right hand, taken from a bunch under her left arm. Her dress is shot pink with 'Austrian' brown and sea-green. Her shoes are pink and sea-green and she wears a yellow and golden-fawn hat.

3250
Name   'Ripe 'Speragus'
Introduced 1938
'Speragus' is an old spelling of asparagus. She holds a basket of asparagus under her right arm and wears a sea-green dress with orange and 'old Worcester yellow' cloak. Her shoes are 'Persian' red and clover, and her hat clover and 'French' brown.

3252
Name   'A Merry New Song'
Introduced 1938
The lady holds up a printed music sheet of a popular song. Song sheets were often finely decorated with engravings and were frequently sold by street vendors. She wears a shot-pink dress with yellow and brown stripes and mauve shoes. On her head is a yellow and golden-fawn hat.

3271
Name   'London Gazette Here'
Introduced 1938
The lady holds in each hand a single printed news sheet. The *London Gazette* was one of the first regular newspapers. In the early eighteenth century it comprised little more than a single sheet. The lady's dress is primrose with orange, purple and yellow, and she wears a clover cloak and hat.

3299
Name   'Fine Writing Inks'
Introduced 1940
The girl holds a selection of pens and a bottle of ink with a funnel to pour into the customer's bottle or inkwell. She wears an ultramarine cloak over a mauve dress, sea-green shoes, mauve ribbons and a round white hat.

3300
Name   'Fair Cherryes'
Introduced 1940
The girl holds two baskets of ripe red cherries and wears a clover dress with yellow. Her basket is painted golden-fawn.

3228-3233
Name   Sporting Dogs Series
Height   4 ½ in. with bases, 3 ¾ in.
              without
Modeller   Doris Lindner
Introduced 1938
Rarity   F
A set of six models of sporting dogs, that is, breeds used by sportsmen as gun dogs. All are naturalistically modelled and coloured, either running through grasses or pointing towards the game. 3228-3233 are mounted on rectangular bases and sold reasonably well. To cut costs, the series was reissued in 1940 at a slightly cheaper price without bases, as numbers 3307-3312. These proved even more popular and were only withdrawn between 1955 and 1957. They were reintroduced in the 1970s in matt colours on rectangular bases and were sold with wooden plinths, if required. This new series has now also been withdrawn. See also page 22.

3228
Name Red Setter
(Without base, shape 3307.)

3229
Name Pointer
(Without base, shape 3308.)

3230
Name Golden Retriever
(Without base, shape 3309.)

3231
Name Cocker Spaniel
(Without base, shape 3310.)

3232
Name Clumber Spaniel
(Without base, shape 3311.)

3233
Name Labrador Retriever
(Without base, shape 3312.)
(3308, 3309 3311, *Colour plate 106*)

3234-3236 and **3238-3240**
Name: Small British Bird Series
(*See* 3197 for description.)

3243
Name: Welsh Corgi
(*See* 2941 for description.)

3246 and 3247

Name   Autumn and Spring Busts
Height   9in.
Modeller Rachel Greaves
Introduced 1938
Rarity   A

3246

A pair of female busts, modelled half-length. Autumn gathers vines in her hands, which are crossed in front of her, and Spring, with head raised, has her hands behind her head and scarf around her. It is likely that these busts were never produced.

3248 and 3429

Name Small British Bird Series
(*See* 3197 for description.)

3250

Name 'Ripe 'Speragus'
(*See* 3227 for description.)

3252

Name 'A Merry New Song'
(*See* 3227 for description.)

3256-3262

Name   The Days of the Week
Introduced 1938
Rarity   G

The first seven of what was to become a total of fourteen figures of children, a boy and a girl representing each day of the week in accordance with the well-known rhyme:

Monday's child is fair of face,
Tuesday's child is full of grace,
Wednesday's child is full of woe,
Thursday's child has far to go,
Friday's child is loving and giving,
Saturday's child works hard for its living,
And the child that is born on the Sabbath day,
Is fair and wise and good and gay.

All the figures are still in production at the time of writing and some have been issued in different colourings with new names. Recently some of the figures have also been made in miniature. A further set of seven figures was modelled in 1954 to complete the set, making a boy and a girl for each day. (*See* 3518-3524 and 3534).

3256

Name   Sunday's Boy
Height   4 ¾ in.

A small boy wearing a blue bathing suit sitting on the beach, his brightly coloured bucket and spade beside him. The blonde-haired boy holds a green ball in his left hand and looks upwards. The sandy base is edged in blue. (*Colour plate 46*)

3257

Name   Monday's Girl
Height   6 ½ in.

A girl wearing a pretty light blue dress with a darker blue edge and waistband. The blonde-haired girl stands on a light blue square base, her shoes covered by the bottom of her dress. The figure was also sold under the name 'Susie'.
(*Colour plate 67*)

3258

Name   Tuesday's Girl
Height   8 ½ in.

A young ballet dancer wearing a yellow and white tutu, her arms widely outstretched as she looks directly upwards. Her pretty yellow and red shoes point towards the white and yellow square base as she carefully balances herself. The figure was also issued in the 1960s in different colours, one version being retitled 'Red Shoes'. (*Colour plate 72*)

3259
Name   Wednesday's Girl
Height   7in.
A girl wearing a deep pink dress has broken one of her shoes, which is beside her on the side of a mound which forms the base. The mound is green with a white top and the girl is crying, with her hands held to her face to wipe away the tears. Wednesday's Girl was slightly re-modelled in 1957 to make it less unhappy, and re-numbered 3638, but this new version does not seem to have been put into production. Some later examples were sold under the title 'Wednesday's child knows little woe', although the child still cries in the same way. (*Colour plate 46*)

3260
Name   Thursday's Boy
Height   6 ½ in.
A boy wearing a light blue coat walks determinedly along the grass which forms the top of the roughly circular base. he wears a red hat and a multicoloured scarf, a dark brown staff held in his left hand. This figure was also sold under the name 'Smilin' thro'. (*Colour plate 67*)

3261
Name   Friday's Boy
Height   6 ⅞ in.
A boy wearing a white shirt and green shorts, holding a white bowl with a red rim in his left hand. In his right hand he holds a small grey kitten drinking milk from the bowl. The boy wears red sandals and stands on a green base with white top. This figure was also sold under the name 'My Pet'. (*Colour plate 46*)

3262
Name   Saturday's Girl
Height   5 ¾ in.
A girl sits on grey steps knitting a scarf from a ball of red wool which lies on the bottom step next to her bare feet. She has dark brown hair and wears a light blue dress with blue and pink edging. A black and white kitten looks inquisitively up at her from her right-hand side.

(*Colour plate 46*)

3263-3266, 3273 and 3274
Name   Zoo Babies
Height   4 ¾ in. with bases, 3 ½ in.
              without
Modeller   Doris Lindner
Introduced 1938
Rarity   B
A charming set of six animal studies showing clearly the modeller's remarkable talent for capturing all kinds of animals so realistically, and often humorously. Doris spent some time at London Zoo sketching and modelling at a time when there were several young animals in residence. Fortunately she made a note of some of the animals' names and records at the Zoo confirm these. Where there is no doubt about the identities of the studies we have given brief details of the animals. The series is amongst the most appealing of all of Doris Lindner's works, and it seems very surprising that it failed to sell in any great numbers. In 1940 all six models were reintroduced without bases, as numbers 3313-3318, and these were a little more successful, but still failed to appeal to the public during wartime. The versions without bases were still available in 1948 at £2. 10s each, and all were withdrawn soon afterwards. The moulds were destroyed in June 1953. Doris Lindner's original water-colour designs for the series are illustrated in Colour plate 136.

3263
Name: Leopards, or Nelson and Norah
A pair of young leopard cubs huddled playfully together and both looking forward. They were painted naturalistically, the base shaded pale green. Issued without a base as 3313.

Nelson and Norah were brother and sister born at Regents Park Zoo on 10th January 1938. Their parents were Ruby and Mick, who died in 1939 and 1943, Mick having been adopted during the war by the comedian Jimmy Dyrenforth. Norah herself died on 30th June 1953 and Nelson, adopted during the war by Mr and Mrs A. J. R. Moore-Sibson, was sent on deposit to Maidstone Zoo, Kent, in 1957.
(*Colour plates 33 and 136*)

3264
Name: Lions, or Oliver and October
A pair of lion cubs playfully fighting. They were issued without a base as 3314.

Oliver and October were born at Regents Park Zoo on 9th October 1937; their parents' names are not recorded. Sadly, they both died on 8th November 1938, and Worcester's model is the only record of their short lives. (*Colour plates 93 and 136*)

3265
Name: Bears, or Mick and Mack
A pair of brown bear cubs, fighting in a friendly fashion. Without a base, they were numbered 3315.

Although various species of bears are recorded as having been at London Zoo during the 1930s, none of them appears to have been named Mick or Mack.
(*Colour plates 93 and 136*)

3266
Name: Fawns, or Young Spotted Deer
A pair of young deer standing on their thin legs on a rectangular base. One raises its head alertly, the other curves its neck around to lick its hind leg. They were re-issued on an oval base as 3316. They were intended as part of the Zoo Babies series and cost the same as the other models in 1938 and 1948. The moulds were noted as destroyed in 1953, although in the following year shape 3259 was listed as 'young spotted deer, no base' selling for £2. 7s. 6d. in 1955. No photograph of this latter version exists. (3316, *Colour plate 105*)

3273
Name: Koala Bears, or Billy Bluegums
A group of three koala bear cubs playfully huddled together on a rectangular base. Sold without a base as 3317.

The only koalas recorded at London Zoo which might have been seen by Miss Lindner were purchased on 10th November 1927. Sadly, they died within two days of each other in December 1927, and there are at present no zoos in this country which keep koalas. A newspaper cutting and photograph in Doris's scrapbook must surely have influenced her. It reads:

'Koalas, commonly called native bears or Billy Bluegums because they live in the eucalyptus or blue gum of Australia. They are protected by law in the Koala Park Reserve near Sydney, as the race is threatened with extinction. These animals are prototypes of the famous toy teddy bears. There are forty-one koalas in this reserve.' (*Colour plates 96 and 136*)

3274
Name: Tigers, or Maurice and Sonia
Two young tiger cubs lying together, pretending to be ferocious. They were issued without a base as 3318.

Quintuplet tigers, three females and two males, were born at Regents Park on 5th September 1938. The name of only one of the five, Rosie, is recorded, and Maurice and Sonia must have been two of the others. Sadly, the three females died in December 1938 aged only three months, and the males survived only until January and April 1939. (*Colour plates 33 and 136*)

3270

Name	Playmates
Height	6 ¾ in.
Modeller	Freda Doughty
Introduced	1938
Rarity	E

A figure of a young girl playing with her pet dog. The girl wears a bright red dress which she holds with her left hand, her right hand touching her dog. Both the barefooted girl and the dog stand on naturalistically coloured grass above a light brown base. The records show that the girl's dress could also be turquoise-blue. The figure proved reasonably popular and was made until the late 1950s. (*Colour plate 2*)

3271

Name: 'London Gazette Here'
(*See 3227* for description.)

3272

Name	Repose
Height	7in.
Modeller	Dorothea Charol
Introduced	1938
Rarity	A

A figure of a young actress dressed in an elaborate tiered skirt with frilled-front bodice, seated in an elegant pose with her legs crossed and her right arm resting on her knee. The slightly saucy nature of this very continental figure is totally alien to Worcester's style, and it is surprising that Joseph Gimson approved of it. Repose was made in two colourings, however:
  1. clover dress, golden hair, golden-fawn skin;
  2. sea-green and turquoise dress, pink bodice, golden-fawn hair.
The latter colouring was still selling in 1945 for £1. 8s. It was withdrawn by 1948. (*Colour plate 131*)

3273
Name: Koala Bears, or Billy Bluegums
(*See* 3263 for description)

3274
Name: Tigers, or Maurice and Sonia
(*See* 3263 for description)

3288
Name	The Necklace or Girl with Beads
Height	4in.
Modeller	Dorothea Charol
Introduced	1939
Rarity	A

A figure of a nude woman kneeling, her hands reaching down to place a necklace on the oval base in front of her. The figure was painted in golden-fawn with shot-tan hair and features, the necklace No. 4 green. It sold for 9s. 6d. in Janaury 1940, rising quickly to 16s. in July 1940. It was withdrawn soon afterwards. (*Colour plate 131*)

3289
Name	Hesitation or Bathing Girl
Height	8 ¼ in.
Modeller	Dorothea Charol
Introduced	1939
Rarity	A

A figure of a girl in tight-fitting bathing costume, leaning forward with her hands on her knees, building up courage before diving into a pool. Two colourings are recorded:
  1. blue-shot costume, suntan features by paintress, blue headband and sandals, golden hair.
  2. white costume, red headband and sandals, brown hair.
Like 3288, it sold in July 1940 for 16s. and was withdrawn soon afterwards. (*Colour plate 131*)

3293-3295
Name	Small Dogs Series

(*see* 2941 for description.)

3296
Name	Hacking in the park
Height	6 ¾ in.
Modeller	Doris Lindner
Introduced	1939
Rarity	F

An equestrian study of a lady enjoying a leisurely stroll with her mount, whose head is bowed. The figure stands on a rectangular base. It seems to have been withdrawn rather earlier than other similar models (*See* 3314-3317)

3299
Name	'Fine Writing Inks'

(*see* 3227 for description.)

3300
Name	'Fair Cherryes'

(*see* 3227 for description.)

3301-3306
Name	Nursery Rhymes Series
Modeller	Freda Doughty
Introduced	1940

A series of six children representing nursery rhyme characters, with the exception of Babes in the Wood which was always intended to be included with the others. Surprisingly, only Polly Put the Kettle On seems to have been popular over many years until the 1980s.

3301
Name	Little Miss Muffet
Height	4 ½ in.
Rarity	E

A figure of a young girl frightened by a spider, causing her bowl to spill. The girl wears a red outer garment with yellow sleeves and a pretty white dress with pink and green patterns. The bowl is blue and the curds and whey spill over the naturalistically coloured grass tuffet. The rather large spider is brown with black spots. The rhyme on which the figure is based reads:

Little Miss Muffet,
She sat on a tuffet,
Eating of curds and whey;
There came a big spider,
And sat down beside her,
And frightened Miss Muffet away.

(*Colour plate 30*)

3302

Name   Babes in the Wood
Height   6 ⅛ in.
Rarity   E

A group of two young children, a boy wearing a pink and purple smock holding his arm around a smaller girl in a light blue dress. The children seem lost and stand on a naturalistically coloured grass base of roughly circular form. (Not to be confused with the model of Sister, 3149, which is somewhat similar, although more complicated.)

(*Colour plate 30*)

3303

Name   Polly Put the Kettle On
Height   6in.
Rarity   G

A figure of a young girl wearing a pink and white dress and a green apron. On her head is a white bonnet with pink and green patterns and she wears brown shoes with green bows. Her right hand holds the handle and her left the spout of a large kettle which can be decorated either in silver or gold. The rhyme on which the figure is based reads:

Polly put the Kettle on
Polly put the Kettle on
Polly put the Kettle on
We'll all have tea.

(*Colour plate 90*)

3304

Name   Goosey Goosey Gander
Height   6in.
Rarity   E

A figure of a young boy wearing a yellow smock, speaking to a goose which stands almost as tall as himself, its orange beak touching his face. The orange webbed feet of the goose and the child's brown shoes stand on naturalistically coloured grass above a light brown roughly circular base. The rhyme on which the figure is based reads:

Goosey goosey gander,
Whither shall I wander?
Upstairs, downstairs,
And in my lady's chamber;
There I met an old man
That would not say his prayers;
I took him by the left leg,
And threw him downstairs.

(*Colour plate 30*)

3305

Name   Little Jack Horner
Height   4 ½ in.
Rarity   D

A figure of a blonde-haired boy sitting on a brown stool in the corner. He is eating from a bowl, and wears a green and yellow striped smock with green stockings. His shoes are orange with yellow bobbles on top. Unlike the other five models in the set, this one does not have a base. The rhyme on which the figure is based reads:

Little Jack Horner sat in the corner,
Eating a Christmas pie:
He put in his thumb,
And he took out a plum,
And said, "What a good boy am I."

(*Colour plate 90*)

3306

Name   Little Boy Blue
Height   3 ½ in.
Rarity   D

A figure of a young boy lying against a white sheep, a little larger than himself. The boy wears a blue coat, hat and shoes and holds a yellow horn to his mouth. The grass is naturalistically coloured above a light, roughly rectangular base. The rhyme on which the figure is based reads:

Little boy blue, come blow up your horn,
The sheep's in the meadow, the cow's in the corn:

Where's the little boy that looks after
   the sheep?
He's under the haycock fast asleep.
(*Colour plate 9*)

3307-3312
Name   Sporting Dog Series
(*See* 3228 for description.)

3313-3318
Name   Zoo Babies
(*See* 3263 for description.)

3319-3322
Name   Dogs' Heads for wall
              mounting
Height   5in. – 7in.
Modeller   Unknown
Introduced 1940
Rarity   A
Four dogs' heads formed as a Scottie,
Bulldog, Spaniel and Peke. These may
never have gone into full production.

3330
Name   Bogskar
Height   9in.
Modeller   Doris Lindner
Introduced 1940
Rarity   A

A fine study of Bogskar, winner of the
Grand National Steeplechase at Aintree in
1940, the last running of the race until
1946. Mervyn Jones, the twenty-five-year-
old jockey having his first Aintree ride, is
in the saddle. He was, at the time, serving
with the Royal Air Force, and sadly, was
killed in action two years later. Bogskar,
owned and trained by Lord Stalbridge, a
steward of the National Hunt Committee,
came from some way behind to join the
leader MacMoffat at the last fence and,
despite making a mistake there, drew clear
to win quite comfortably. Seventeen of the
fifty-seven starters completed the race and
Bogskar returned a 25/1 outsider. The
horse was hardly a popular winner with
the public, and seems a strange choice of
subject. Not surprisingly, only one or two
examples seem to have been sold. Despite

3330

this rather inauspicious start with racehorses, Doris Lindner was to model some
most impressive studies as Limited
Editions in the future, and this early
example certainly should not have failed
on account of the superb modelling and
detail. See also page 23.

3331
Name   Toto, Cairn Terrier
Height   3 ½ in.
Modeller   Aline Ellis
Introduced 1940
Rarity   B

A charming small model of Toto, Dorothy's
dog from *The Wizard of Oz*. The dog walks,
tail upright, along a rectangular base
representing the yellow brick road. He is
black, his red tongue visible in his mouth,
and the name 'Toto' is painted in brown
letters on one side of the yellow base. An
unusual orange mark below the base of an
example we have seen includes the printed
words 'Made only for U.S.A.', as at this time
much ware was produced for export only.
The film of *The Wizard of Oz* came out in
1939 and was still a big hit in the United
States when Alex Dickens commissioned
this model. (*Colour plate 113*)

3333-3338
Name   Small British Birds Series
(*See* 3197 for description.)

3339-3342
Name   The Four Seasons
Height   4 ¾ in. – 5in.
Modeller   Gwendoline Parnell
Introduced 1941
Rarity   B

A set of four figures, each of a young girl surrounded by flowers representative of the different seasons. Inspired by eighteenth-century porcelain figures and produced in full colours. Production was very limited.

3339
Name   Summer
The dress could be either pink or yellow with white scarf and ribbon.

3340
Name   Winter
Pink cloak with emerald-green surround, white snow.

3341
Name   Autumn
Mauve dress, emerald-green surround and orange flowers. Red shoes.

3342
Name   Spring (second version)
Pink dress with white top and red shoes

3346, 3347, 3351, 3352, 3369, 3370, 3382
Name   Wartime Series
Height   4 ½ in. – 6 ½ in.
Modeller   Eileen Soper
Introduced 1941 and 1942
Rarity   A

A set of seven models capturing the sadness and frightening realities of the war, seen through the events in the lives of childen in wartime Britain. These were some of the most appealing and effective studies ever made by Worcester, and it at first seems rather surprising that the figures proved so unpopular. The reason, however, almost certainly lies in their striking realism together with the often painful and sad portrayal of the effect that the war had on the children. Nobody wanted to buy the models and Daisy Rea even recalls the paintresses being given one each, just to be rid of them. The bright colours and the detail so accurately modelled by Eileen Soper make these figures very desirable now, and it would seem that they were merely introduced at the least opportune time, when people were actually experiencing the same sad events. The colourings are shown in the original drawings, illustrated in Colour plate 129. An eighth figure, Missing, showing a distraught mother holding an official letter bringing bad news from the front, was felt to be too tragic a subject and was not produced. See also page 24.

3346
Name   The Rescue
A girl kneels on a roughly circular base and attempts to rescue a small black and white kitten sitting on a wall next to a sign which reads 'Danger, Unexploded Bomb'. The proposed title for this figure was 'The Unexploded Bomb' but 'Rescue' was thought to be more appealing. It sold for a guinea. *(Colour plate 129)*

3347
Name   Evacuees
Two children are together, a girl with her arm around her younger brother as they await collection by their temporary family. Both have name-tags, with 'Jenny Smith, London' and 'Tommy Smith, London' painted on them. Their belongings are beside them. It sold for a guinea
(Colour plate 129)

3351
Name   Take Cover
A boy and a girl shelter behind a wall, the boy clutching a rather frightened brown and white puppy, the girl's left hand raised to her face to express her fear. it cost £1. 10s. *(Colour plate 129)*

3352
Name   Spitfire
Two boys stand and look up to the sky as a Spitfire passes overhead. The taller boy waves his cap as he cheers the popular British fighter plane. The largest group in the set at 6 ½ in., it cost £1. 12s. 6d.
(Colour plate 129)

3369
Name   Stowaways
A girl, with a name-tag reading, 'Bessie Brown', sits on a bench, her brown suitcase by her side, also with her name on it. Partially hidden by her coat and scarf are two tiny kittens, one black and one brown. These are the 'stowaways' as the girl waits for the train which will evacuate her from London. She smiles, content with the knowledge that her pets are safe. It sold for 17s. 6d. *(Colour plate 64)*

3370
Name   Salvage
Any surplus metal and re-usable materials were collected to help the war effort. A boy has been gathering his toys together and carries them, with his dog running alongside. A sign on the wall reads 'Wanted – Scrap Metal, Rags, Bones and Waste paper'. It sold for 17s. 6d. *(Colour plate 129)*

3382
Name   The Letter
A figure of a young mother seated with her arm around her little daughter. Together they read from a letter received from the father, serving with the forces overseas. It sold for £1. 10s.

3348, 3354 and 3362
Name   Chinoiserie Children
Height   4 ⅞ in. – 6 ¼ in.
Modeller   Gwendoline Parnell
Introduced 1941
Rarity   E
Three models of oriental children. 3348 is a girl sitting on a tree stump, her left arm outstretched. 3354 is a small boy standing with his hands in his pockets and a smile on his face. 3362 is another girl, also standing, her hands held upwards. These three models were painted in black and 'duck egg' green and marketed by Worcester together with four models of older chinoiserie characters, which were decorated in the same way. Shoes and features were painted 'Chinese' red *(see 3397-3400) (3348 and 3362 Colour plate 37)*

3349
Name   Boy and Dolphin
Height   Unknown
Modeller   Frederick Gertner
Introduced 1941
Rarity   A
No details survive in any of the factory records, and it is therefore unlikely that the figure was produced.

3350
Name   Rats, Cairn Terrier
Height   3 ¼ in.
Modeller   Aline Ellis
Introduced 1941
Rarity   B
A model of a Cairn Terrier, Rats, one of a series of dog studies by Aline Ellis probably made exclusively for the American market. Rather similar to Toto (3331), the dog's name is painted on one side of the rectangular base. Whilst Toto walks along the ground, Rats stands alertly with his tail upright. All examples we have seen bear the mark of Alex Dickens, who probably commissioned the series.

3351 and 3352
Name   Wartime Series
(See 3346 for description.)

3353
Name   Seaweed
Height   7in.
Modeller   Frederick Gertner
Introduced 1941
Rarity   A
A figure of a naked boy with a faun-like face, standing, his lower part draped in flowing seaweed. No details of colouring or cost price exist, and production was probably very limited.

3354
Name   Chinoiserie Boy
(See 3348 for description.)

3355
Name   Mack, West Highland Terrier
Height   3in.
Modeller   Aline Ellis
Introduced 1941
Rarity   B

A model of a West Highland terrier named Mack, one of a series of small dogs by Aline Ellis, probably made exclusively for Alex Dickens and the American market. Mack is a white dog sitting on a green rectangular base which has his name painted on one side. (*Colour plate 107*)

3356

Name	Ranter, Standing Hound
Height	4in.
Modeller	Aline Ellis
Introduced	1941
Rarity	B

A model of a hound stalking in rough grass, his head lowered near the ground. The long grass forms the top of a green rectangular base with the name 'Ranter' painted on one side. One of six models probably made exclusively for the American market at the request of Alex Dickens. (*Colour plate 107*)

3359 and 3360

Name	The Bow and The Curtsey or Masquerade Boy and Girl
Height	7 ½ in. and 6 ¼ in.
Modeller	Freda Doughty
Introduced	1941
Rarity	G

A very popular pair of figures of a boy bowing and a girl curtseying, both dressed elegantly. In the 1950s the original names of The Bow and The Curtsey were changed to Masquerade Boy and Girl. We do not know the reason for this, but the pair always retained their popularity and were continued well into the 1970s, amongst the most successful of Freda Doughty's many studies of children.

The recorded colourings are as follows.
The Bow:
1. turquoise blue and yellow with yellow-ivory ribbon, golden-fawn and yellow hair.
2. yellow, scarlet red ribbon.
3. ultramarine and yellow, scarlet red ribbon, fair hair.

The Curtsey:
1. turquoise-blue, ultramarine and yellow with pink highlights.
2. letter pink and white with green and pink flowers, brown hair.

(*Colour plate 108*)

3361

Name	Tony, Sitting Spaniel Puppy
Height	3in.
Modeller	Aline Ellis
Introduced	1941
Rarity	B

A charming model of Tony, a young spaniel puppy, one of six models by Aline Ellis probably made exclusively for the American market. Tony is a black and white spaniel with large black ears who sits, an inquisitive expression on his face, on a rectangular green base with his name painted on one side. (*Colour plate 107*)

3362

Name	Chinoiserie Girl

(*See* 3348 for description.)

3363-3365 and 3375-3377

Name	Double Birds on Tree Stumps (First Series)
Height	about 4 ¾ in.
Modeller	Eva Soper
Introduced	1942
Rarity	G

A set of six models made to complement the series of single small birds by the same modeller. Each depicts a pair of popular British garden birds in natural settings. They were realistically coloured, originally with glost finish, but subsequently changed to matt. All proved to be very popular and at the time of writing are still available.

3363
Name	Pied Woodpeckers on Stump

3364
Name	Chaffinches on Stump

3365
Name	Linnets on Stump

3375
Name	Blue Tits on Stump

3376
Name	Cole Tits on Stump

3377
Name	Yellow Hammers on Stump

(*3365 and 3377 Colour plate 100*)

3366

Name   Taffy, Welsh Corgi
Height   3in.
Modeller   Aline Ellis
Introduced   1942
Rarity   B

3366

A model of a Welsh corgi standing on a roughly rectangular base with his name, 'Taffy', on one side. This is one of six studies by Aline Ellis, probably made exclusively for the American market at the request of Alex Dickens.

3369 and 3370

Name   Wartime Series
(*See* 3346 for description.)

3371 and 3372

Name   Nude Boy and Nude Girl
Height   Unknown
Modeller   Frederick Gertner
Introduced   1942
Rarity   A

No details exist other than the names and a note that the moulds were destroyed in 1953. They were possibly not put into production.

3373

Name   Nude Boy with Cornucopia and Nude Girl with Cornucopia (second version)
Height   7 ¾ in.
Modeller   Frederick Gertner
Introduced   1942
Rarity   A

A pair of figures of boys with short curly hair, both naked and holding a large cornucopia overflowing with fruit. They stand on a roughly circular textured base. No details or prices of colouring exist, and production was probably very limited.

3375-3377

Name   Double Birds on Tree Stumps
(*See* 3363 for description.)

3380 and 3381

Name   Sitting Child and Crawling Child
Height   4in. and 3 ¾ in.
Modeller   Freda Doughty
Introduced   1942
Rarity   C

A pair of young babies, one sitting on the floor and the other crawling along. Daisy Rea often remembered how she enjoyed these models, and how simple the flesh colouring on the naked bodies was for the paintresses. It is perhaps surprising that we have seen so few examples of either figure. Both were withdrawn in the early 1950s.

3382

Name   War Group
(*See* 3346 for description.)

3383 and 3384

Name   Blue Tit on Plinth and Goldfinch on Plinth
Height   3 ¾ in. and 3 ¼ in.
Modeller   Doris Lindner
Introduced   1942
Rarity   A

No photograph or any other details survive. It is therefore unlikely that these models were put into full production.

3385 and 3386

Name   Foxhounds Standing
Height   7in.
Modeller   Aline Ellis
Introduced   1942
Rarity   B

Two models of foxhounds standing on rectangular grassy bases, their tails raised. Painted with red-brown patches on a white ground, they were produced in matt colouring and were made especially for export only at the request of Alex Dickens. They cost £1. 16s. each and were withdrawn by 1948. (*Colour plate 60*)

3387

Name   Fox
Height   5in.
Modeller   Aline Ellis
Introduced 1942
Rarity   B

A powerful model of a fox seated alertly on an overgrown log, painted in matt colours and raised on a pale green rectangular base. The fox was made for the American market at the request of Alex Dickens and was probably not offered for sale in England. It cost £2 and was withdrawn by 1948. (*Colour plate 61*)

3388 and 3396

Name   Southwind and Westwind
Height   7¼ in. and 7in.
Modeller   Agnes Pinder-Davis
Introduced 1942 and 1944
Rarity   A

Two distinctive sculptures in a striking Art Deco style, these were Mrs. Pinder-Davis's first work for Worcester. Southwind depicts a lady holding on to her hat and the hand of a child by her side, a toy on a string dragged behind him. Westwind also depicts a lady, this time with a child clinging to her side and holding an umbrella in front of her, her dress with pronounced buttons and a spreading skirt. Introduced in wartime, the figures were possibly not put into production. No colour schemes or prices are recorded.

3397 and 3398

Name   Chinoiserie Figures Kneeling
Height   5⅜ in. and 5⅝ in.
Modeller   Agnes Pinder-Davis
Introduced 1944 and 1946
Rarity   D

A pair of chinoiserie figures, both kneeling on rectangular white bases. The male (3397) looks upwards with hands held with palms facing the sky. The female (3398) holds a fan towards her face. Two colour schemes are recorded for this and the following pair. By far the more popular was a combination of 'duck-egg' green and 'Chinese' black, but examples have been seen in the second colouring of 'letter' pink, yellow and 'Chinese Norse' blue. The

3397   **3398**

figures were sold just in white and were first shown at the 'Britain Can Make It' Exhibition at the Victoria and Albert Museum in 1948. A note in the catalogue for the white figures records that at that time they were only available for export. They cost 15s. in white or £1. 10s. each coloured, rising to £2. 19s. each in 1955

3399 and 3400

Name   Chinoiserie Figures Standing
Height   7⅞ in. and 7½ in.
Modeller   Agnes Pinder-Davis
Introduced 1944
Rarity   D

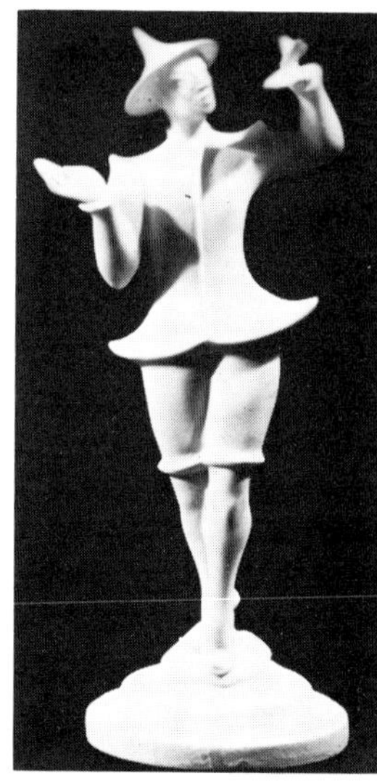

3399   **3400**

A pair of chinoiserie figures, intended to go with the previous pair and coloured in the same way. Both stand on a leaf on top of a circular white base and also balance their hands as a butterfly, generally painted orange, lands on the left hand of each. Like 3397 and 3398 the pair were shown, in white, at the 'Britain Can Make It' Exhibition in 1948, and both were withdrawn in 1958.

3402-3405

Name	Four Watteau Figures, two Male and two Female
Height	8in., 7½in., 6in., 6in.
Modeller	Agnes Pinder-Davis
Introduced	1946
Rarity	A

A set of four figures in eighteenth-century style. 3402 and 3403 are both standing, the former a young man in a wide circular hat, short smart jacket and tight stockings. The lady, dressed in a bell-like fluted skirt, holds a basket of flowers under one arm. 3404 is a man seated on a log, wearing a fitted sleeveless waistcoat, a jabot round his neck and his legs crossed, a dog by his side. His companion is a lady (3405), also seated on a tree stump, dressed in a petticoat and open robe, a cornucopia of fruit by her side. The figures were all brightly coloured, mainly turquoise, blues, greens and yellows. No prices are listed for any of these figures and it is likely that they were not put into full production. The moulds were destroyed in 1953.

3414 and 3415

Name	Pair of Regency Figures
Height	10in.
Modeller	Agnes Pinder-Davis
Introduced	1947
Rarity	B

An imposing pair of rather elegant ladies dressed in long gowns of the Regency period with *décolleté* necklines. 3414 has a sash wrapped around her shoulders and arms, 3415 holds a similar sash in her right hand. Both stand on circular bases. The dresses are usually white with peacock and indigo but the records show that 3414 was also issued in a pale pink dress with light chrome-green and sea-green decoration, whilst 3415 was issued with a pale turquoise-blue dress with yellow decoration. Like Mrs. Pinder-Davis' other departures from the Chinese theme, the figures were not a success, and it is probable that very few were made. The moulds were destroyed in 1953.

3416-3418, 3440, 3441 and 3452-3458

Name	The Months of the Year
Modeller	Freda Doughty
Introduced	1947 and 1949
Rarity	G

A set of twelve figures of children, each representing one of the months of the year. Along with the Days of the Week series by the same modeller, these figures must rank as the most popular to have been made by the factory. All are still in production at the time of writing and some of the figures have also been sold under other names. In the 1980s miniature versions of many of the models have been made, and some of the later versions have been tried in different colourings to those listed here, including an experimental series with matt finishes which was not put into full production.

3416

Name	April
Height	6⅜in.

A girl playing happily with a frisky young lamb, the rough, naturalistically coloured base representing the field through which they run. The girl wears a yellow top and a white dress with lilac and yellow stripes. Miss Doughty gave specific instructions to the casters to make sure the figure was assembled at the correct angle, and her drawing still survives. See illustration on page 30. *(Colour plate 69)*

3417

Name	October
Height	7½in.

A boy playing in the woods with two squirrels, one climbing up his leg and the other on the naturalistically coloured green mound which forms the base. The boy wears a yellow sweater and ultramarine shorts with 'Donville' black shoes. His hair is golden-fawn and 'French' brown. Miss Doughty's original instructions to the casters indicating the positioning of the heads and body still survive and are illustrated on page 30. (*Colour plate 71*)

3418
Name November
Height 7⅜ in.
A boy, standing with a white dove eating from his left hand whilst three more gather around his feet on a grey, roughly rectangular base. He is well-wrapped in a coat painted 'New Beige' with mauve shadows. His pointed hat and trousers are 'Persian' red. The figure was slightly altered by removing the dove perched on his right foot and issued as shape No. 3760 under the name 'Fantails', introduced in 1963. November continued to be made with the additional dove.
(*Colour plate 71.* Fantails, *Colour plate 7*)

3440
Name July
Height 7in.
A girl wearing a 'pillement' pink swimming costume and paddling in the sea. The base on which she stands is decorated light sea-green and white and shaped to represent the waves. Her hair blows in the breeze and is painted golden-fawn and yellow. (*Colour plate 98*)

3441
Name August
Height 5in.
A naked girl resembling a sea nymph, seated peering down into the sea water which forms the base to the figure, a small fish looking up at her. The records show that the base was to be painted sea-green, ultramarine and water-green, and the girl's skin golden-fawn. (*Colour plate 98*)

3452
Name January
Height 6in.
A blonde-haired boy wearing a coat and scarf, sliding on the ice which forms the base of the figure. The boy's shoes are brown and he wears 'New Austrian' brown stockings. The coat was painted 'Boardman's' crimson and the scarf 'Paddy' green. (*Colour plate 69*)

3453
Name February
Height 6¼ in.
A boy wearing a long sea-green raincoat with 'Donville' black wellington boots on his feet and a similarly coloured sou'wester on his head. His right arm is extended in front of him and he stands on a roughly circular white base, the upper part of which is painted blue. (*Colour plate 69*)

3454
Name March
Height 5⅞ in.
A girl running happily through the countryside. She wears a pink dress and holds an ultramarine hat in her left hand. Her shoes are yellow and her golden-fawn hair blows in the wind. The irregularly shaped based is painted green and light brown. (*Colour plate 69*)

3455
Name May
Height 5in.
A girl kneeling in the woods picking large daisies. She wears an ultramarine dress and the irregularly shaped base is decorated deep green. Her hair is yellow and golden-fawn. The original colour standard painted by Freda Doughty is illustrated on Colour plate 91. (*Colour plate 98*)

3456
Name June (second version)
Height 6¼ in.
A boy sitting on a grey rock partially covered with grass, his bare legs crossed. A brown and white dog lies on the rock, its head resting on the yellow shorts of the boy, who wears a white shirt with a striped tie. He holds to his mouth a small harmonica. (*Colour plate 98, also plate 91 for the original colour standard painted by Freda Doughty.*)

3457
Name   September or Snowy
Height   4 ½ in.
A small boy plays with a white kitten on a green and golden-fawn base. The boy wears a white shirt with ultramarine hat, shorts and shoes, his dark brown hair showing below the brim of the hat. The figure was issued in a slightly different colouring from 1963 and was renamed 'Snowy', although September continued to be made. *(Colour plate 71)*

3458
Name   December
Height   6 ⅜ in.
A girl plays in the snow which covers the roughly circular base, a pile of snowballs collected around her red shoes. In her arms she holds more snowballs, which she is cheerfully throwing. She is warmly wrapped in a golden-fawn and yellow coat with 'New Austrian' brown edges and a hood protecting her brown hair. Beneath her coat is a red dress, and she wears red shoes. *(Colour plate 71)*

3419 and **3420**
Name   Female Chinese Figures
Height   11in.
Modeller   *Agnes Pinder-Davis*
Introduced 1947
Rarity   D
A pair of tall standing figures of women in chinoiserie style, with strongly moulded angular costumes, one with a short coat and the other a long one. Their hands, modelled with strongly pointed fingers, are outstretched, one holding a rose. Both figures stand on stepped circular bases. The most usual colouring is green and black, but they were also painted in green, yellow and pink. Both cost £6. 15s. in turquoise and coloured sheen in 1953, and £7. 8s. 6d. in 1954. They were in addition sold in biscuit for £4.5s. each in March 1958. *(3420, Colour plate 22)*

3421 and 3422
Name   Pair of Pigeons, Wings
             Crossed
Height   7in.
Modeller   Doris Lindner
Introduced 1947
Rarity   B
Two models of wood pigeons realistically modelled on rocky mounds. The glossy finish makes the naturalistic colouring seem unusually bright. Doris Lindner's bird models always seemed to lack the realism of those of Dorothy Doughty or Eva Soper, and few were ever sold. They were still listed in 1952, selling for up to £8. 5s. each.

3425, 3426, 3462 and 3463
Name   Large Dog Series
Height   About 8in.
Modeller   Doris Lindner
Introduced 1947 (3425, 3426) and 1950
             (3462, 3463)
Rarity   B
A series of four models of show dogs on a much larger scale than Miss Lindner's normal dog models. All stand and have no bases. They were naturalistically coloured, although more usually are seen just in white.

3425
Name   Afghanistan Hound
3426
Name   Borzoi
3462
Name   Alsatian (second version)
3463
Name   Setter
The model of the Setter (3463) could be coloured differently to depict either an English Setter or an Irish Setter. All cost £7. 10s in 1952 and £8. 5s. in August 1955. They were withdrawn soon afterwards.

3433
Name   Johnnie or Farmer's Boy, or
             Young Farmer
Height   6 ½ in.
Modeller   Freda Doughty

Introduced 1947
Rarity Johnnie E., others G
A figure of a boy wearing a white shirt and green shorts playing with a number of yellow ducklings. The model was redesigned with one of the ducks removed, and named 'Farmer's Boy'. The records show blue shorts instead of green. For details of the original model *see* 3226. Farmer's Boy was very popular and remained in production into the 1980s. Young Farmer was an alternative name. (*Colour plate 6*)

3435

Name Happy Days
Height 7 ½ in.
Modeller Freda Doughty
Introduced 1948
Rarity D
A model of a boy riding a brown and white pony. The golden-haired boy wears a light green shirt and blue-grey trousers. This was not one of Freda Doughty's most successful models. She is seen at her best when modelling children, but in this figure the pony tends to dominate and lacks the movement and realism captured in Doris Lindner's studies. it cost £4. 8s. in 1952 and was withdrawn by 1955.

3440 and 3441

Name July and August
(*See* 3416 for description.)

3442-3445

Name Double Birds on Tree Stumps
      (second series)
Height Unknown
Modeller Doris Lindner
Introduced 1949
Rarity A
A set of four groups, each depicting two birds on a tree stump with sprigs of leaves, on stepped circular bases. They resembled Dorothy Doughty's bird models but have less elaborate flowers. The type of bird in each case is not recorded. They were priced at a hefty 11 guineas each fully coloured, and very few seem to have been sold.

3446 and 3447

Name Chinoiserie Figures with
      Birds
Height About 13in.
Modeller Agnes Pinder-Davis
Introduced 1949
Rarity D
A pair of large figures of a Chinese man and woman in long spreading angular robes, both holding a bird on one hand, their heads turned to face each other. A particularly fine pair which was often sold in white but fully marked. The models are recorded as having been painted with strong shining black hair and aerographed bronze coat, fawn-pink sleeves and yellow sash. Alternatively they were decorated with shot-gold on a black coat, turquoise hat and crimson dress with gold edge and tassle. The price varied depending on the colour variations, rising to £12. 13s. each in powdered colouring in 1954. They continued into the early 1960s.

3448 and 3449

Name Hamlet and Romeo and Juliet
Height Unknown
Modeller Agnes Pinder-Davis
Introduced 1949
Rarity A
One photograph book in the factory records these two numbers as Shakespearean groups by Mrs. Pinder-Davis. No further details are noted and it is likely that the figures were never proceeded with.

3452-3458

Name Months of the Year
(*See* 3416 for description.)

3459 and 3460

Name Pair of Ducks (second
      version)
Height Unknown
Modeller Doris Lindner
Introduced 1950
Rarity A
Two large realistic models of ducks, one on an angled base with tufts of grass, the other on a rocky base. Naturalistically coloured,

they sold for £12. 10s. each, rising to £14 in 1952. They were withdrawn soon afterwards.

3461

Name   Girl Skipping thro' Roses
Height   Unknown
Modeller   Unknown
Introduced 1950
Rarity   A

One factory photograph book records 3461 as 'to come – Girl skipping thro' roses'. This has been crossed out and replaced by 'July'. The figure was probably not proceeded with.

3462 and 3463

Name   Alsatian and Setter (second
                   versions)
(*See* 3425 for description.)

3466

Name   Wild Horses or Galloping
                   Horses
Height   16 ¼ in.
Modeller   Doris Lindner
Introduced 1950
Rarity   F

A magnificent large group of two galloping wild horses on an oval base. The horses were predominantly white and were finished in matt enamels known as white vellum. Originally made in unlimited forms, they were produced until the early 1970s and came with wooden plinths. In 1978 Doris Lindner re-designed the group, eliminating the plinth supporting the horses in the middle, and it was issued in colour as a Limited Edition of 250 under the name 'Galloping in Winter'.

3471 and 3472

Name   Battledore and Shuttlecock
Height   Unknown
Modeller   Freda Doughty
Introduced 1951
Rarity   A

The names Shuttlecock and Battledore refer to the sport later called Badminton. One factory book lists 3471 as 'Badminton Player, F. G. Doughty'. A photograph of Shuttlecock survives and it depicts a lady in nineteenth-century costume holding a shuttlecock and a racket, standing on a

roughly circular base edged with modelled and gilt scrolls. The pair are a complete departure from Miss Doughty's children figures, and it is possible that the factory did not find them worthwhile and never put them into production. No prices are listed, and no colour scheme was apparently devised.

3473 and 3474

Name   Balinese and Siamese Dancers
Modeller   Agnes Pinder-Davis
Introduced 1951

Issued as a Limited Edition of twenty-five and discussed in Chapter 2, page 24. A smaller version of each was proposed, *see* 3550 and 3551.

3475

Name   Angel Fish
Height   Unknown
Modeller   Doris Lindner
Introduced 1951
Rarity   A

A group of three angel fish swimming among aquatic plants and grasses, on an irregular base. For this unusual departure from her dog and horse models, Miss Lindner was possibly inspired by a somewhat similar group made by the Rosenthal factory. The model was clever, with considerable charm, but caused many technical problems. Coloured, the model sold for £27. 10s. in 1955, or only £18 in the matt white finish known as Pencilled Vellum. In 1958, in white glost only, it cost £13. A certain number must have been sold, but it is a very fragile group and one wonders how many can have survived.

3479 and 3480

Name   Paul and Priscilla
Height   Unknown
Modeller   Freda Doughty
Introduced 1952
Rarity   A

A pair of figures of a youth and a girl gathering apples. The boy is smartly dressed with arms outstretched, an apple held in each hand, further apples on the base beside him. The girl stands also with arms outstretched, waiting to catch apples thrown by her friend, a single fruit by her feet. Both stand on square step-moulded bases, and represent a strange style of modelling which lacks the charm of Miss Doughty's usual work. No prices or colourings are listed and they were probably withdrawn before full production commenced.

3481 and 3482
Name   Chinese Goddesses
Height   Unknown
Modeller Agnes Pinder-Davis
Introduced 1952
Rarity   A

Two very angular models, one of an Oriental lady seated in contemplative pose on a circular tasselled cushion, her hands folded in front of her; the other is in a similar style on a plain circular base, her left hand holding a flower. They sold for £11 each coloured in 1954, or £12. 2s. with gold lustre. Production was very limited.

3483
Name   Jester (second version)
Height   Unknown
Modeller Miss Stevens
Introduced 1952
Rarity   A

A figure of a man with jester-style pointed hair, dressed in a tiered costume resembling a tutu, a stick held in front of his face, standing on a stepped circular base. This is a very strange figure with little to commend it, and it is not really surprising that it never went into full production.

3488 and 3489
Name   Punch and Judy
Height   6in.
Modeller Freda Doughty
Introduced 1952
Rarity   B

A pair of figures of kneeling children. Punch is a little boy with curly hair, his hands on his lap, his shirt open at the top. Judy is a girl with long hair, kneeling with her feet to one side, her left hand touching the ground. She wears a short plain dress.

With this model Freda Doughty returned to her simple child-figure style which started her at Worcester, but here she failed to get the scale just right, with the result that sales were very disappointing and the figures were withdrawn very soon after introduction.

3491-3502
Name   Chinoiserie Sayings Series
Height   About 5in. to 6in.
Modeller Agnes Pinder-Davis
Introduced 1953
Rarity   C

A set of twelve figures of chinoiserie children representing sayings and proverbs. By far the largest series from Agnes Pinder-Davis, and one of the largest from any of the Worcester modellers. It must be said, however, that the figures are all rather strange and, since they were introduced at a time when Freda Doughty's popular children were selling very well, it is easy to see why these chinoiseries were failures. They were painted in bright colours contrasting with hard white and each figure has its name printed in black around the base. They sold for £1. 16s. each in July 1953 and were all still available in August 1955 in black and white only, priced at £2. 5s. each. Many have been seen just in white with the title printed in black. All were withdrawn by 1957.

3491
Name   Sea Scout
A smiling child sits on the shoulders of a giant sea-horse, her hands on its head to steer, the creature's tail adjoining a roughly circular base. (*see* illustration on page 47).

3492
Name   Lucky Spider
A child sits on an irregularly shaped rock with feet to either side. The child looks away to the right, having been startled by the large spider crawling up in front of it.

3493
Name   Funny Fish
A laughing child sits on a rock with head looking upwards to the sky. The child's left

leg is raised and a large, rather odd-looking fish is held with both hands. Clearly the child is somewhat amused by the fish.

3494
Name   Don't Let the Cat out of the
               Bag
A child stands on a roughly circular base with one finger of his left hand raised to his mouth. A small cat emerges from a sack behind him and it is clear that he knows something that for the moment he is unwilling to reveal. (*see* illustration on page 47).

3495
Name   Slow Coach
A child sits astride a tortoise which is roughly the same size as himself, waving with his right hand, and seemingly unconcerned at his mount's lack of speed.

3496
Name   Joy Ride
A naked child sits astride a stylized dolphin riding on top of the waves, clinging firmly to the creature's tail.

3497
Name   Apple of Your Eye
A child has been picking apples and holds one in his right hand raised level with his right eye; this causes him to drop the remaining apples, which he has been holding in his other arm.

3498
Name   Early Bird
A child stands with his left foot on a rock just above the ground and looks up to the sky. On his left shoulder sits a small bird. (*see* illustration on page 47).

3499
Name   Two's Company, Three's None
A child sits with her head supported by her left hand, which is raised to her chin. She looks down at two lovebirds perched happily on her knee.

3500
Name   Wise as an Owl
A young girl, sitting studying an open book held in her hands, looks to her left shoulder, on which sits an owl. (*see* illustration on page 47).

3501
Name   Hen Party
A girl sits on the ground, her right hand raised to her mouth as she talks to a large hen standing on a rock by her side. (*see* illustration on page 47).

3502
Name   Mad as a Hatter, or, Mad as a
               March Hare
A child stands with both hands held up level with his head as he gazes upwards. Beside him and to his left a hare stands on its hind legs, its ears pointing upwards, its stance resembling that of the child. (*see* illustration on page 47).

3503
Name   The Queen's Beasts (two
               models)
Height   5 ½ in.
Modeller   Frederick Gertner
Introduced   1953
Rarity   A
Two models of heraldic beasts intended to form part of the Queen's Coronation Vase (*see* page 25). Worcester's two figures comprised a white dog holding a shield emblazoned with the Tudor Rose, and a white horse, the shield with quartered Royal Arms. The animals are upright on circular bases. Eleven pairs were made to be mounted into the vases and it is known that a few extra models were made. The painting was by Harry Davis.

3504 and 3505
Name   Little Rock Temple and
               Summer House on the Hill
Height   Unknown
Modeller   Agnes Pinder-Davis
Introduced   1953
Rarity   A
No photographs or any other details survive except the note in one book for 3504

'Chinese Garden Temple on the Hill, P. Davis'. 'Little Rock Temple' is written over this. It is unlikely that they were produced.

3510 and 3511
Name   Red Riding Hood and Wolf
Height   8in.
Modeller   Miss Stevens
Introduced 1954
Rarity   A
Red Riding Hood is a girl in a patterned dress partly covered by a cloak, a frightened look on her face. The Wolf is dressed as Red Riding Hood's grand-mother in a large patterned dress and leaps towards the little girl. Both are on irregular bases picked out with rococo scrolls. The figures were felt to be too frightening by the workers in the factory and this view was shared by the public, who bought very few.

3514-3517
Name   Farm Animal Series (without bases)
(*See* 3123, 3146, 3152 and 3153.)

3518, 3519, 3521-3524 and 3534
Name   The Days of the Week
Modeller   Freda Doughty
Introduced 1954
Rarity   G
A second set of figures, one representing each of the days of the week and making a girl and a boy for each day. For the first seven figures and the nursery rhyme on which the series was based, *see* 3256.

3518
Name   Sunday's Girl
Height   7in.
A young girl, who wears a light blue hat, stands with her right arm outstretched holding a brightly coloured windmill. She wears a blue top and a white dress with red spots. Her shoes are blue and she stands on a circular base.(*Colour plate 67*)

3519
Name   Monday's Boy
Height   7¼in.
A boy stands, feet together, on a circular base. He holds a brown and white puppy in each arm, against his bluish-mauve shirt. His shorts and shoes are also bluish-mauve and his hair is golden-yellow. This figure was also sold under the name of 'All Mine'.(*Colour plate 72*)

3521
Name   Wednesday's Boy
Height   6⅞in.
A boy stands barefoot on a circular base. He holds a broken teddy bear and wears a green smock.(*Colour plate 72*)

3522
Name   Thursday's Girl
Height   7¼in.
A girl walks along the ground, her reddish shoes on a roughly oval-shaped base. She wears a brown satchel over her blue-green dress and her right arm is held out before her.(*Colour plate 72*)

3523
Name   Friday's Girl
Height   6in.
A girl sits on a green rock, a bird on her right knee looking up at her. She wears a yellow dress, and her hair is dark brown. (*See Colour plate 46 for the original standard painted by Freda Doughty*)

3524
Name   Saturday's Boy
Height   6⅛in.
A boy leans on a spade as he digs the garden, naturally coloured brown and green and forming the roughly oval-shaped base. He wears a white hat and shirt and light blue trousers.(*Colour plate 67*)

3534
Name   Tuesday's Boy
Height   8⅛in.
A boy skates on ice, which forms a circular base. He wears a yellow and red jumper and hat and light blue trousers. His hands are in his pockets.(*Colour plate 72*)

3527 and 3528
Name   Fox and Hound Lying
(*See* 2872 and 2873 for description).

3529
Name   Young Spotted Deer
(*See* 3266 for description.)

3530 and 3531
Name   Goats
(*See* 3124 for description.)

3534
Name   Tuesday's Boy
(*See* 3518 or description.)

3535
Name   Officer of the 29th Foot
(Worcestershire Regt.)
Height   12in.
Modeller   Frederick Gertner
Introduced   1954
Rarity   G

3535

A model of an Officer of the Worcestershire Regiment in the uniform of 1812, standing on a stepped black base. It was, no doubt, produced following local demand as an addition to the popular series begun forty years earlier. The model is virtually identical to 2676, Coldstream Guards Officer, but with minor differences to the uniform. It was sold in 1955 for 15 guineas and is still available at the time of writing.

3538 and 3557
Name   Isabella and Philip
Height   Unknown
Modeller   Miss Mitchell-Smith
Introduced   1955
Rarity   A

No records exist except for single written entries dated April 1955 and October of the same year. It is likely neither figure was ever produced.

3541-3543
Name   Set of Three London Cries
(second series)
Height   Unknown
Modeller   Agnes Pinder-Davis
Introduced   1955
Rarity   A
3541   Rose (second version)
3542   Violets
3543   Heather

No photographs survive of these models and no other details are listed. It is possible that, following the failure of Gwendoline Parnell's 'Cries of London' series modelled in 1938-40, it was felt that a further series would also fail, and no moulds were made.

3546 and 3547
Name   Spring Morning and Summer Day
Height   6in. and about 7½in.
Modeller   Freda Doughty
Introduced   1955
Rarity   3546 C, 3547 B

Two figures of young ladies in wide-brimmed hats. 3546 wears a long skirt and holds a basket of daffodils in her left hand. 3547 wears a swirling skirt and holds a basket in front of her. Both figures were made in two different sizes, all enjoyed only limited success and have been seen in both pale blue or green dresses. An experimental matt colouring was also tried out in 1958 but is very rare. Spring Morning continued until the early 1960s, although Summer Day was withdrawn by 1957-58. Spring Morning, was also known as Spring Morn and both were reintroduced in the 1980s.
(3546, *Colour plate 14*).

3550 and 3551
Name   Balinese Dancers (small size)
Height   Unknown
Modeller   Agnes Pinder-Davis
Introduced   1955
Rarity   A

Smaller-sized versions of the larger Balinese and Siamese dancers (3473 and 3474), which had proved so difficult to make. George Morris was responsible for reducing the size and he believes only two of each were made. It is not known if these were coloured.

3552-3556

Name	Brer Fox and Brer Rabbit (second version)
Height	Unknown
Modeller	Peggy Foy
Introduced	1955
Rarity	A

A set of five models of which no details exist except a single entry listing the name and modeller. 3552 is Brer Fox, while 3553-3556 are all of Brer Rabbit. Like the following figures by Peggy Foy, it is unlikely that the models were ever cast for production. Brer Fox and Brer Rabbit were both characters in the Uncle Remus stories by Joel Chandler Harris.

3558 and 3559

Name	White Boy and Piccaninny
Height	Unknown
Modeller	Peggy Foy
Introduced	1955
Rarity	A

Two figures listed only by a single entry in one book, no photographs or details surviving. The figures were probably not produced. 'Piccaninny' derives from the Spanish *Pequeno* meaning 'small' and was used in the West Indies and the American South to describe coloured children. The figures may well have been companions to the Brer Fox and Brer Rabbit series, also not put into production.

3560

Name	Daisy
Height	Unknown
Modeller	Agnes Pinder-Davis
Introduced	1955
Rarity	A

Probably a fourth suggested model in Miss Pinder-Davis's London Cries series (3541-3543). Again no photograph or details survive and the figure was probably not produced. The date 28th November 1955 is pencilled against the entry.

3561 and 3562

Name	Chanticleer and Gamecock
Height	Unknown
Modeller	Doris Lindner
Introduced	1955
Rarity	B

Two elaborate models of cockerels on circular bases. Both have high looped tails and Chanticleer has a prominent comb and wattle. Chanticleer is a traditional name for a cockerel and was used by Chaucer. A small number were made and sold only in white. Also made in unglazed biscuit selling for £3. 15s. each in 1955.

3569

Name	The Seamstress
Height	6in.
Modeller	Freda Doughty
Introduced	1956
Rarity	C

A figure of a young lady in an old-fashioned long dress with a stole draped over her arms and shoulders and held in her raised hand, a pair of scissors hung from her waist. Few factory records exist, and one of the few examples we have seen is that illustrated with yellow dress and bright gold edging to her stole and scissors. (*Colour plate 79*)

3570 and 3571

Name	Pair of Fox and Hounds Lying

(*See* 2997 and 2998 for description.)

3572-3576 and 3579

Name	Tropical Fish Series
Height	Approx. 5½in.
Modeller	Ronald Van Ruyckevelt
Introduced	1956
Rarity	G

A series of six realistic models of fish in their natural setting, the coral-floored lagoons of Bermuda. Ronald Van Ruyckevelt visited the coral reefs to see for himself the colourful fish and his sketches and models became an important series of porcelain studies. He modelled seven large groups issued as Limited Editions and therefore falling outside the scope of this book, but at the same time he produced six smaller versions, each of a single fish or several small fish among coral. All were naturalistically coloured with a matt finish and could also be bought in a white glazed version. See also page 49.

3572
Name   Red Hind
A small compressed sea-bass found off Bermuda, the West Indies and the American Atlantic coast. Usually reddish with red spots, it has black-edged fins and grows up to 18in.

3573
Name   Four-Eyed Butterfly fish
So called because of a black spot near the tail resembling an eye. Delicately coloured in pinky brown and yellow, it is found off Bermuda, the West Indies, Florida and Panama, and grows to 6in. The model depicts two fish with spiky coral and brain coral.

3574
Name   Blue Angel Fish
A medium-sized fish with streamer-like extensions of dorsal and anal fins, it exhibits a blueish tinge and grows to about 18in. It is found off Bermuda, the West Indies and Florida. (*Colour plate 20*)

3575
Name   Sergeant-Major Fish
A small compressed fish of bluish-green colour shading to yellow with black vertical stripes which give it its name. It is found widely distributed around America and the Caribbean. It grows to 6in. and is an inquisitive fish, unafraid of man.

3576
Name   Yellow Grunt Fish
A model of three small fish among tall coral. The Yellow Grunt is an elongated, compressed fish, yellowish with horizontal blue stripes, and so-called because of the deep muffled sound it makes. It grows to 18in. and is common off Bermuda and the West Indies, and from Florida to Brazil.

3579
Name   Spade Fish
A large compressed deep-bodied fish of pearly-grey colour, with dark vertical stripes. It grows up to three feet and is found off Bermuda, the West Indies and parts of the American Atlantic coast. (*Colour plate 20*)

3581 - 3584
Name   The Azori Cockerels
Height   Unknown
Modeller   A. Azori
Introduced 1956
Rarity   B
A set of four models on rectangular bases moulded with leaves and grasses. Little is known about the series or their exotic names. They were made in glazed white, or with limited colouring, selling for £3. 6s. each in February 1957. Production was fairly limited.

3581
Name   Liserion
A cockerel, upright with beak raised.

3582
Name   Marguerite
A hen, looking downwards.

3583
Name   Coquelicot
A cockerel, upright.

3584
Name   Anemone
A cockerel, upright with beak raised.

3585-3588
Name   Chinoiserie Figures on Plinths
Height   11¼″
Modeller   A. Azori
Introduced 1956
Rarity   D
A set of four figures, each of a man or a woman seated on a cylindrical plinth raised on a square base. They resemble the eighteenth-century chinoiserie style of terracotta figures and were made in totally unglazed white biscuit bone china. It is possible that the figures represent four of the five senses: taste, smell, touch and sight. (3586 and 3588 *See* illustration on page 38).

3585
Name   Le Panier
A man holding fruit in a basket.

3586
Name   La Fleur
A lady with flowers in a basket.

3587
Name   L'Oiseau
A man holding a bird and a birdcage.

3588
Name   La Miroir
A lady looking in a mirror and adjusting her hair.

3597-3601
A pencil note in one book records that these numbers were reserved for Freda Doughty's models Chamberlain, Cardinal, Archbishop, etc. These models were probably never delivered or the moulds not completed.

3607 and 3620
Name   Clarissa and Amanda
Height   About 7"
Modeller   Neal French
Introduced   1956 and 1957
Rarity   B
A pair of figures of ladies in Victorian style modelled from actual costumes in the Victoria and Albert Museum. Clarissa looks longingly at a single rose held in her left hand whilst Amanda looks upwards with her right hand raised pointing over her shoulder. Both wear open robes over long petticoats, Amanda's sleeveless dress with a *décolleté* neckline. Neal French came to the Worcester factory fresh from art college and brought a figure of a violinist he had modelled as a student. Joseph Gimson saw this and said that the factory needed to produce a series of 'fashion' figures in the style of the violinist, to be sold cheaply. Neal produced Clarissa and Amanda, but in the meantime Freda Doughty had modelled Invitation and Red Ribbons (3698 and 3699) and Ruth van Ruyckevelt was working on figures of ladies in similar style. It seems quite likely that Mr. Gimson asked his various modellers to work on the same theme to see who came up with the best figures. At this time, however, Ronald van Ruyckevelt suggested that his wife's figures would go well as Limited Editions and Mr. Gimson agreed, but did not want two series of similar models. Neal French's figures, therefore, were produced in only small numbers and Clarissa probably failed also because the girl looks downwards, never a good selling point. Clarissa was decorated white, green and red, Amanda with a green top to her blue dress. Several other colourings were also tried out. *(Colour plate 84)*

3608-3614
Name   Alice in Wonderland Series
Modeller   Freda Doughty
Introduced   1957
Rarity   B
A set of seven figures of characters appearing in the popular stories of Lewis Carroll. The last major series to be modelled by Freda Doughty, and certainly very different in style from her popular models of children, it was clearly inspired by the original book illustrations by Tenniel. Miss Doughty updated the characters, producing charming and inexpensive figures. Rather surprisingly, the models do not appear to have sold well and were possibly not even sold in England. We have seen more of them in the United States, which leads us to suspect that the few that were made were intended for export. The colourings are as illustrated in Colour plate 73, and most of those shown are the original colour standards painted by Freda Doughty. See also page 26.

3608
Name   Alice
Height   4in.
Alice kneels on the ground, her left hand by her side and her right hand touching her chin. Her hair is golden-yellow and her dress blue, her white apron having red pockets and edges. *(Colour plate 73)*

3609
Name   Cheshire Cat
Height   3½ in.
A cat sits with tail curled around his feet,

a very wide grin on his face. His fur is purplish-blue and his mouth bright red with teeth showing. He has green and black eyes. (*Colour plate 73*)

3610
Name   Mock Turtle
Height   3 ⅛ in.
A comical figure with a cow's head and turtle's carapace, sitting upright and wiping away the tears with his green flippers. (*Colour plate 73*)

3611
Name   White Rabbit
Height   4in.
The elegantly dressed rabbit stands, his hands holding his white gloves to his waist. He wears a pale red coat and yellow waistcoat with black buttons. He also wears a black bow tie and his ears and features are tinted pink. (*Colour plate 73*)

3612
Name   The Duchess
Height   4in.
The Duchess stands, a smile on her face, holding her bright purple and yellow robes to her chest. Her golden-yellow hair is adorned with a purple and white head-dress. (*Colour plate 73*)

3613
Name   The Dodo
Height   3 ¼ in.
The rather peculiar Dodo stands with its hands by its side, a brown stick in the left hand but modelled on the yellow front of the body. The back is brown and the face light green with red bill, features and feet. (*Colour plate 73*)

3614
Name   Father William
Height   3 ¼ in.
Father William sits on a black stool, a white pipe held in his right hand. He wears a blue coat, yellow waistcoat with black buttons and light brown trousers. His necktie is red and small tufts of white hair are on each side of his face. (*Colour plate 73*)

3615
Name   Long-Haired Cat
Height   3 ½ in.
Modeller   Freda Doughty
Introduced 1957
Rarity   F
A model of a cat with long fur, sitting upright, its tail curled underneath. The cat could be painted either in ginger and white or as a grey Persian, and was a popular model. it was still in production in the mid-1970s. (*Colour plate 4 for the original standard painted by Miss Doughty*)

3616
Name   Short-haired Cat
Height   3in.
Modeller   Freda Doughty
Introduced 1957
Rarity   F
A model of a cat with short fur, also sitting upright with its tail curled underneath. It could be painted in a number of styles, including tortoise-shell, grey or ginger. Again proving very popular, it was still made in the mid-1970s

3620
Name   Amanda
(See 3607 for description.)

3629
Name   First Dance
Height   7in.
Modeller   Freda Doughty
Introduced 1957
Rarity   G
A figure of a young lady nervously accepting an invitation to dance. She wears a long wide skirt hitched up by her left hand. By far the most successful of Freda Doughty's 1950s models of children, First Dance was still being produced in 1979. The records give the colouring as a green dress and pink shawl with blue and yellow spots and black tassels. Other colourings are known. (*Colour plate 15*)

3630
Name   Sweet Anne
Height   7in.
Modeller   Freda Doughty
Introduced 1957
Rarity   G

A figure of a young girl in a long skirt, her hands held in front of her. Miss Doughty's last successful figure, it sold very well and at the time of writing is still in production. The dress is coloured blue. (*Colour plate 15*)

3638

Name	Wednesday's Child (new version)
Height	Unknown
Modeller	Freda Doughty
Introduced	1957
Rarity	A

A note in the factory records reads 'New Wednesday's Child to replace 3259'. (*See* entry under the original shape number.)

3645-3650

Name	Small American Bird Series
Height	Approx. 3in.
Modeller	Ronald Van Ruyckevelt
Introduced	1958
Rarity	F

A series of six small models of popular American birds, each on a simple leaf-moulded base. They are naturalistically coloured and finished in matt enamels to give a more realistic look. Following the success of the British Bird series by Eva Soper, the factory asked Van Ruyckevelt for similar models aimed at the important American market. They sold well at first, being much cheaper than the American Doughty Birds, but never proved as popular as Miss Soper's English birds, being withdrawn in the early 1970s

3645

Name	Cardinal

3646

Name	Jay (American version)

3647

Name	Robin (American version)

3648

Name	Waxwing

3649

Name	Bluebird

3650

Name	Western Tanager

3654

Name	Spanish Beauty
Height	Unknown
Modeller	Freda Doughty
Introduced	1958
Rarity	A

A note written in one of the shape books lists 'Spanish Girl', crossed out and replaced by the name 'Spanish Beauty' with the date 29th May 1958. Ruth Van Ruyckevelt's name has been crossed out and replaced by that of Freda Doughty. No other details are recorded and it is unlikely that the figure was produced.

3655

Name	Surprise
Height	7 ½ in.
Modeller	Freda Doughty
Introduced	1958
Rarity	B

A figure of a girl in a wide skirt tied with a sash around her waist, her gloved hands held up in front of her. The figure tries to convey an expression of surprise on the girl's face, but it has to be said that the effect has not really been strikingly achieved. A certain number were made but the figure was soon withdrawn.

3656

Name	Mayflower
Height	7 ½ in.
Modeller	Freda Doughty
Introduced	1958
Rarity	B

A figure of a boy dressed in naval costume of the eighteenth century, a blue jacket with yellow buttons and epaulettes, a yellow waistcoat and brown knee-length breeches. His hair is in a pigtail tied by a black bow, a tricorn hat and a telescope by his side on the shaped base. He holds a model of a ship in full sail in his arms. it is a finely modelled figure, and an unusual attempt at an historical subject for Miss Doughty. The cheerful young face, however, was more suited to her Worcester Children and the figure sadly proved unpopular. To help sell the model it was redesigned in 1963 on a plain base without hat or telescope, as shape 3761. This does not seem to have been put into production, and the original version was quickly withdrawn. (*Colour plate 1*)

3667
Name   The Winner, with Stable Boy
Height   11¼in.
Modeller   Doris Lindner
Introduced   1959
Rarity   A

We illustrate in Colour plate 134 the original colour design for this impressive equestrian study as it was intended to be produced. A stable boy dressed in a smart grey suit leads a racehorse back to the paddock after a successful race. The jockey, still mounted, holds his whip and lifts the peak of his cap to acknowledge the cheers of the crowd. The green base is oval and fits into a wooden plinth. It proved a very complicated group to support and fire, with intricate painted metal fittings, and it was decided that it was too difficult to produce in this form. It is probable that two completed groups were made before the factory decided to drop the stable boy. A note in the shape book reads: 'Cancelled per JDM Memo'. Mr J. D. Milne was the Managing Director, who saw this unlimited model as a financial disaster.
(*Colour plate 134*)

3671
Name   The Winner (Grey or Brown Horse)
Height   11¼in.
Modeller   Doris Lindner
Introduced   1959
Rarity   G

Miss Lindner's model (3667) was altered only by the omission of the stable boy and a slight shortening of the plinth. The group in this form proved much more practical and was an instant success. It was produced in matt colours, the horse painted either grey or brown, the jockey wearing Her Majesty The Queen's racing colours. At an extra cost customers could have the model painted in their own racing colours if desired. At the time of writing The Winner is still in production.

3675 and 3677
Name   Coldstream Guards Officer (third version) and Scots Guards Officer
Height   11¾in. and 11¼in.
Modeller   Frederick Gertner
Introduced   1959
Rarity   G

Aspreys, the London retailers, asked the factory to update some of the Historical Military Figures which Frederick Gertner had modelled in 1918. *See* 2676 for the original Coldstream Guards Officer and 2657 for the Scots Guards Officer, which was originally an Officer of the Seaforth Highlanders.

3679
Name   Falconer
Height   7in.
Modeller   Freda Doughty
Introduced   1959
Rarity   B

Intended as a companion to Mayflower (3656) although in costume of an earlier period. The Falconer is a boy dressed in Elizabethan costume standing with a hawk on his arm. Falconry was a popular sport in the sixteenth century and Freda Doughty's model is very detailed in its historical treatment of the subject. However, like Mayflower, the childish face does not seem to fit in, and very few seem to have sold. It was soon withdrawn.

3684
Name   One Circus Horse
Height   Unknown
Modeller   Doris Lindner
Introduced   1969
Rarity   A

Two written entries in the Factory records list this model as '1 Circus horse, Do. Lindner'. It is possible that the intention was to issue separately one of the horses from the larger groups modelled in 1937 as 3179 and 3180. No further details are noted.

3698

Name	Invitation
Height	8 ¾ in.
Modeller	Freda Doughty
Introduced	1960
Rarity	A

The most elaborate costume figure attempted by Freda Doughty, Invitation depicts a young lady dressed in Victorian costume adorned with ribbons and a full skirt hung with festoons over a finely ribbed petticoat, a bow around her neck. In one hand she holds an envelope, in the other an invitation just received to a ball. A complicated figure to make, involving many different moulds for the skirt and long sleeves, it proved too costly for the public, who preferred the new limited editions series by Ruth van Ruyckevelt. Invitation was probably not put into full production. (*Colour plate 51*)

3699

Name	Red Ribbons
Height	Unknown
Modeller	Freda Doughty
Introduced	1960
Rarity	A

A figure of a girl in a smart dress with wide sleeves and long swirling skirt, tying a bow around her neck, a large bow fixing a sash around her waist. She stands on a circular base. Like 3698, an ambitious model in Victorian costume which was complicated to make and had to be painted with tiny dots. The factory tried the figure out at various times during the 1960s, but it never sold well and was probably not put into full production.

3714

Name	Siamese Cat
Height	Unknown
Modeller	Freda Doughty
Introduced	1961
Rarity	A

Following the success of Miss Doughty's two cat models (3615 and 3616) a further model was intended to be added to the series. No details survive and the Siamese Cat may never have been put into production.

3720

Name	Will You, Won't You?
Height	Unknown
Modeller	Freda Doughty
Introduced	1961
Rarity	A

A large figure of a young lady in a long swirling skirt which is appliquéd with fine floral festoons. She holds in her outstretched hands a pair of silver sugar tongs and seems to be asking if sugar is to be taken in the tea. With its complicated Victorian costume requring detailed flower modelling, it failed for the same reasons as did Miss Doughty's similar large figures of the previous year (3698 and 3699). This series was Miss Doughty's last work for Worcester before she retired to nurse her ailing sister Dorothy. It is a shame that her last models were failures, as her little children still sold in great numbers and were to continue to do so for many years to come.

3747, 3748 and 3754-3757

Name	Playtime Series
Height	5in. – 5 ¼ in.
Modeller	Neal French
Introduced	1962
Rarity	B

A set of six models of children, the modeller's instructions being to bring the Freda Doughty children up to date and show children doing the things that they really do in modern times. The series was a failure and is discussed at length on pages 27 and 29. A small number of sets were sold fully coloured, and many single figures were sold off in white.

3747

Name	Young England

A boy sits on a box, a football in front of his feet and football boots to the left of the box. He dreams of playing for England in the future. (*Colour plate 45*)

3748

Name	Treasure Trove

The most expensive of the set to produce, a girl kneels beside her jewellery box placed on a cushion. She holds her hands out in front of her as she tries on a bracelet. (*Colour plate 45*)

3754
Name   Poupée
A girl kneels on one leg and holds a doll in her hands, cradling it against her body. (*Colour plate 45*)

3755
Name   Master Mariner
A boy crouches down upon the ground, holding a toy boat in his hands.

3756
Name   First Aid
A girl sits on a stool lovingly caring for her teddy bear, who is clearly unwell. She wears a white band painted with a red cross around her head. (*Colour plate 45*)

3757
Name   Sheriff
A boy sits on a rock, a gun held in his right hand aimed in front of him and a cowboy hat on his back. (*Colour plate 45*)

3760
Name   Fantails
(See 3418 for description.)

3809 and 3810
Name   Kate Greenaway figures (new version)
Height   Unknown
Modeller   Ronald Van Ruyckevelt
Introduced 1966
Rarity   A
A pair of figures of smartly dressed Victorian children. The boy holds a boater by his side, and the girl also holds a hat beside her. A photograph in the shape books is of the plasticine models only, and the figures almost certainly did not go into production.

No Shape Number
Name   Fontainebleau series
Height   About 4 ½ in.
Modeller   Neal French
Introduced 1970 or 1971
Rarity   D
A set of six different figures, each available in two colourings, making twelve named

models in all. After the eighteenth-century German style, particularly that of Bustelli, they depict young men and women in simple costumes. They were painted in bright colours and stand on rock bases. The figures were made in hard true porcelain in a new factory at Diglis, near to the existing works. This new factory was intended for the mass production of hard porcelain for 'oven-to-tableware' and the Art Director, Professor Baker, was concerned that Royal Worcester was 'using the finest ceramic materials in the world known to man to make chamberpots'. He felt that it should be possible to produce the chamberpots but make much more effective use of the kiln per cubic inch by placing small thin figures in spaces in the kiln. Following the successful introduction of Limited Edition models 'Day and Night' and 'The Seasons' by Arnold Machin, Professor Baker asked Neal French to model a set of figures, intending them to be left white with Ormolu bases. When the Directors saw them they liked them but insisted that they be coloured. This annoyed Professor Baker because the object of the exercise was to produce cheap figures. Neal himself considered that colouring much improved them, but it did defeat the original intention.

The series was originally to be called 'Glyndebourne' but one of the Directors was also a Director of Glyndebourne and made it clear that this would be quite unacceptable. Fontainebleau was the second choice, and Neal chose the twelve individual names from a book. They were intended to be grouped as table decorations, the idea being that people would want to buy more than one of them. Unfortunately they were not bought as table decorations and Neal felt that they really needed to be raised well above the table level as they were in too dangerous a position on the table top. Probably only fifty coloured sets were sold, although as many white models were issued, generally unmarked. The name given to each figure is recorded in the photograph (*Colour plate 128*).

Introduction to Colour Plates

The following pages of colour illustrate an enormous number of the Royal Worcester figures recorded in this book. These superb photographs, all taken specially, will give the reader an idea of the standard of modelling and decoration that epitomizes the figures. Particular attention should be paid to the exceptional quality of painting to be seen on the figures made in the 1930s, and also to the range of different colour schemes that can be found on the same figure.

Generally speaking, the standard of painting declined after the 1950s and, partly for this reason, we have as far as possible indicated the date code appearing on each figure illustrated. The collector should always look carefully at the quality of decoration and prefer a nicely painted example to one which may not have received the same level of attention and detail from the paintress. The photographs will assist and are worth close examination. Are the details of the faces carefully and sensitively done, or just blobs of colour? Are the clothes beautifully shaded down the folds, or just a plain overall colour? Look for the special effects of shot gold and shot silks.

The colour photographs are, therefore, of the greatest importance and form a very significant part of the book. We hope that you will enjoy looking at these lovely things and learn from them.

All are in private collections unless stated otherwise.

Plate 1. Shape 3656, Mayflower, modelled by Freda Doughty, black mark with copyright 1962.

Plate 2. Shape 3270, Playmates, modelled by Freda Doughty, black mark, dated 1949.

Plate 3. Shape 3160, Bubbles, modelled by Freda Doughty, black mark, dated 1956. (Bygones of Worcester)

Plate 4. Shape 3615, Long-Haired Cat, original colour standard painted by Freda Doughty, dated 1957. (Dyson Perrins Museum)

Plate 5. Shape 2993, Sitting Fox, modelled by Doris Lindner, black mark, dated after 1960.

Plate 6. Shape 3433, Young Farmer, modelled by Freda Doughty, black mark, dated after 1960.

Plate 7. Shape 3760, Fantails, modelled by Freda Doughty, black mark, dated after 1960.

Plate 8. Shape 2881, Sauce, modelled by Phoebe Stabler, puce mark and title, dated 1935.

Plate 9. Shape 3306, Little Boy Blue, modelled by Freda Doughty, black mark, dated 1952.

Plate 10. Shape 3133, Puppy, modelled by Doris Lindner, puce mark, dated 1940.

Plate 11. Shape 2393, Pierrot with Ruff modelled by Ernest Evans, impressed mark, unglazed biscuit porcelain, c. 1905.

Plate 12. Shape 3087, Boy with Parakeet, modelled by Freda Doughty, black mark, dated after 1960.

Plate 13. Shape 3091, Bust of George V, modelled by Gwendoline Parnell, unmarked, 1935.

Plate 14. Shape 3546, Spring Morning, modelled by Freda Doughty, unmarked, c. 1955.

Plate 15. Left: shape 3630, Sweet Anne, modelled by Freda Doughty. Right: shape 3629, First Dance, modelled by Freda Doughty. Both with black marks, dated after 1960.

Plate 16. Shape 2697, Nude Bather Seated on Plinth, modeller unknown, printed Crownware mark, date code for 1919. (Dyson Perrins Museum)

Plate 17. Left: shape 3008, Sea Breeze, modelled by Freda Doughty. Right: shape 3225, Dancing Waves, also by Freda Doughty. Both with black marks, dated 1951.

Plate 18. Left: shape 2900, Barbara, Polar Bear, modelled by Ethelwyn Baker, puce mark and title, dated 1932. Right: shape 3063, Polar Bear Looking Up, modelled by Doris Lindner, unmarked.

Plate 19. The Victorian Musicians Series, modelled by Ethelwyn Baker. Left: shape 2898, The Harpist. Centre: shape 2899, The Lute Player. Right: shape 2902, The Song. All with puce marks and titles, dated 1931.

Plate 20. Tropical Fish Series, modelled by Ronald Van Ruyckevelt. Left: shape 3574, Blue Angel Fish, dated 1968, unfinished. Right: shape 3579, Spade Fish, dated 1968.

Plate 21. Shape 2582, French Soldier, from the First World War Series, modeller unknown, green mark, dated 1916.

Plate 22. Shape 3420, Female Chinese Figure, modelled by Agnes Pinder-Davis, black mark, dated 1955. (Dyson Perrins Museum)

Plate 23. Shape 2924, modelled by Freda Doughty. Left: titled Mother Machree, black mark, dated 1951. Right: titled The Fortune Teller, puce mark, dated 1933. (Bygones of Worcester)

Plate 24. Shape 3096, Elephant, modelled by E. Evans, puce mark, dated 1935. (Dyson Perrins Museum)

Plate 25. The Small Dogs Series modelled by Doris Lindner. Top row: shape 3243, Welsh Corgi; shape 2946, Scottie; shape 3034, Pekinese sitting; shape 3294, Dachsund (dark). Second row: shape 3026, Airedale Terrier standing; shape 3293, Dalmatian; shape 3295, Alsatian. Third row: shape 2943, Dandie Dinmont; shape 2942, Terrier seated, as Airedale, and as Wire-haired; shape 3033, Cocker Spaniel; shape 3029, Scottie (light colouring). Bottom row: shape 2941, Pekinese standing; shape 3294, Dachsund (light); shape 2945, Bulldog; shape 3028, Sealyham. Various date codes.

Plate 26. Shape 2936, Argentina, modelled by Anne Acheson, puce mark and title, dated 1933.

Plate 27. Shape 2886, The Old Goat Woman, modelled by Phoebe Stabler, puce mark and title, dated 1931.

Plate 28. Shape 2949, The Dancers, modelled by Doris Lindner, puce mark and title, dated 1932. (Dyson Perrins Museum)

Plate 29. Shape 2645, Standing Soldier, First World War Series, modelled by William Pointon, green mark, dated 1916.

Plate 30. Nursery Rhymes Series, modelled by Freda Doughty. Left: shape 3301, Little Miss Muffet, black mark 1943-1948. Centre: shape 3304, Goosey Goosey Gander, black mark, 1943-1948. Right: shape 3302, Babes in the Wood, puce mark and title, dated 1940.

Plate 31. Shapes 2906 and 2905, June and Noel, modelled by Sybil Williams and Jessamine Bray. From left: large June, dated 1936; small June, dated 1934; small Noel, dated 1932; large Noel, dated 1936. (Bygones of Worcester and Private Collections)

Plate 32. Shape 3082, The First Cuckoo, modelled by Freda Doughty. Left and centre: black marks with puce titles, 1943-1948. Right: puce mark and title, dated 1936. (Bygones of Worcester and Private Collection)

Plate 33. Zoo Babies Series, modelled by Doris Lindner. Top: shape 3318, Tigers – Maurice and Sonia, black mark, 1943-1948. Bottom: shape 3313, Leopards – Nelson and Norah, puce mark, 1943-1948.

Plate 34. Children of the Nations Series, modelled by Freda Doughty. Left: shape 3069, Greece, black mark, dated 1953. Centre: shape 3074, Holland, black mark, dated 1949. Right: shape 3066, Egypt, black mark, dated 1950.

Plate 35. Shapes 2903 and 2904, Bluebeard and Fatima, modelled by Sybil Williams and Jessamine Bray, puce marks and titles, dated 1931. (Bygones of Worcester)

Plate 36. Shapes 3194 and 3195, Chinese Dancers, modelled by Gwendoline Parnell, black marks, dated 1935. (Bygones of Worcester)

Plate 37. Chinoiserie Children, modelled by Gwendoline Parnell. Left: shape 3348, black mark, with no date code. Right: shape 3362, black mark, dated 1959.

Plate 38. Children of the Nations Series, modelled by Freda Doughty, Left: shape 3103, Wales, black smark, dated 1954. Centre: shape 3104, Scotland, black mark dated 1955. Right: shape 3178, Ireland, puce mark, dated 1940.

Plate 39. Shape 3108, Amaryllis, modelled by Gwendoline Parnell, black mark, dated 1955. (Dyson Perrins Museum)

Plate 40. Shapes 2869 and 2868, Pierrot and Harlequin, modelled by Doris Lindner, puce marks and titles, dated 1931 and 1934.

Plate 41. Shape 3106, The Duchess's Dress, modelled by Freda Doughty. Left: small size, puce mark and title, dated 1940. Right: large size, puce mark and title, dated 1937.

Plate 42. Left: shape 2884, Coquette. Right: shape 2883, Little Dancer. Both modelled by Phoebe Stabler, puce marks and titles, dated 1932.

Plate 43. Shape 3088, Dance, modelled by Doris Lindner, puce mark and title, dated 1936.

Plate 44. Group of white Nudes. From left: shape 3030, Naiad, modelled by Doris Lindner; shape 2689, Nude Female with Slipper; shape 2698, Nude Bather Kneeling; shape 2805, Female Nude Seated, in Crownware. All unmarked.

Plate 45. The Playtime Series, modelled by Neal French. From left: shape 3757, Sheriff; shape 3754, Poupée; shape 3756, First Aid; shape 3748, Treasure Trove; shape 3747, Young England; black marks with copyright 1963. (Bygones of Worcester)

Plate 46. Days of the Week Series, modelled by Freda Doughty. From left: shape 3523, Friday's Girl (bird missing), original colour standard painted by Miss Doughty, 1954; shape 3262, Saturday's Girl, dated after 1960; shape 3259, Wednesday's Girl, dated after 1960; shape 3256, Sunday's Boy, dated 1955; shape 3261, Friday's Boy, dated after 1960.

Plate 47. Shape 3116, Over the Sticks, modelled by Doris Lindner, black mark, dated 1962.

Plate 48. Left: shape 3150, Two Babies, modelled by Freda Doughty, puce mark dated 1940. Right: shape 3076, Woodland Dance, also by Freda Doughty, black mark, dated after 1960.

Plate 49. Shape 3149, Sister, modelled by Freda Doughty, black mark dated 1951.

Plate 50. Shape 3141, Kittens, modelled by Doris Lindner, puce mark, dated 1936. Right: shape 3130, Spaniel Puppy Group, black mark dated 1952.

Plate 51. Shape 3698, Invitation, modelled by Freda Doughty, unmarked, c.1960.

Plate 52. Shapes 3145 and 3144, The Thief and Magnolia Bud, modelled by Gwendoline Parnell, black marks dated 1958. (Bygones of Worcester and Private Collection)

Plate 53. Shape 2887, Pick-a-Back, modelled by Phoebe Stabler, puce mark and title, dated 1931.

Plate 54. Shape 3083, Sunshine, modelled by Freda Doughty, black mark with puce script, 1943-1948.

Plate 55. Shape 2855, Bonzo, modeller unknown, puce mark, dated 1930.

Plate 56. Shape 3085, Poodle, Champion Spriggan Bell, modelled by Doris Lindner, gold mark, dated 1935.

Plate 57. The Netsuke Animals Series. Left: shape 2636, Double Mouse, green mark, dated 1916. Right: shape 2624, Toad, dated 1916, date code unknown.

Plate 58. Netsuke Animals Series. Top row: shape 2612, Ape, gold mark, dated 1916; shape 2623, Quail, black mark, dated 1931; shape 2605, Snail, unmarked. Bottom row: shape 2606, Cheetah, green mark dated 1916; shape 2609, Cow, gold mark, dated 1916.

Plate 59. Shape 2877. Young Horse, modelled by Eric Aumonier, puce mark and title, dated 1934.

Plate 60. Foxhounds, modelled by Aline Ellis. Top: shape 3385, puce mark with mark of Alex Dickens dated 1943. Bottom: shape 3386, black mark, no date code.

Plate 61. Shape 3387, Fox, modelled by Aline Ellis, puce printed mark and title, mark of Alex Dickens, dated 1943.

Plate 62. Shape 2917. Sea Urchin, modelled by Margaret Cane, puce mark and title. dated 1936.

Plate 63. Shape 3012, Spring, modelled by Freda Doughty, puce mark, dated 1937. (Bygones of Worcester)

Plate 64. Shape 3369, Stowaways, modelled by Eillen Soper, puce mark with no date code. (Photograph Giles Padmore)

Plate 65. Shape 3127, Looking Over Shoulder, modelled by Henri Bargas, puce mark and title, dated 1936.

Plate 66. Left: shape 2914. Mischief, modelled by Freda Doughty, puce mark dated 1941. Right: shape 2912, Michael, also modelled by Freda Doughty, black mark, dated 1951.

Plate 67. Days of the Week Series, modelled by Freda Doughty. From left: shape 3257, Monday's Girl; shape 3260, Thursday's Boy; shape 3518, Sunday's Girl; shape 3524, Saturday's Boy. All with black marks, dated after 1960.

Plate 68. Shape 2918, Sleepy Boy, modelled by Margaret Cane, puce marks. Top: 1931. Left: 1938. Right: 1935. (Bygones of Worcester)

Plate 69. Months of the Year Series, modelled by Freda Doughty. From left: shape 3416, April, dated after 1960; shape 3452, January, dated 1958; shape 3453, February, dated 1955; shape 3454, March, dated after 1960.

Plate 70. Children of the Nations Series, modelled by Freda Doughty. Left: shape 3068, Burmah, black mark, dated 1950. Centre: shape 3073, China, black mark, dated after 1960. Right: shape 3071, India, puce mark, dated 1934.

Plate 71. Months of the Year Series, modelled by Freda Doughty. From left: shape 3417, October, dated after 1960; shape 3458, December, dated 1956; shape 3457, September, dated 1955; shape 3418, November, dated 1956.

Plate 72. Days of the Week series, modelled by Freda Doughty. From left: shape 3258, Tuesday's Girl, dated after 1960; shape 3534, Tuesday's Boy, dated 1955; shape 3521, Wednesday's Boy, dated after 1960; shape 3519, Monday's Boy, dated after 1960; shape 3522, Thursday's Girl, dated after 1960.

Plate 73. Alice in Wonderland Series, modelled by Freda Doughty. Top row: shape 3611, White Rabbit; shape 3608, Alice; shape 3613, The Dodo. Bottom row: shape 3612, The Duchess; shape 3609, Cheshire Cat; shape 3610, Mock Turtle; shape 3614, Father William. The last with black mark, dated 1958, all others original factory standards, each signed 'Pattern 1957 F.G.D.'

Plate 74. Shape 2895, Giraffes, modelled by Stella Crofts, puce mark and title, dated 1931. (Dyson Perrins Museum)

Plate 75. Shape 2728, Kate Greenaway Girl (second version), probably modelled by James Hadley, unmarked circa 1920.

Plate 76. Shape 3226, Only Me, modelled by Freda Doughty, black mark, dated 1949.

Plate 77. Shape 2213, Jester (first version), 'modelled by E. Evans 1902' in puce script. Blue mark, dated 1931, original factory price code CH/E (i.e. 12s. 3d.) on base.

Plate 78. Shape 3081, Grandmother's Dress, modelled by Freda Doughty, black mark, dated 1954.

Plate 79. Shape 3569, The Seamstress, modelled by Freda Doughty, black mark, dated 1958.

Plate 80. Shape 3006. Sweet Nell of Old Drury, modelled by Anne Acheson, puce mark and title, dated 1936.

Plate 81. Shape 3224, The Bridesmaid, modelled by Freda Doughty, black mark, dated 1949.

Plate 82. Shapes 2831 and 2841, Mr and Mrs Toby, middle size, modeller unknown, puce marks, dated 1941.

Plate 83. Shapes 2621 and 2620, Crinoline figures, modeller unknown. Left: brown mark, dated 1919. Right: green mark, dated 1918.

Plate 84. Left: shape 3620, Amanda. Right: shape 3607, Clarissa. Modelled by Neal French, both unmarked and painted by the modeller, c.1957.

Plate 85. Left: shape 2915, Joan. Right: shape 2913, Tommy, both modelled by Freda Doughty, puce marks and titles, dated 1939 and 1940.

Plate 86. Shapes 2922 and 2923, Dutch Girl and Dutch Boy, modelled by Frederick Gertner. Left: unmarked,. but with puce title. Right: puce mark, dated 1941.

Plate 87. Left: shape 3154, The Drum, modelled by Gwendoline Parnell, black mark with puce title, dated 1950. Right: shape 3097, Lady Bountiful, also by Gwendoline Parnell, puce mark and title, dated 1938. (Bygones of Worcester)

Plate 88. 3132 and 3131, Young Foxhounds and Young Foxes, modelled by Doris Lindner. Left: in underglaze colours, unmarked. Right: black mark, dated 1953.

Plate 89. Birds on Stumps modelled by Frederick Gertner. Left: shape 2662, Bullfinch. Right shape 2667, Goldfinch. Black marks, dated after 1960.

Plate 90. Nursery Rhymes Series, modelled by Freda Doughty. Left: shape 3305, Little Jack Horner, black mark, dated 1953. Right: shape 3303, Polly Put the Kettle On, black mark, dated after 1960.

Plate 91. Two original colour standards painted and signed by Freda Doughty. Left: shape 3456. June (second version), dated 1949. Right: shape 3455, May, not dated.

Plate 92. Shape 3094. Penguin Looking Down, modelled by Doris Lindner, puce mark and title, dated 1935. (Phillips)

Plate 93. Zoo Babies Series, modelled by Doris Lindner. Top: shape 3315, Bears – Mick and Mack, puce mark, 1943-1948. Bottom: shape 3314, Lions – Oliver and October, puce mark, dated 1940.

Plate 94. Shape 2875, Book-end Horsemen, modelled by Eric Aumonier, date code unknown.

Plate 95. Shape 3111, Bal Masqué, modelled by Gwendoline Parnell. Left: later oval base, black mark dated after 1960. Right: puce mark and title, dated 1936. (Bygones of Worcester)

Plate 96. Shape 3273, Billy Bluegums, from the Zoo Babies series modelled by Doris Lindner; puce mark with green title, dated 1939.

Plate 97. Two models in Crownware by Frederick Gertner. Left: shape CW 156, Female Budgerigar. Right: shape CW 236, Male Budgerigar. Green marks, dated 1925.

Plate 98. Months of the Year Series. modelled by Freda Doughty. From left: shape 3440. July, dated after 1960; shape 3441. August, dated after 1960; shape 3456. June (second version), dated 1959; shape 3455, May, dated after 1960.

Plate 99. Shape 2930, modelled by Anne Acheson. Top: Lavender, puce mark and script 'Lavender, B. Bragg'. Left: Marigold, puce mark and title, dated 1934. Right: Pansy, puce mark and title, dated 1934. (Bygones of Worcester and Private Collection)

Plate 100. Small British Birds, modelled by Eva Soper. Top: shape 3365, Linnets on Stump, and shape 3377, Yellow Hammers on Stump. Bottom: shape 3197, Robin; shape 3238, Bullfinch; shape 3336, Marsh Tit. All with black marks, after 1960.

Plate 101. Columbine, Harlequin and Pierrot, modeller unknown. From left: shape 2681, dated 1921, shape 2680, dated 1920; shape 2679, dated 1920; shape 2682, dated 1919. All marked in puce.

Plate 102. Shape 3138, The Planter's Daughter, modelled by Gwendoline Parnell, puce mark and title, dated 1936. (Phillips)

Plate 103. The Netsuke Animals, in white and tinted colouring, all marked in green. Top row: shape 2622, Blackcock, dated 1933; shape 2624, Toad, dated 1916; shape 2613, Ram, dated 1916; shape 2612, Ape, unmarked. Second row: shape 2623, Quail, dated 1916; shape 2607, Rabbit, dated 1916; shape 2606, Cheetah, dated 1916. Bottom row: shape 2608, Snake, recast in 1970s; shape 2604, Tortoise, no date code; shape 2610, Mouse, dated 1916.

Plate 104. The Netsuke Animals in Stained Ivory colouring. Top left: shape 2623, Quail, Top right: shape 2607, Rabbit. Bottom left: shape 2611, Fish. Bottom right, shape 2613, Ram. All with green marks dated 1916. Top centre is a small tortoise (no shape number) from an earlier birdcage by George Evans (*see* page 11), gold mark, dated 1908.

Plate 105. Farm animals and Zoo Babies Series, modelled by Doris Lindner. Top left: shape 3146, Calves, green mark, dated 1956. Right: shape 3123, Maytime, green mark, dated 1957. Bottom left: shape 3153, Kids at Play, green mark, dated 1952. Right: shape 3316, Zoo Babies – Fawns, puce mark, dated 1940.

Plate 106. Sporting Dogs Series, modelled by Doris Lindner. Top: shape 3308, Pointer, dated 1949. Left: shape 3309, Golden Retriever, dated 1950. Right: shape 3311, Clumber Spaniel, dated 1954. All marked in black.

Plate 107. Three dogs, modelled by Aline Ellis. Top: shape 3356, Ranter, puce mark and mark of Alex Dickens, dated 1942. Left: shape 3355, Mack, black mark dated 1941, original factory colour standard. Right: shape 3361, Tony, puce mark, titled in brown, dated 1941.

Plate 108. Left: shape 3360, Masquerade Girls, modelled by Freda Doughty, black mark, dated after 1960. Right: shape 3359, The Bow, also by Freda Doughty, black mark, dated 1950.

Plate 109. Shapes 3089 and 3090, Jubilee Statuettes of King George V and Queen Mary, modelled by Gwendoline Parnell, puce marks, dated 1935.

Plate 110. Shapes 3014, My Favourite, modelled by Freda Doughty, puce mark, dated 1940.

Plate 111. Four Candle Extinguishers. Left: shape 2543, Witch, puce mark, dated 1913; shape 2844, Hush, puce mark, dated 1928; shape 2568, Mandarin, puce mark, dated 1916. Right: Japanese Girl, a nineteenth-century model still produced until the 1950s as a companion to Mandarin; green mark, dated 1901.

Plate 112. Shapes 2663 and 2664, Female (left) and Male Budgerigars on Stumps, modelled by Frederick Gertner, black marks, dated after 1960.

Plate 113. Shape 3331, Toto, the cairn terrier from *The Wizard of Oz*, modelled by Aline Ellis, black mark, dated 1941.

Plate 114. Shape 3107, Applause, modelled by Gwendoline Parnell, puce mark, dated 1935. (Phillips)

Plate 115. Shape 3149, Sister, modelled by Freda Doughty, puce mark, date code unknown.

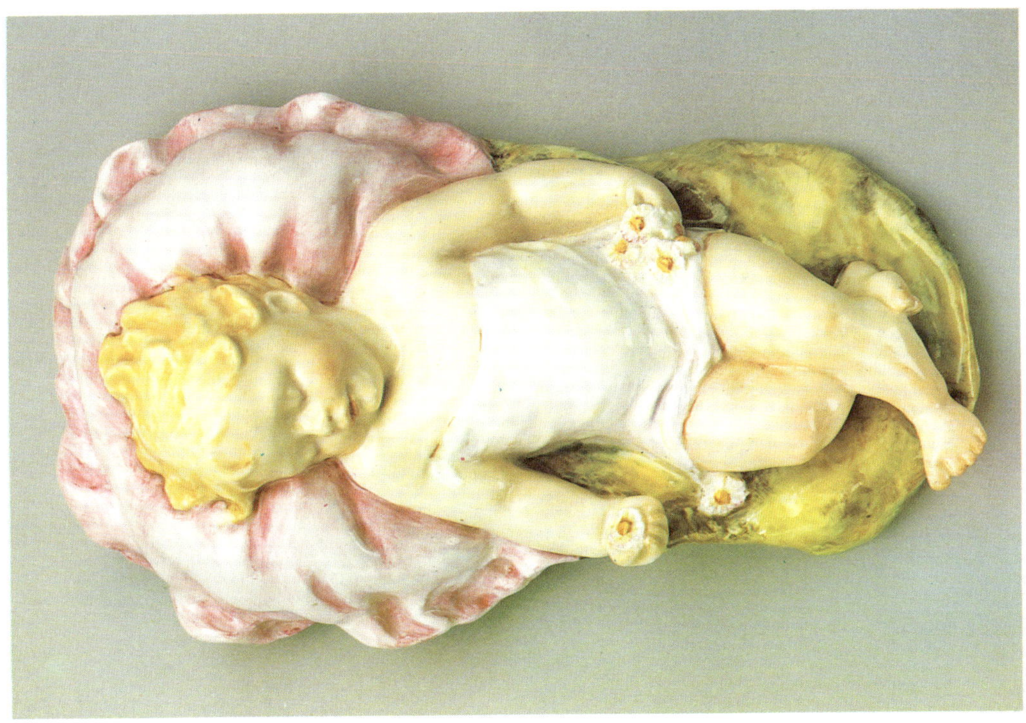

Plate 116. Shape 3009, Baby on Cushion, modelled by Frederick Gertner, puce mark, dated 1932.

Plate 117. Shape 3088, Dance, modelled by Doris Lindner, in original mottled grey colouring, dated 1935.

Plate 118. Shape 3157, Child with Butterfly, modelled by Anne Acheson, date code unknown.

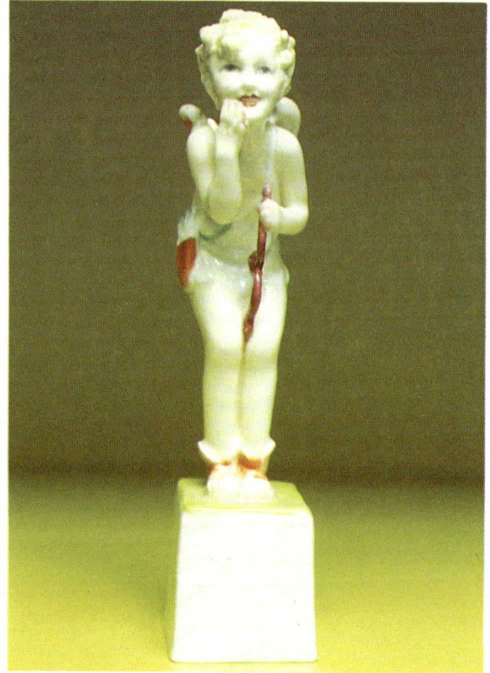

Plate 119. Shape 3105, Hit!, modelled by Gwendoline Parnell, date code unknown.

Plate 120. Shape 2633, Gentleman with Cloak and Opera Hat, modeller unknown, dated 1917.

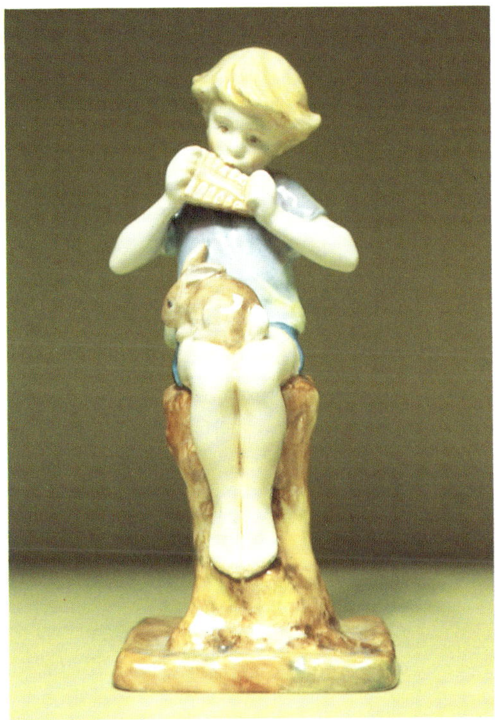

Plate 121. Shape 3011, Peter Pan, modelled by Frederick Gertner, date code unknown.

Plate 122. Shape 2907, Indian Chief, modelled by Frederick Gertner, date code unknown.

Plate 123. Shape 3142, The Frog, modelled by Gwendoline Parnell, date code unknown.

Plate 124. Shape 3114, At The Meet, modelled by Doris Lindner, date code unknown.

Plate 125. Shape 2894, Boy With Donkey, modelled by Stella Crofts, date code unknown.

Plate 126. Shape 3010, Happy Boy, modelled by Frederick Gertner, date code unknown.

Plate 127. The Boer War Soldiers Series (from l. to r.) Shape 2108, Colonial Trooper: Shape 2109 Soldier of the Black Watch: Shape 2107, Imperial Yeoman, probably modelled by George Evans.

Plate 128. The full set of Fontainebleau figures modelled by Neal French. The Figures in this original factory photograph have been identified by the same stickers which were attached to the undersides of the plinths. (see page 149)

Introduction to Colour Sketches

The following illustrations have been taken from drawings housed in the archives of the Worcester Royal Porcelain Company. In many cases these pencil and water-colour sketches are the work of the modellers themselves, and show their preferred colour schemes for their figures. The sketches would usually be sent to the factory together with the original plasticine model, and assisted in the preparation of a 'colour standard' to ensure that the intended colourings were faithfully reproduced by the paintresses. Sometimes Daisy Rea, or internal factory designers such as Neal French, worked alongside the modeller to produce the colour sketches.

The finely detailed drawings have provided invaluable assistance in the writing of this book, and we have chosen to illustrate a representative selection. The authors have yet to see a coloured example of any of the Ballet Dancers of Rachel Greaves, or Dorothy Charol's Bathing Girls, and these sketches provide our only indication of the appearance originally intended for the models. The proposed series of figures celebrating Peace in 1945 was probably never produced, but we felt the wonderful water-colour designs for them should be recorded here, if only to illustrate the visions or dreams of an unidentified figure modeller. Doris Lindner's own sketches are in themselves a joy to the eye, and pay further tribute to an outstanding craftswoman.

Plate 129. Original colour designs for the Wartime Series modelled by Eileen Soper. Top row: 'Missing', design not produced; shape 3370, Salvage; shape 3352, Spitfire. Bottom: shape 3347, Evacuees; shape 3351, Take Cover; shape 3346, The Rescue. (WRPC)

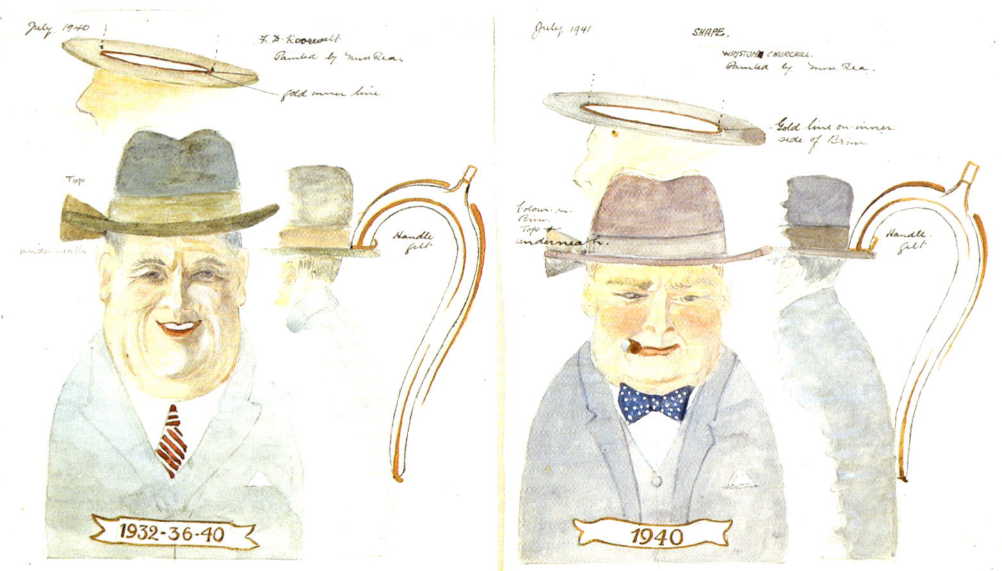

Plate 130. Original colour designs by Daisy Rea for the Roosevelt and Churchill Toby Jugs, dated 1940 and 1941, modeller unknown. It is probable that only two of each jug were produced. (WRPC).

Plate 131. Original colour designs for Dorothea Charol's figures. Top left: shape 3289, Hesitation. Centre: shape 3272, Repose. Bottom row: shapes 3186 and 3192, Ballet Dancers. Right: shape 3288, The Necklace. Top right is the design for shape 3040. The Kiss, probably by Doris Lindner. (WRPC)

Plate 132. Three watercolour designs for a proposed series of figures commemorating Victory and Peace in 1945. The series was never put into production. (WRPC)

Plate 133. Three original colour designs. Top: shape 3202, Pierrot Group, modelled by Dorothea Charol, dated January 1937. Left: shape 3193, The Queen in the Parlour, modelled by Anne Acheson, dated April 1937. Right: shape 3126, Pierrot Puff Bowl, modelled by Henri Bargas, dated January 1936.

Plate 134. Shape 3667, The Winner with Stable Boy, original colour design. (Worcester Royal Porcelain Company)

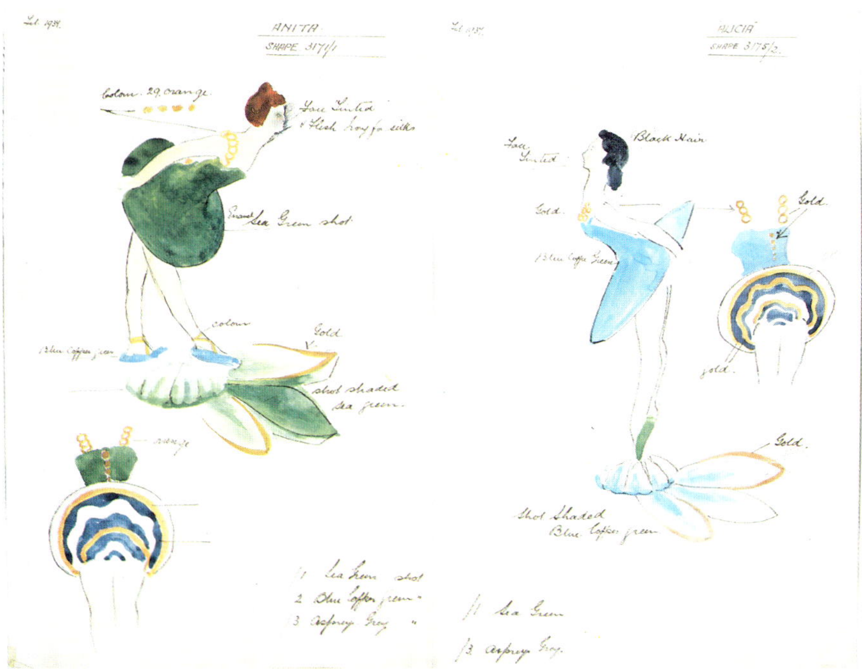

Plate 135. Original colour designs for Rachel Greaves' Ballet Dancers, dated February 1937. The bases were not produced in this form. Top: shape 3171, Arita; shape 3175, Alicia. Bottom: shape 3174, Anna; shape 3177, Irina. (WRPC)

Plate 136. Original water-colour designs by Doris Lindner for the colouring of her Zoo Babies series, shapes 3263-3265, and 3273 and 3274. Centre right: a colour design for shape 2780, Tigers Couchant, modeller unknown. (WRPC).

Plate 137. A range of original colour designs for Doris Lindner's small groups, including shape 3119, Sealyham Cigarette Box; below is a watercolour sketch by Miss Lindner for the colouring of shape 2943, Dandie Dinmont, not actually produced in this form. (WRPC)